COTTON REELS AND SO FORTH
Who's going to milk the cow then?

*To Margaret
with love
Sally x*

Dedicated to Mum and Dad

And for my precious grandchildren
Tom, Althea, Joe, Jack and Sally

ACKNOWLEDGEMENTS

I must express here my sincere and grateful thanks to my family without whose help, encouragement and assistance with the complexities of publication, this book would not have got beyond the first draft. A special thanks to Paula for the artwork.

My grateful thanks also to all the friends with whom I have reminisced over the years, providing me with a collection of little anecdotes which hopefully have added the extra dimension to this book. Thanks guys. Your participation has been invaluable.

Sally Cotton

COTTON REELS AND SO FORTH
Who's going to milk the cow then?

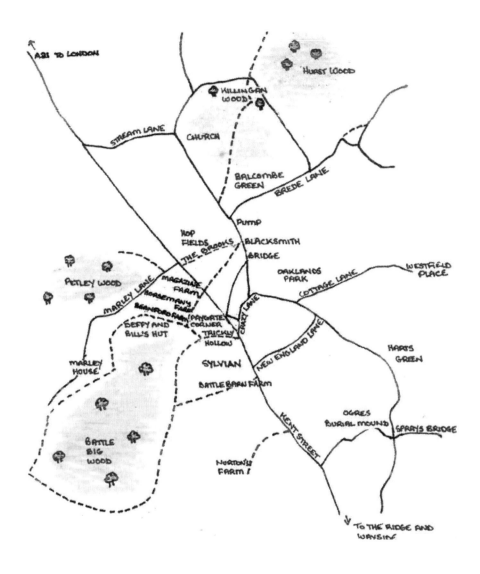

INTRODUCTION

Cotton Reels and So-forth is the third book in the series by Sally Cotton about childhood in the Sussex village of Sedlescombe.

It is now 1948 and the country is still struggling with the aftermath of WW2.

In spite of having to pay off massive war loans to America, Aneurin Bevan and the Labour Government are moving heaven and earth to implement the Welfare State and the National Health Service, as devised by the Liberal, William Beveridge, in his famous report. Ghandi, much to the sadness of Pop Cotton, has just been assassinated.

At the start of this book, Sally is nearing her 13th birthday. Life in the village continues to move at a steady pace absorbing the inevitable changes with each passing year. Sally and her friends continue with their adventures increasingly aware of, but choosing to ignore, the approach of that final change that lies ahead - adulthood. Theirs is still a world of adventure peppered with unavoidable chores. Responsibility is still in the future, harsh reality breaks through only occasionally.

All the old colourful characters are still there with some new ones entering the story, the Reverend Smith and his family being the most notable. There is an addition to the family called Rosebud, a Guernsey cow Pop Cotton has purchased. Little do Pat and Dorothy know that milking her will become their responsibility, a chore Sally mercifully escapes thanks to her allergy to Udsall, the disinfectant used on Rosebud's teats.

We see Sally and her sisters, plus the much-loved Hilary, joining in with the Beating the Bounds, enjoying Carnival time in Hastings and winning first prize for their Waxwork Show in the little market town of Robertsbridge, plus many more of their less eventful, but still memorable, childhood experiences. Towards the end of the book, however, the more adult interests of dancing and speedway enter their world. Their transition to womanhood has already begun. Hazel marries Albert Soan and Hilary has already caught the eye of David Burt, the man she will eventually marry. As for Sally, she is about to take that huge step from child to adult – she is to start work at Buttons Grocery Store.

Sally would like to point out and apologise for the following errors in her second book, More Cotton Reels:

Error on page 180, Sir Hartley Shawcross was Chief Prosecutor and not Presiding Judge as stated. The Presiding Judge was Colonel Sir Geoffrey Lawrence, President of the Tribunal.

Error on the photo of the railway workers – the third main line driver should read Horace not Aubrey Woollet.

Chapter 1
Spring 1948

The trees were beginning to lose their skeletal aspect. Above their lichen-covered trunks, embryonic buds that had lain dormant on twig and branch throughout the long, cold winter were now slowly emerging to decorate their hosts with a fine tracery of the palest green. And the wood anemone, with its delicate mantle, was transforming the brown leaf- littered ground around the base of their gnarled trunks, into a sea of cool green and white that stretched as far as the eye could see. Mother Nature armed with her multi coloured palette, was busy now, gently awakening the landscape and all that stood within it, from its seemingly dull and lifeless condition into a living entity as she began to fulfil this crucial phase in her yearly cycle.

The cloud streaked sky, for now clearly visible through the sparse canopy, would soon be obscured by millions of leaves as each one vied for a share of light with which to carry on its age old and vital purpose of photosynthesis.

Pat, Hilary and Sally were in Battle Big Wood collecting firewood for the old copper. As they worked mechanically through the task of carefully extricating suitable lengths of wood from the entanglement of old and new vegetation, Sally's thoughts were a million miles away. She was thinking about the assassination of Gandhi, which had taken place at the end of January. She remembered her dad's exact words as the dramatic news came over the airways. 'It was bound to happen sooner or later,' he had said. That was all. As he turned around however, she had seen the expression on his face and noticed the moistening around his eyes as he moved to exit through the scullery door. She had read various articles in the newspaper since then about Gandhi, and was beginning to build up a picture of this remarkable man, born in the Land of Far Beyond. She knew that he had been and was still referred to as 'Mahatma,' or Great Soul by his followers, and that he had been a pacifist. And yet he was often referred to as an agitator. True enough, he had spoken up in support of the untouchables, those lowest in the pecking order and other outcasts in India, (the land of his birth) seeking to gain for them political equality with other Castes. He had also stuck his neck out in support of other disaffected people, in South Africa in particular. As she bent and automatically wrestled another reluctant lump of wood from its resting place, an image of Gandhi, his body covered in a white sheet and surrounded by leaves and flowers uppermost in her mind's eye, she felt a tap on her shoulder and shot up as though old Beelzebub himself had touched her.

"You were miles away you were. I've been talking to you for ages and ages and all I've got from you is an occasional grunt," said Pat. "All I'm after is someone to scratch my back for me and Hilary's miles away. A bit of dead leaf or something's got down under me vest and it's driving me mad. Pity I didn't think to bring old Silus with me then I wouldn't have needed to bother you," she added with just a hint of sarcasm in her voice Sally thought, her heart beating rather rapidly after the shock she had just received. Old Silus, the resident back scratcher that Pat had referred to was the best implement in the world for chasing and catching those elusive back itches that played hide and seek with human finger nails. After use it was always returned to its position in the scullery where it hung suspended by its ancient and dirty piece of string, from a cup hook that had been screwed into the side of the dresser.

When a hurried and cursory rub failed to relieve the irritation between Pats shoulder blades, Sally pulled aside jumper and vest from the back of Pats neck and in a short time had retrieved the irritant, a piece of brown, shrivelled leaf, from the affected area.

"That better? Look that's all it was," said Sally, holding the offending piece of leaf up for inspection. Then in one movement she released the desiccated fragment to the four winds and stooped to gather together the higgledy piggledy pieces of assorted wood she had scattered around her. "Looks like between us we've got enough to keep the old copper fed for a day or two at least," she said as she looked around at what the three of them had managed to wrestle from the trees and undergrowth.

"Wonder what we've got for dinner today? I forgot to ask mum before we came up here," said Pat, following her sister's example and now endeavouring to arrange her assorted lengths of 'wood' into some semblance of order.

Cotton Reels and so Forth

"Inky stinky spider, snot and bogey pie.
All mixed up with a dead dog's eye.
With bread and butter, spread it on thick.
Then wash it down with a cup of cold sick."

Replied Sally quick as a flash and then immediately regretted having recited this yucky bit of nonsense, which the boys at school were very fond of coming out with at dinner times, wickedly trying to put the girls off their food. It always made her feel queasy, no matter how hard she tried not to let it do so. The trouble was she had such a vivid imagination with a capacity for seeing just about everything in Technicolor detail.

Pat and Hilary just shrugged without replying and then, taking a deep breath they stooped in unison and gathered their precious gleanings up into their arms, thick ends uppermost, leaving the twiggy end bits to drag along behind at their own pace - all with the same well practiced gait.

"Look, there's Miss Collins up there," said Pat as they moved from wood to pathway, and she indicated the solitary figure moving around the cow shed, with a slight movement of her head. "She's not seen us, well not yet anyway. I reckon they're a bit posh, the Collins's you know. I had to use their lavvy up there the other day and they've got something called Bronco paper in there. Mind you, newspaper's better. It's not so rough and it gives you something to do while you're in there, like going through the bits until you find something worth reading sort of thing." Then she stopped for a moment bringing the other two girls to a sudden halt behind her. "What does that remind you of, those sheets blowing in the wind on the line up there?" she asked indicating the area where the skeletons of lots of domestic animals had been found many years ago. "Ships sailing in the wind that's what," she said as she contemplated the puzzled silence from the other two.

The tricky manoeuvre of lifting the bundles of wood over the stile at the top of the field having been accomplished with the minimum of fuss, they proceeded to drag the wood across the field. As they walked, the twiggy end bits snagged up at times in the coarse and tufty clumps of grass that proliferated throughout the field, but they automatically pulled it through these minor obstacles with an almost imperceptible tightening of pressure from their arms, which were encircling this precious harvest.

"Look there's even more ships sailing in the wind down there," said Hilary pointing ahead to where the four lines in the back garden had been filled to overflowing with fresh washing of every size, colour and description. "Looks like your fairies have been hard at work again Sally," she added "I just hope they've waved their magic wands and so forth so's it doesn't rain today, that's all. We've got a busy day ahead of us lot."

As they dropped the wood beside the old chopping horse with sighs of relief, dad came round the side of the house to meet them.

3

"Your mum's got you a drink in there. Don't forget you've got to go to the village for me to pick up those pieces of leather from old Silks place," he said as he came up alongside. "I've got several orders for bags and things that I need to get on with."

"Yes dad," replied Sally automatically. As if they could forget a thing like that, she thought, but decided to keep thoughts like this to herself.

After supping their cocoa, Pat, Hilary and Sally hurried along the main road towards the village. As they were passing Farrows steps, they saw old Sniff'n' spit coming towards them on his large framed ladies bicycle, looking more like a wounded bean-stick than ever. He was sitting very upright and peddling along slowly, puffing away on a cigarette, which smouldered then glowed as he dragged on the thing, taking the smoke laden air right down into his lungs. They moved onto the grass verge as he drew level with them, and as he passed by, he removed the offending missile from his mouth, nodded vaguely in their direction and continued on his way. Sally looked back over her shoulder as he peddled off slowly along the road, and was just in time to see him spit sideways into the grass verge and she felt her stomach heave. Why did so many men have to do that, she thought to herself. It was disgusting, and she voiced her opinion to the other two girls.

"Yes I know, but he's a very old man and he probably can't help it," said Hilary. "I know some of the boys at School do it but that's to wind us up, that's all, especially you Sally. If only you'd ignore them they'd get fed up doing it. You should see your face sometimes. If looks could kill they'd be dead as a doughnut. Anyway, we shouldn't complain. He smokes Turf cigarettes, doesn't he and gets packets of twenty at a time. That means he gets two cards in each packet and the doubles from the ones the boys cadge from him, come to us, don't they. You didn't think of that, did you," she added as she stooped to pull up her lazy socks.

Even before they lifted the knocker on the door of Mr Silks house beside the Bridge Garage, they realised that he was not around and that they would have to walk up through the village to his workshop at the top end of the village. They lingered awhile beside Gregory's bakery, perusing the cakes, pastries and variously shaped loaves of bread displayed inside the large plate glass window, sniffing appreciatively, before moving off reluctantly, determinedly setting their sights on the pathway ahead.

There was a lone figure sitting on the pump seat and even from the bottom of the village green, there was no mistaking its identity. Still as a statue, back straight as a ramrod and looking as though he were contemplating the origins of the universe, sat Henry Maplesden his old clay pipe stuck firmly and comfortably into the side of his mouth.

"You're quiet today," said Hilary as having walked across the green, they were now standing in front of him.

"Me tractors broke," he replied without removing his pipe. And then he lapsed back into silence once more, and no amount of gentle coaxing could entice another syllable from him. After a while, they left this complex youth to his contemplation of the universe or whatever and moved away towards the top end of the green, chatting away about inconsequential things.

They saw Mr Hobden, the Cobbler sitting near the window of his little shop at the top of the village, puffing away on his old pipe, and paused momentarily to watch this craftsman ply his trade. He had a man's boot positioned firmly over one limb of the three footed shoe iron he was using, and was tapping away with the same tip-o tap-o movement favoured by Mr Taylor, the blacksmith in whose Smithy down at the bottom of the village, they had spent many a happy hour. As he tapped rhythmically away, he spat tacks out of his mouth one by one into the palm of his left hand, picked them up deftly with the thumb and middle finger of his right hand and then pinned them, neatly spaced around the sole of the old boot. Each movement was performed with the utmost precision and done within the blink of an eye-lid. Sally wondered what would happen if he sneezed suddenly. And she grinned to herself as she pictured the old man on all fours, searching among the parings and shavings and general debris, which cluttered the floor space within this tiny room. As they moved away, he looked up and gave them a tight lipped smile, then immediately turned his attention back to the job in hand.

A bell rang out shrilly as they opened the door into the building referred to as the Minor Hall, and the girls jumped at the sudden onslaught on their ears. Almost immediately, Mr Silk came through from the back room and walked towards them. As Sally peeped through the door from which he had appeared, she got a brief glimpse of his large industrial sewing machine before the door closed slowly behind him. It was almost identical to the one used by her dad for the stitching of handbags and any other heavy sewing jobs that came his way.

The Minor Hall, now used by this leather merchant come artisan, had been the venue for various village functions in the past, but Sally had no idea when it had changed from a parochial meeting place to one of singular employment.

The overall impression of Mr Arthur Silk, the brisk and business like little man who stood before them, was one of overall neatness and attention to detail. Beneath the large leather apron and the light jacket he was wearing, peeped a white shirt with collar and tie, and the brown leather shoes on his feet had been polished to the same shade and shine as the hair on his head. Sally understood that he had come to live and work in Sedlescombe after his home and warehouse in Hastings had been destroyed by enemy action during the war, and had just decided to stay here after the war had ended. She had heard recently however, that he now intended to move back to Hastings sometime in the near future. She would be sorry to see him go.

"We've come for dad's leather," said Sally as he stood looking at them one at a time with the hint of a smile hovering around his lips.

"Your dad? And who might that be," he replied mischievously. Then before she had time to elaborate, he patted her on the shoulder, "as if I didn't know," he said. "Just wait here for a moment will you and I'll fetch it from the back room" After a short while, he came back through the doorway carrying two packages tied up with brown paper, and handed one to Hilary and one to Sally. "They're not that heavy. The two of you should manage them without having to involve the little one." And he smiled at Pat as he moved over to open the door for them, the shrill jangling of the bell making them all jump for a second time. The little tongue twister, 'red leather, yellow leather,' popped up into Sally's mind as she passed through the doorway, and she grinned. She still tripped over the words of this simple bit of nonsense no matter how hard she tried.

As they walked toward Wilton's, they saw Kate Furner coming through the doorway of the paper shop and stopped to pass the time of day with her. She was a tall, thick-set lady and Sally had never once seen her dressed in anything but a pair of serge trousers, which would be accompanied by anything from a baggy cotton shirt to the thickest tweed jacket, varying only with the prevailing weather conditions – hence one of her nick names, 'Arse 'n Trousers. The boys however, always referred to her as Dumph.

"What you got in them parcels then?" she asked and moved towards Hilary to examine more closely the size and shape of the package she was carrying. "Now let me guess," she continued without waiting for an answer. "You've just come from old Silk's place, haven't you, so likely you've got leather or some such thing for Pop Cotton in there. Tell him don't forget to let me know when he's made up that bag I've ordered from him. It'll last me for the rest of me life and likely into the next if I'm not mistaken. Quality stuff he turns out." The girls just nodded and after a short pause, they turned to move away. They turned back however, when she started to talk again and stood there listening politely to the rest of the conversation. "He copped it Old Silk during the war you know, he wouldna been here in Sedlescombe but for that," she was saying. "No he were living in Hastin's up to the time he were bombed out. It weren't just his warehouse and shop in Queen's road (No 25) that went up, his house in Havelock road went same way. Still their loss is our'n gain as I say's and he's taken to village life like a duck to water. Now get along with you, you've likely got the leather in there what your dad needs to do me bag with." Then she turned determinedly away from them and walked away towards the old village pump.

A cursory glance into the window of the paper shop, showed the usual adverts for cigarettes and tobacco and two tins displayed right by the doorway caught Sally's eye. One was clearly marked with the words, 'Bondman Tobacco,' and had a red lid. The other, with the words, 'Skipper Tobacco' inscribed on its surface, had a bright green lid. She wouldn't mind a couple of these colourful tins, she thought to herself. Perhaps she could find out from the boys, who smoked the stuff and get them to cadge one of each for her. It was worth a try she thought as she turned away from the display and followed Hilary and Pat as they walked towards the green and then on to the bottom of the village.

"Mr Taylor's shoeing a horse in there," said Pat taking a deep and satisfying sniff as she pointed towards the old Smithy. "Let's have a quick look in there. Please, please, it won't take a minute. I just want to see if it's one from Gotway's farm or if it's one of Mr Budgen's old Cart Horses. They know me those horses, I know they do, and they're always good as gold if we just stand quietly and watch them being shod. I think they enjoy us being around and Mr Taylor certainly does."

Having accepted the inevitable, Hilary and Sally crossed over the road and followed Pat towards the Smithy. In truth, they were not averse to watching a re-inaction of this age old craft, this display of vernacular workmanship, which was taking place within the rustic shed and Mr Taylor they reckoned had to be was the best Blacksmith for miles around.

Mr Taylor looked up as they entered his domain and smiled his weather-beaten smile as they grouped around him. Even though they had watched this procedure countless times before, it never failed to fascinate them. In the hands of this skilled craftsman, the performance itself was an art form - in its own right.

As Sally watched, anticipating each sleight of hand of this artisan with an accuracy born out of years of observation, she thought about the man plying his trade in front of his uninvited audience. Not only did he tend to the needs of horses, but could fashion a piece of iron into any shape, be it a nail or a wrought iron gate and anything in between. As she took her eyes away from contemplation of the skilled operation on which Pat and Hilary were fixated, she could see examples of his handiwork hanging or standing around the Smithy awaiting collection and she marvelled at the complexity, the scale and variety of the items, mostly vernacular, that were in this modest shed. Only very rarely did dad need to cycle into Battle to pick up one of the ready-made products available from Till's the hardware store in the High Street. This man, who could knock up a piece of simple hardware or a work of art, with the same skill and attention to detail, was the most important man in the village, dad reckoned. As she remembered his words, her eyes and attention returned to the work of this master craftsman, and she began to hum the Twanky Dillo song to herself:

> 'Here's a health to the jolly Blacksmith the best of all fellows.
> He works at his anvil while the boy blows the bellows.
> Which makes his bright hammer to rise and to fall.
> There's the old Cole and the young Cole and the old Cole of all.
> Twanky dillo, Twanky Dillo, Twanky Dillo Dillo Dillo Dillo.
> And the roaring pair of bagpipes made from the green willow.'

7

Until recently, she realised, she had taken Mr Taylor for granted, along with his ability to make each skilled operation look easy, now she began to appreciate his skill. She had also assumed that his roots were as firmly in the soil of this village as were those of Bangy Smith, old Fred and old George. She had heard recently however, that he had started life in a cottage somewhere up country, in a place called Cranbrook if her memory served her right. The cottage in question was one of a pair and had housed between them twenty-four children, thirteen in one and eleven in the other. He had spread his wings, escaping from these cramped conditions in the year 1912, and with the Princely sum of seven pounds ten shillings, had secured a berth on a ship, which was heading for Canada. She clearly remembered the name of the town in which he had settled and smiled to herself, running the word around in her mind as she stood in silent contemplation of the interaction between man and horse taking place before her. Moosejaw it was called and she understood that the origins of its name, was connected with some kind of animal. She had tried to visualise these creatures from the time she had heard the name and the best her imagination could come up with was a cross between a horse and a camel. In actual fact, she had no idea what the animals looked like. What she did know however, was that the Blacksmith had returned to England in 1914, enlisting in the British Army at the onset of The Great War, and had spent the next four years fighting a war which had claimed the lives of so many men, including her Uncle Bill and her mum's two cousins. The names of the places in which they fought were a blur, even though they had been mentioned several times within her hearing. That this man had survived the carnage though was something of a miracle as far as she could make out, and for this miracle, plus the fact that he had chosen the village of Sedlescombe in which to ply his trade, she was very grateful. His cut throat razor had also survived the war but had come to grief later at the hands of his youngest son Tony, who had borrowed the thing to whittle bits of wood about and hack himself through the brambles and stinging nettles in and around the local woods. But that was another story.

She came back to the here and now as Mr Taylor was relinquishing his hold on one of the horse's feet then as he lowered it to the ground he stood up slowly, arching his back as he did so. "There' that fits like a stocking on a chickens lip," he said, a satisfied grin on his face. As the horse shuffled around and snorted, Pat moved forward instinctively to stroke his muzzle. The creature turned its aquiline profile slowly towards her and looked at her with his big brown eyes. "There, what did I tell you? He recognises me he does," she said grinning from ear to ear.

"Come on then," said Sally, hoisting up her parcel to a more comfortable position as she moved over towards the open doorway. "Don't forget we're going over to Stafford's wood soon as we get this stuff home, so we'd best get a move on Thanks Mr Taylor," she added looking back hurriedly over her shoulder. Then after lingering for a few seconds, the other girls followed reluctantly in her footsteps. Once out into the fresh air again, they all took a deep breath, exhaled noisily then followed their feet towards home. By the time they reached Pay Gate corner, they had sung a couple of simple ditties, put the world to rights and now they were hungry enough to eat a scabby donkey.

As they walked up across the field, Whitey the cat came running down to meet them. Nuggly their old cat was long gone but this pale replacement was as good a mouser as her predecessor and apart from a bit of milk and a few scraps of food, was pretty well self-sufficient. Gruesome evidence of her sorties in and around her territory scavenging for prey, were often to be seen deposited in the scullery, and Sally shuddered as she pictured the mangled heads and assortment of other unidentifiable scraps of anatomy and contemplated the lingering deaths of these unfortunate little creatures. As Whitey wound herself around their feet, they bent and fondled her and she purred away contentedly.

As Sally stood up, she saw her dad coming through the top gate carrying the large saucepan with the wobbly bottom in his hands. He walked a few paces into the field then emptied the contents of the saucepan onto the ground and was immediately surrounded by a flock of cackling hens. After placing the saucepan just inside the gate, he walked down to meet them and relieved them of the parcels they were carrying. He smiled as Pat recounted the message from Kate Furner and just replied, "I'll do me best." Then he turned and made his way back across the field with the girls following behind, the cat still rubbing itself around their ankles.

Sally stood at the kitchen table pouring flour into mum's old mixing bowl. "Can I have a bit of suet now please mum," she asked. "And would you grate it for me please, only I don't want to grate my knuckles this time." Mum duly obliged, adding a good handful of sultanas to the bowl, which Sally mixed in with her hand before binding the whole lot together with a bit of cold water. She could see a delicious suet pudding taking shape and her mouth watered in anticipation of seeing this lump of grey dough transformed into a pudding made in Heaven. She wrapped the pudding carefully in greaseproof paper followed by a bit of white rag, then tied the whole lot up with a piece of string, as she had seen mum do time and again. "There, even you couldn't do much better than that, could you mum, she said patting it proudly. What she had failed to mention was that the actual boiling of the pudding would not be taking place in the comparative safety of The Windy Ridge kitchen as she had intimated, but on a less predictable, open fire in Stafford's wood.

As she moved towards the scullery door with Pat and Hilary, dad came down the stairs and moved towards the old range. "Any chance of a cup of tea?" he asked looking towards the simmering kettles on the top plate. Then he tut-tutted as he caught his hair in the hooks on one of the brassieres that were hanging over the line. "Damn and blast these bosom things," he said as he tried to extricate himself from the thing, and Sally saw her mum grin as she moved to give him a hand.

As the girls hurried down the field, the words, 'now is the winter of our discontent' popped into Sally's mind and she could not think for the life of her where they had come from. She had no idea where she had heard or even read them and yet for some reason they had chosen this moment to pop up into her mind. Winter was done for, she told herself. There was now a fresh green hue creeping across the neutral landscape, interspersed here and there with dots of astonishingly bright colours as the first flush of flowers offered up their heads to the thin rays of early spring sunshine. Ah, now she remembered. Those words were connected somewhere along the line with Jumbo James, their headmaster. He had quoted them along with some other lines of prose in one of their English lessons a few weeks ago. It was something Shakespeare had written if she remembered rightly, though she was not absolutely sure. She would have to ask him sometime.

Before they set off on their travels, they called into Windy Ridge for just long enough to collect a saucepan, and all the paraphernalia they needed to get a good fire going, plus an old bit of blanket to sit on while they waited for their meal.. They hurried across the back of the Winchesters garden, into Crazy Lane, and within a short while were walking along the track leading to Stafford's wood. Rolling grey clouds now hid the skeletal clouds that had decorated the early morning sky, and stirred up the trees and long grasses around them, as it steadily increased in volume. As they walked up to the narrow wooden walkway, which crossed this narrow stream, Sally looked into the water then paused momentarily. She was fascinated by the action of the water as it wobbled up to one particular boulder in the bed of the stream then seemed to pause for a split second before going into free fall over the miniature obstacle. It looked for all the world like a fairy waterfall, she thought as she bent down and peered closely into the light misty spray If she looked long and hard enough, she would surely catch a glimpse of some small fairy like creature within its orbit, she reckoned. Not today though, she thought as she stood up reluctantly and removed her gaze and person from the magical scene. She just did not have the time.

Once they had crossed the walkway into the wood, Hilary stooped down and scooped up a measure of the cold running water from the stream and into the saucepan she was carrying, holding back her skirt out of harm's way as she did so. They then moved off together towards a clearing in the wood, used by them and other youngsters in the area as a meeting place, a venue for all sorts of motley gatherings. As they walked, Sally looked towards the Cyclops tree, standing just off the beaten track, and smiled to herself. She remembered the countless times she had swung through its branches, along with as many as a dozen other youngsters at times. They had had a lot of fun in this wood over the years there was no doubt about that, and with any luck would have lots more. From time to time, they picked up suitable lengths of fallen branches with which they would feed the fire once they had stirred it into life with the sticks,

10

newspaper and matches they had brought with them. It was fun when some of the other youngsters were around, but it did get a bit noisy at times and once they had got a fire going today, they did not want to attract too much attention to themselves.

"At least you won't have to climb up there and rob the pigeons of their eggs, Sally," said Hilary pointing towards the edge of the wood where the trees, tall and willowy stood sentinel like a line of mute, oversized toy soldiers. "It's much too early for that. We'll just have to make do with this pudding," Then she began to set the rolled up newspaper and bits of kindling wood into a cone shape around a couple of charred bricks before striking and touching a match carefully to the whole thing. Once the little fire had spat and spluttered into life, she began to apply the thicker pieces of wood carefully, one piece at a time. She then waited a short while before poking the charred and half burned pieces of wood back into the heart of the fire with the aid of a long stick, and added just a few more lengths for good measure. Once the thick smoke began to lessen and the blaze had died down to a decent glow, she placed the saucepan of water over the bricks, then settled back on her haunches and waited for it to come to the boil. Before long, she was up on her feet and placing the precious bundle carefully down through the vacillating steam and into the rolling water.

Before sitting back down again, Hilary spread the bit of old blanket over the ground, far enough but not too far from the fire and steaming saucepan, and they shuffled around until they managed to minimise the discomfort from the cold, lumpy ground. After a while, Hilary took a tin of Snowfire cream from her pocket, scooped up a glob of the salve with her fore finger and placed the sticky ointment into the palm of her hand. Then after passing the tin over to Pat and Sally, she began to rub the stuff into and all over her grubby fingers. "There, that's better, that'll stop us getting chapped hands," she said, as Sally passed the open tin carefully back to her. Then as she replaced the lid and popped it back into her pocket, a satisfied grin spread across her face.

While they waited for the pudding to cook, they chatted about this and that, chuckling from time to time as they recounted shared experiences. They grimaced and dragged the backs of their hands across their mouths as they recalled the acrid taste of some of the tannin drenched tea they had brewed here in the wood from time to time, then forced down their throats. From the time Basil Winchester had remarked that it looked and tasted as though it had been strained through an old sock, and a dirty one at that, their imaginations had run amok, and they had vowed never to expose their taste buds to the stuff again. What if that sock were one of old Sniff and Spit's, and had been attached to one of his dirty old feet, they'd said and very nearly retched at the thought. If they wanted tea these days, they brought it along in a bottle from home, all sweet and milky and delicious. Then they talked about the time they had been chased out of here by an irate Gamekeeper, and had very nearly been caught by him. They had been collecting pigeons' eggs at the time and it was while they were testing the things to see if they were addled or not, that he had crept up on them. It was their own fault, however, they had been making one hell of a noise at the time.

Uncle Fred Sansom was next on the verbal menu, with an appraisal of his unique interpretation and articulation of jokes, and even more interesting, the way he regaled the girls with tales of a lifetimes experiences, albeit with a bit added on here and there for effect. One incident in particular, though not really humorous when they really thought about it, always amused them. It had happened when he was serving with the troops in Burma and a close mate of his was seriously injured. 'Don't you dare die here, the grounds too bloody hard,' he'd told his friend and the man had survived against all the odds.

After recalling other tales and jokes that their Uncle always seemed to be awash with, it was inevitable that the conversation would return at some time to the death of Len Masters, a friend of theirs from school, who had fallen down the stairs while sleep walking. As they spoke about this gentle boy, Sally felt the tears well up into her eyes and she brushed them away, aware that the other two girls were doing the same thing. It seemed that he had fallen onto a large glass vase that stood on a table at the bottom of the stairs, shattering the thing, the shards of glass severing a jugular vein, whatever that was, and he had bled to death. Thoughts and memories of the terrible death of this amiable lad, this gentle giant, had haunted her dreams on and off since this had happened and had changed her attitude to glass forever.

To take their minds off this painful subject, they began to talk about Deffy and Bill, the two old men who lived a hermit style life at the edge of Battle big wood. The last time they had visited these old men, Bill had showed them how to make a kite out of sticks, string and bits of brown paper. They had yet to try it out. He had also made them a bow, which had just the right combination of spring and resistance. The handful of arrows to go with it, were straight and true. They were even more accurate than the burnt tipped ones made for them by Mr Elkins, Hilary's dad. They knew they were as they had already given them and the bow, a bit of practice. The kite was still awaiting its maiden voyage.

From time to time, Hilary moved forward and carefully placed more wood onto the embers and then watched as the fire sparked into flame again before dying back down to a satisfactory glow, while the saucepan with its precious contents, continued to simmer away satisfactorily.

"There were hop fields all over there at one time," said Pat after the silence that followed Hilary's ministrations and her examination of the pudding simmering away on the fire. And she pointed south towards fields that were obscured from their view by this wooded area. "Bangy Smith was telling us all about it the other day. He said that before Jaybez Winter was even knee high to grasshopper, his dad had hops growing all around here, and that even the field at the back of Luck's Ness, where the Linchs's used to live, was covered with them. Well you were there Sal, it was after you told him about getting shot at as you walked across that field back in the war.

"Yes, I remember. I was there and so was Hilary," replied Sally and she grinned as she recalled the lively conversation and the actions of the old man on that occasion. As well as talking about the hops that had adorned so many fields in the area in the past, and the reason for their demise, he had also spoken to them for the first time about his father. It seemed that his dad had been one of only a handful of people around who still knew the steps and more importantly, the movements of an ancient country dance called step dancing. On special occasions, old Spenser Smith would be persuaded or cajoled into performing these dances on the village green and Bangy would always accompany his old dad on that squeeze box of his. Bangy reckoned that he had tried but never really got the hang of these dances himself, with their strange irregular movements. He had, however, given the girls a demonstration and Sally, unable to resist the challenge, rose to her feet and tried to mimic his movements. She bent her knees ever so slightly and moved from one foot to the other, just as he had done. But no matter how hard she tried she could not recreate the bow legged gyrations of the old man.

She sat down again very carefully, still chuckling to herself, and drew her knees up under her chin, sub consciously copying the other two girls and they sat in silence for a few moments, each occupied with their own but most likely, similar thoughts. They were brought back to the here and now suddenly by the sound of a disturbance in a nearby tree and as they looked upwards, they saw a squirrel falling down at a rate of knots from its top most branches, followed closely by a piece of rotten wood, which it had obviously grasped on to and which had collapsed under its weight. It was stabbing out with its little hands, trying to grab and hold on to any twig or branch that would halt its rapid descent to the ground – without success. They held their breath as it crashed through the branches, landing on all fours, tail held high and quivering. It looked at them for a split second with its beady little eyes, with a mixture of fear and embarrassment, before scuttling off into the undergrowth and then up into a nearby tree.

It was only when they sat back laughing their heads off with the spectacle of the incident, coupled with relief that the creature had survived its swift, undignified exit from the tree, that they realised it had begun to rain. They quickly sobered up, scanning the heavens as far as the trees allowed and the rolling dark clouds told their own story. This was not just a shower. This weather was here to stay, for a few hours at least. They rose quickly to their feet and Hilary removed the blanket from the ground, rolling it up unceremoniously and tucking it under her arm. Then she moved forward and removed the steaming saucepan and its contents from the bed of the fire.

"We can't eat this yet, it's not done," she said examining the thick roll of suet, which had expanded and was straining at its covering of greaseproof and rag. "We'll just have to leave it here. I must take this saucepan home though or mum'll be looking all over for it. It'll need a bit of cleaning up and so forth as well where it's got scorched up with smoke, but a bit of Vim will soon take care of that. Stand back then," she ordered as she walked back to the fire and tipped the saucepan up very carefully, sloshing some of the steaming water from the pan on to the fire, which sizzled and shot out snots of smoke before coming back to life again. "It's no good, I'll have to get a bit more water to put this thing out," she said as she tipped the half cooked pudding on to the ground. "Hang on, I'll pop back down to the stream and fill this saucepan up again. That should do it."

Once the fire had been extinguished, they hurried down through the wood and, as they walked back along the track towards Crazy Lane, Sally looked for the fairy waterfall that had caught her attention on the way to the wood. It was still there but already the water generated by this heavy rain was threatening to overwhelm this miniature wonderland. She felt a little sad, struck once again by the transient nature of things. Her low spirits were short lived however, when her thoughts led to contemplation of the change to their plans for the rest of the day due to the early arrival of this band of rain. With any luck she would get a bit of time to peruse the Rupert Album that had recently come her way, and she grinned to herself as she thought about this little bear and his exciting adventures. If she closed her eyes ever so slightly, she could see its cover in every detail. Rupert was pictured centre stage, grinning and waving down to his mates, Algy and Pug as he flew over their heads on his little flying bicycle. He was wearing a red jumper, yellow and brown check trousers and his scarf was streaming out behind him in the wind. He was surrounded by other unidentifiable creatures that were soaring up and around him, decorating the elevated area on this lofty plane. There was also a castle with its inevitable deep dark dungeon in the background, which suggested excitement here. If things got a bit scary though, she could always put the book to one side until she found the courage to read on.

"I wish we'd worn our wellies. My feet are getting soaked in these old plimsolls," Pat was saying, bringing Sally back to the here and now. And she stomped and squelched through the muddy pathway to emphasise her discomfort.

"You mean Wellingtons, don't you? You remember what old Fred said the other day when he was wearing the things. He said 'these ere boots, they goes back to the Duke of Wellington they does, the man who were named after his boots,' replied Hilary mimicking the old man's accent, but not quite getting it right. "When I told him he'd got it back to front, he grinned and wagged his finger at me, didn't he. He said, 'I says what I means and means what I says, young lady,' that's all and then he walked back off up the road again. He does say some strange things sometimes when you think about it. Anyway, I'd best take this saucepan home and give it a bit of attention and then we'll go up to your place."

***

As Pat, Hilary and Sally hurried up Crazy Lane on their way to the village one Sunday morning, they decided to visit the cellars of the Chapel en route, something they had been planning to do for some time now. They had been told by some of the boys that there was a huge library down there and they reckoned that today was as good a day as any to explore this region and peruse some of the books it contained. The Smith family were due to take up residence here shortly and although their advent into the community was anticipated with enthusiasm, an opportunity to explore these books to their hearts content would be lost. Time was on their side for a change. They had arranged to meet up with Willie and Roy in the village this morning but not until the two boys had had their hair cut, which from past experience meant that they had at least an hour to spare.

As they crept around the back of the Chapel, they looked furtively around them even though the place was still as a grave and the likelihood of them being apprehended seemed very unlikely.

"This couldn't half do with a bit of oil," said Hilary as the rusty old bolt across the doorway squeaked as it resisted then reluctantly acquiesced to Hilary's attempts to draw it back. "I'd better go first," she added peering down into the gloomy interior. "These steps are a bit slippery so for goodness sake hold on to this rail at the side here," she warned. "The water runs off the bank at the back here and under this old door and we have had a lot of rain recently." Then she began to descend the steep and narrow brick steps very carefully, holding on to the rail on the right hand side of the wall with both hands as she did so, followed closely by Pat, with Sally bringing up the rear.

The only light that penetrated this dark, damp place came from a small window that had been let into the wall, where the natural slope of the ground exposed the lower bricked area. It was sufficient however, once their eyes had become accustomed to the gloom, to enable them to examine the contents of the room. Some of the books mentioned by the boys were on shelves while others had been left in untidy heaps on a couple of heavy wooden tables beneath the window, as though they had been leafed through then casually and hastily set aside. Trust boys. It would take ages to sort this lot out, Sally thought to herself and tut-tutted as she tried to bring one of the piles into some semblance of order. The covers felt slightly damp to the touch and as she turned one or two over, she noticed that the pages had assumed brown and wavy, almost lacy edges to them. Most of the books here were on a religious theme, which was understandable, she reckoned. A few however, were from the pen of novelists, albeit mostly on a solemn theme. A couple of Charles Dickens books were amongst the ones in the pile she was perusing and she smiled as she recognised the titles and flicked through the pages with a satisfying feeling of familiarity. There were similar copies in the bookcase in the front room at home, and although she still had not read all of them from cover to cover, she was familiar with the stories contained within. After a while, having casually perused several books, her eyes alighted on one in a brown paper cover. As she picked it up then opened it, an image of a Saint in his death throes, his body pierced with arrows, stared up at her. Then as she flicked over the pages, other and similar images afflicted her eyes and she closed the book with a shudder. This was too much like the exhibits in the chamber of horrors at Madame Tausauds for her liking she thought as she replaced the book back down onto the table, wiping her hands instinctively down her dress as she did so. She would not revisit that place, not in a million years, she told herself.

"Let's go then," she announced suddenly and Pat and Hilary looked up at her in puzzlement as she made her way towards the slippery steps leading back up and into the outside world. Without comment, they replaced their books and followed her retreating back. Once outside and with the old wooden door bolted behind them, they all took a deep breath, then moved around to the front of the building together and onto Chapel Hill. "Doesn't the village look nice from here?" Sally remarked and sighed with relief as she set her sights on the familiar scene that she almost always took for granted.

The girls made straight for Mrs Harris's little cottage beside the village green and along the track, which ran down beside it, to the shed used as a barbers shop on a Sunday morning. The usual notice, 6d for men. 3d for boys was pinned to the door, and as they peered through, they could see Mr Jack Playford, linesman during the week and barber on Sundays, busily fulfilling his Sabbath duties. One of his roll up cigarettes was perched precariously on an old saucer beside him, which he picked up and puffed on every now and again. He was putting the finishing touches to one of his customers and as Sally watched him run the clippers up the back of the man's neck, splayed fingers controlling the angle of his victims head as he did so, she shivered, remembering her own experiences with dad's ancient clippers.

Willie and Roy were amongst the line-up of men and boys waiting their turn for a short back and sides, the only style available from this establishment. They were sitting quietly in their chairs, grinning back at the girls, obviously having been aware of their presence from the time they had arrived there.

"They're going to be ages, the boys," said Pat turning away and looking back along the track towards the village green. "Let's go and sit on the pump seat for a bit and see who else is about."

The girls wandered back down the track and up across the green, then decided to cross over to the other side of the road to have a look in Button's shop window rather than sit around on a cold damp seat. As they approached the shop, Sally's eyes went straight to a drawing that had been chalked up on the wall of the building. This hastily scrawled interpretation of Chad had been around for some time and in spite of many attempts to eradicate the thing, still adhered stubbornly to the rough surface on which it had been chalked. It was classic Chad, with his characteristic twirl of hair and bunched knuckles, peering over a wall and the artist had somehow conveyed humour in the character with just two round beady eyes. The caption, 'Wot no bananas,' had been written underneath, with just a rough outline of this rare fruit to one side of the wall. This character popped up all over the place with assorted messages scrawled underneath, all on a similar theme, usually a reminder of shortages past and present. Sally had practised sketching this cheerful little chap on any spare piece of paper that came her way and could now produce a reasonable likeness of him in record time. She was quite proud of her achievement.

In the window on one side of the doorway, was a display of washing powders. Seen in tall stacks like this, they seemed to take on a different identity, their primary purpose subsumed somehow into something almost artistic. Each pile had become an entity in its own right rather than something merely to remove dirt from garments. The colours, from the dull orange of the Oxydol through the blue's, red's and off white shades of the Persil and Lux flake boxes, seemed to form themselves into something akin to a large, impressionist painting. Even the Omo with its little owl motif seemed to complement this whole arrangement. Partially hidden by this display, was the poster advertising Pears soap, which had been pinned up onto a side wall ages ago and was now a bit raggedy around the edges. The colours however, were still vibrant, with the smile on the girls face as radiant as ever. Her long dark hair still framed her face and her little white fluffy cat still sat there in solemn silent contentment. Even the wording, 'Good morning! Have you used Pears Soap?' was plain to see. Though different in content, this poster was as charming as the one that had decorated the wall in that building in Battle during the war, from where she and her sisters had collected the concentrated orange juice and cod liver oil compound. She grinned as she recalled the chubby legs and radiant smiles of the two children who, in this other poster, were running through fields of wheat and barley. Where was it now, she wondered, this personification of endless summers.

On the other side of the doorway, the display of tinned food was quite dull in comparison, an indication Sally thought that the window dresser had either run out of time or inspiration, or both. Or maybe it was just that these items were in short supply. Who knows, she thought to herself.

As they made their way back down the bricked pathway towards the pavement, they saw Mrs Brooman shuffling down the road towards them wearing a long coat, which had changed from black to a napped clerical grey over years of constant use. The felt hat pulled right down over her ears, was of a similar age and condition. Following closely on her heels, was a man they recognised instantly as Cokey Coleman from Cripps Corner, looking more like a little Leprechaun than ever. He was wearing the same tweed jacket that he had been wearing when they had last seen him, while cycling to Poppinghole Lane, ages ago now. The cap on his head was also familiar, and was still several sizes too big for him. The girls stopped in their tracks, as the figures moved towards them, knowing that it was too late to beat a hasty retreat from the two adults, who would no doubt vie with one another to have the last word.

"Look out, 'ere comes old Cokey Coleman, shivering and shaking like a little dog at shit," said Mrs Brooman as she puffed up beside them, the winner by a whisker. "I bet he's bin sharpening that there sickle of his on the gravestones in Church Yard up yonder. No respecter of the dead he ain't," she added ignoring the man even though he was now standing right beside her and could hear every word she was saying. The girls instinctively moved a few paces away from the old lady. Rumour had it that she took a bath maybe once a year – if she felt like it, and as the boys, who always referred to her as Fanny, would say, 'whiffed' a bit.

"Well, what brings you all the way down here then Cokey? Looks like you be here to swip the green with that old weapon you be carrying, she said, turning round to face the old man as though she had only just realised he was there. "It's no good you looking longingly over to old Buttons either. He ain't got no food to spare and it ain't his fault either. Tell you what, if that Lord Woolton were to walk down here, he'd get me old slop bucket on his head, he would. It's coupons for this and coupons for that, and never a bit of slipper bacon or a nice Quarto loaf to go with me dried mushrooms. That man ain't 'uman."

The girls, feeling that it would be rude to just walk away at this stage, stood around listening to the strange interaction between these two old people. When Cokey could get a word in edgeways, it was to tell tales of his superhuman achievements. He pulled himself up to his full height and smiled around from one face to the next as he talked, looking intently for any sign of admiration. Mrs Brooman however, knowing the man a darned sight better than they did, just interrupted when he went too far, bringing him back down to earth with a tale or two of her own. She was talking now about the Drovers and Carters that used to make their way through the villages in the old days. As she said as she began to give her dissertation, "this were ages ago, before me 'eadache." She mentioned one called Curley Thomas who had lived in Brede. He always had his dogs with him, she said, which ran around and in between the wheels of his old trap as it clopped along. It was a miracle that they were never killed or injured, she reckoned. She cupped her hand to her mouth here and leaned towards the girls and whispered something about him tending to take a bit more than dram or two of whisky than was good for him. She reckoned it was down to his old horses, who knew every bend in every lane for miles around here, that he got home safely from his regular forays into the large towns, mostly Hastings and Battle. She mentioned old Mr Drury, Bill's Father, who before he became a linesman, had also been a Carter. Also a Gordon Thomas who had plied a similar trade. These were mostly men they had heard about but who's occupations they had not really appreciated or concerned themselves with.

She smiled around at the girls as she spoke about Charlie Soan and George Kenward, Nurse Kenward's husband, whose enthusiasm for make do and mending had got a bit out of hand The two men had hatched this ambitious plan to build a large hand cart out of bits and pieces of wood that they had begged borrowed or stolen from in and around the area. The trouble was that by the time they had finished building the thing, they were unable to get it out of Charlie's back garden where this mammoth task had taken place. It had had to be dismantled and re-erected in George's garden where the gateway was wide enough by a whisker to enable them to wheel their pride and joy in and out.

Old Cokey clearly feeling a bit left out of things by this time, thought it was about time he was allowed to put in his own two pen'orth. Unable to contain his apparent hero worship of one fellow in particular it seemed and determined not to be silenced by Mrs Brooman this time, he started talking about a fellow called Jack Hunter, who lived in Bodiam. From the start it was apparent that he was more interested in the man's mode of transportation, a Model T Ford, than he was in the man himself, this modern day Carter. Now she came to think about it, Sally did remember having seen a vehicle fitting the description so glowingly detailed by Cokey, it was sometimes to be seen or heard chugging up Whydown Hill. Also, on one occasion, when she Pat and Hilary had been walking up Ebdens Hill towards Wayside, it had passed them, turning off near the top as it made its way towards the Ridge, the steep bit that had tested dad's leg muscles when he had had to cycle up there to the munitions factory during the war.

After a while Sally's thoughts began to wander as they were wont to do, and she suddenly realised that she had not seen Mrs Brooman's husband Bert for ages now. That man both repelled yet fascinated her with his habit of chewing tobacco, then expelling the residual black liquid from pursed lips in a neat spume of black liquid. She was not sure whether this habit was better or worse than his wife's habit of snorting snuff. She would have to give that question some thought. She had learned recently, that he had done a bit of brick laying at Sylvian, alongside Jessie Kenward, all those years ago. She wondered what he was up to these days.

"We'll have to go now," said Hilary suddenly as she looked across the Green and saw the two boys emerging from the track. Mrs Brooman paused momentarily in her deliberations, her eye following the direction in which Hilary's arm was now pointing. "Well blow me down, if that ain't ole Fred over there Cokey. It's im you've come to see I'll be bound," she said, suddenly noticing the wrinkled old villager standing on the grass. "Silly ole bugger. Now you know why coppers wear chin straps," she uttered, looking back over her shoulder towards her old adversary. He however, remained silent for once, not taking the slightest notice of her comments.

As the girls walked across the road and down over the Green to where Willie and Roy were waiting for them, Mrs Brooman decided not to follow them after all. She probably needed a bit of peace and quiet after all the talking, Sally reckoned and would probably go along to the brooks or just as far as the waterfall to find it. She might even be lucky enough to catch Mr Taylor at the Smithy. He was often to be seen there on a Sunday morning shoeing horses or just working away on an intricate piece of ironwork. Sally looked over her shoulder just the once at the back of the squat figure, retreating slowly down the pathway and for some reason was reminded of what her mum and dad had been talking about only a few days ago. They had mentioned some people -The Wandering Minstrels of old, they had called them and she had been fascinated by the way these people had kept history alive in poetry and song. This was in the days when very few ordinary people were able to read and write, so their contribution to what was now known about ordinary folk, was largely down to them, plus a handful of Diarists according to her parents. By the time they reached the boys, they were talking to old Fred, his flat cap now back on his head and covering his new haircut.

"Old Cokey's on his way, he's been looking for you," said Hilary. And she pointed to the little figure, laden down with the tools of his perceived trade, who was now struggling across the green towards them.

Fred removed his cap and scratched his head as though seeking inspiration for the task that lay ahead. "Er, ah," he said, and then fell silent for a few moments, which was most unusual for this normally garrulous man. "Looks like he be here to swip the grass then," he added after a while, repeating what Mrs Brooman had said when the little man had first made his appearance.

"Well, we'll leave you to it then," said Roy moving hastily away from the old man as Cokey came within spitting distance of the little group. Then he lifted his arm in a kind of salutation as he turned and followed the other youngsters who were now making their way up towards the old pump house. After a quick examination of the seating on both north and south sides of this vernacular building, they decided not to risk their bums on these cold damp surfaces, but would walk up to the Church and back instead. It made more sense to keep on the move in this weather anyway, they told themselves.

They caught a brief glimpse of Mrs Flint in the garden of her little house, which nestled behind Old School Cottage as they walked briskly along the pathway, but had passed by before the little old lady had had even a chance to blink in their direction. As they passed their old School building, they could see Bill Smith hurrying along towards the Church, where he performed some important duties and guessed by the rate at which his long legs were covering the ground that he had cut things a bit fine. The last time Sally had seen this kindly man, he had been suffering from a bout of something called the ague and was shivering uncontrollably. She and Pat had been talking about this man only yesterday if she remembered rightly. She understood that, like Uncle Fred her mum's brother, he had spent part of his war years both in the Middle and the Far East and had caught something called Malaria, a disease spread by a type of mosquito. Once infected with the virus evidently, the effects stayed around and plagued its unfortunate host for many years. It just popped up unannounced catching the person unawares and unprepared.

At one time this man had lived with his grandparents on Church Hill, in one of the old cottages that had decorated the hillside here, but that for some unknown reason had been demolished. Sally reckoned that if they looked closely into the tangle of vegetation that had grown up over the years and taken over the gardens, they would probably find some remnants of these ancient dwellings. She had no idea what had happened to his parents, but what she did know was that when he was demobbed after the war, he had followed in his grandfather George's steps and had become a Postman. Like the old King, he had a speech impediment, a stutter as it was commonly referred to. In spite of this however, this well informed and friendly man, always took the time to pass on his knowledge and experiences of life, using that unique turn of phrase of his. Sally would challenge anyone, be it child or grown up, to resist that chuckle of his; or to ignore that characteristic way he had of angling his head towards the Heavens as he did so.

As the youngster paused briefly beside the steps leading up into the precincts of the Church, they saw Dr Locke and his sisters, Connie and Margaret hurrying up the slope towards them to take part in the morning service, and they moved aside to let them pass. Sally wondered if these two ladies still ran a Sunday School class in the front room of their house in the village. She knew that Freda and Betty had received their religious instruction from them at one time, along with other local youngsters, but that was ages ago now. This family belonged to the higher echelons of village society and as such were treated with a certain degree of respect. They briefly acknowledged the children as they ascended the steps, which led into the house of God and were quickly lost to sight.

After a brief consultation, the youngsters decided to make their way through the Churchyard to the small gate at the far end, and then homeward via Balcombe Green. As they made their way towards this exit, Sally knew without looking at Pat and Hilary that their thoughts were on the same plane as her own. She was aware of the almost imperceptible movement of their heads towards an area of unsanctified ground where their little sister had been buried, and she felt the sadness they were feeling. It was probably her imagination, but the trees and shrubs around here seemed different, as though united by a common bond to protect the innocent victims of this edict on original sin.

It was worth getting a bit scratched and muddied up by taking this route home, Sally reckoned, if only for the spirit lifting beauty of this rural scenery. The pale grey of the sky was accentuated by the early spring sunshine, as were the fields and wooded areas around them. The village itself was lost to their sight from here but as they walked towards Balcombe Green, a view of the imposing building and magnificent grounds of Oak lands Park opened up before them, and before long the village itself came into view.

Thankfully, Cokey Coleman was nowhere to be seen as they walked down through the village and old Fred had also made himself scarce. Mrs Naomi Go Farter however, was walking slowly towards them and although she was profoundly deaf, she could lip read so they stopped to pass the time of day with her. Sally had no idea what her real name was, but guessed that her nick-name had come about either because she seemed unable to control her wind or because she moved everywhere at a snail's pace. Her profound deafness affected her speech, but Willie and Roy who knew this kindly lady well, were able to follow and interpret her words, and to emphasise their own responses with exaggerated lip movements. After a short while, the girls became restless. The time was getting on and they were anxious to be on their way again. As they and the boys took their leave of her, she treated them to one of her widest grins and after responding in kind, they turned and walked away.

Once they reached the bottom of the village, there was a parting of the ways, with the boys making their way towards the footpath at the side of the Tythe Barn, and the girls moving off homewards. They walked briskly passed the Smithy, guiding Pat purposefully away from contemplation of this modest building with its lone occupant, and were soon to and over the river bridge, deciding at this stage to take the low road home. As they passed cow shit corner, the ancient dividing of the ways, Sally looked instinctively to her right where, tucked away in the corner of Mr Farrow's field, a cluster of sweet smelling violets would soon be decorating and perfuming this small area.

When they reached Farrow's steps, the pure clear sound of singing reached their ears, and they knew immediately who the vocalist was. Sure enough, following the sound with their eyes and ears to the garden of Uplyme, they could see Amy pottering around in the front garden As she sang, she snipped off bits of twig here and there from some of the scrubby bushes in its borders, revealing fresh shoots that were already beginning to burst into life. As they paused beside her gate, she stopped singing and came over to speak to them.

"There's this dead rat under one of the bushes over there," she said turning and pointing towards the resting place of the unfortunate rodent. "I think old Rudge's cat must have killed it. That animal thinks it's a tiger, and it's the only thing that I know of that ever got the better of was that old crow that used to strut around in the garden here. Anyway, it reminded me to give my brother's old jacket another airing," she said looking towards the clothesline on which a solitary garment hung limp and lifeless, almost shamefully it seemed to Sally as she followed the line of the pointing finger. As she was talking, Amy opened the gate and moved on to the pathway to stand beside them. "Trust Tony to leave a dead mole in his pocket. After a while it stank to high heaven, it did and it took us ages to find out where the smell was coming from. And the thing still stinks if you get close enough even though mum's washed it a couple of times. That's why I've brought it out here," she added and grinned. "Mr Farrow gives Tony traps to catch the moles with and thruppence for every one he catches in them, and he's got it off to a fine art. What with that and all the other odd jobs he does around the farm, he earns a lot of pocket money. Even so, he was a bit put out that he'd lost the thruppence for the one he'd left in his pocket, but he didn't volunteer to scrape the mouldy, stinky stuff out I noticed He left mum to do that, and she used best part of a bar of Sunlight soap to do it." They all grinned, seeing the funny side of the situation and for Sally at least with relief that she had not been involved with the disposal of this poor, smelly little creature.

"I saw old sniff and spit cycling along here earlier on and his cough's getting worse by the day He worries me he does. And. guess who else I saw, Denis Crow that's who," she continued glancing at Sally as though to gauge her reaction to this bit of information. Sally had seen this youth only a couple of days ago. She had watched from her elevated position on the underground tank at Sylvian as he had free-wheeled down Whydown hill and along New Road, towards Marley Lane on his bicycle. She would recognise him anywhere, and she grinned as she related this sighting of her nemesis to her friend. Although he had shown no sign of having seen her, just before he reached the Bee House, he had pressed down hard on his peddles, raised his bum off the saddle and wiggled it from side to side a few times. A gesture he often used when she was around. Still, the observation, out of sight out of mind, created its own sense of security, and here amongst friends she felt somehow liberated, freed from his slightly disturbing influence.

Leaving Amy to her gardening and contemplation of the dead rodent, they walked on towards Paygate Corner, pausing for a while beside the little cottage there. Uppermost in their minds was a conversation they had had with Neil Farrow recently, when he'd been telling them about the number of vehicles that had careered out of control and into this little cottage. The girls remembered the time a lorry had misjudged the acute angle in the road here, clipped the side of the house knocking out several bricks, and frightening Rosney Edwards and her Gran who were inside at the time, half to death. According to Mr Farrow however, other and even more serious accidents had occurred from time to time, one in particular, when the Budgen family had lived there. This one had also involved a lorry, which according to an eye witness had been travelling like a bat out of hell along the New Road. The driver had braked suddenly as he approached the junction, lost control of the lorry as he turned into the corner at speed and had demolished the front of the cottage. It was a miracle that nobody had been killed that time, he reckoned.

"I already knew about that tank he was talking about, the one that hit the place during the war," said Hilary. "I've mentioned it before, I know I have. It was Ronald who spotted 'CANADA 1944' etched into one of the concrete steps at the front there while we were fetching water from the spring. It was when the water in our old tank got polluted by a dead bird or something and we had to fetch and carry it until dad got it all sorted out. Anyway he, Ronald, found out that some Canadian soldiers had driven their tank into the place and as they were making good the damage, had put that message in one of the steps for some peculiar reason. It's still there I'm sure. We shall have to check it out sometime."

"Mr Farrow's family haven't always been farmers you know," said Pat, returning to the person who had set them out on this train of thought. "I heard him telling dad that his father had had a bakery business in Slough at one time. I pricked my ears up because I remembered you telling me Sally, that dad had worked in a munitions factory during the war in a place called Slough, and reckoned it must have been the same place. Anyway, he, Mr Farrow was on his way up the track to Battle Barn Farm to see Mr Collin's about some 'livestock,' as he called it and me and dad were over the edge of the field seeing to one of the chicken coops. He said he wondered sometimes why his parents had made that decision when they seemed to have made a good living out of bread and such like. Evidently they just packed up everything they had and piled it on to a big truck of some sort and made their way down to Luff's Farm. That was ages ago, back in the olden days, of course and before Mr Farrow had been born. One of his older brothers, Harold, who'd been looking to coming home and playing the church organ again, was killed in the big war. His other brother, Jack, wasn't interested in farming, so it was left up to his dad but mostly to Neil and the farm workers, to keep the farm going. They'd had hops and things in those days. Before the bakery business, he said his dad's family had bred lots of horses, and had lived in a place called Stebbing. I remember the name because of old Mr Stebbings who lives up the road there. But I wondered then why they had needed to make bread, when they could have stayed looking after horses. That's what I would have done."

"Yes you would, we all know that," said Hilary and grinned as she tapped her on the shoulder. "Sometimes though you can't do just what you want because you have to make a living best way you can. The thing I remember him telling us about was the yew tree that was in the front of the old farm house when they had moved there and had just been ignored until one of the sheep had strayed into the garden and decided to sample the thing. It died of course. That stuff's lethal."

"Talking about trees, I remember Mr Farrow chuckling as he was telling dad about the time he caught Tony Taylor, Len Larkin and Arthur Puxty over there," said Pat pausing for a second while she pointed her finger over in the general direction of the Brooks. It was ages ago now. They were so busy shaking the living daylights out of his old conker trees, that they didn't see him coming until the last minute. They tried to scarper but he caught Len, he said and gave him a good old ticking off for damaging his trees. Then as he, Len ran off, Mr Farrow watched and saw him miss his footing as he tried to jump across the river to join the other boys, and he fell right in. The others did come back to drag him out though, with one eye on Mr Farrow of course, who said he'd had to laugh even though he felt a bit sorry for the lad as he called him. He said he didn't mind them taking the conkers but they had been a bit hard on the old trees." They all chuckled, predictably seeing the funny side of this kind of situation then moved on and before they knew it, were beside the cottages in the lane leading up to Sylvian.

That evening Pat and Sally sat around the kitchen table, idly watching their mum as she minced the remains of the shoulder of lamb, ready for tomorrow's dinner. Yummy, yummy. Sally thought, already seeing in her mind's eye a steaming Shepherd's pie taking place, its flavoursome content topped with delicious, crispy mashed potato. She was also keeping a watchful eye on Dorothy and Jacky, or rather on one of mum's ornaments with which they playing - the precious pig with its quizzical, enigmatic look. The sooner it was returned to its rightful place on the shelf of the ornate mirror in the front room the better, Sally thought to herself grumpily, forgetting that she, as a small child, had spent many happy hours playing with the thing. Her attention was suddenly diverted from the little ones, towards mum and Pat who were talking about Betty. She suddenly remembered that this sister of theirs would be home next weekend and her mood changed instantly. Their sister always had a tale about some or other amusing incident she had witnessed. And she always brought presents down with her. The last time, it had been an embroidered tablecloth for mum. She had whispered to Sally that she was making and dressing a couple of Teddy Bears for Dorothy and Jacky but that Sally was to keep that information a secret. She was also making padded coat hangers for her and the other girls, and that she, Sally could choose from pink or blue satin or from a pretty floral cotton design, all made up from off cuts of material from her place of work. Sally could not wait. For now though, she had more mundane things to do like cleaning her muddy shoes in readiness for school tomorrow.

Chapter 2

There was a blackbird in the garden, its chops full of maggots and worms. Sally watched from the kitchen window as it hopped around moving its little head this way and that, apparently oblivious to all except the task it was performing. This apparent nonchalance was deceptive however, as she well knew. At the first sign of trouble, be it the shape of a human being or their cat, or even a movement from behind a pane of glass, and the little creature would be up and gone in an instant. For the moment though, it seemed content to quarter the garden, picking up the soft squiggly creatures, on which to feed its babies no doubt. She stood very still as she observed the little bird, its scruffy plumage an indication of the relentless nature of the task it was performing - the all-consuming business of feeding its hungry, demanding brood. She had noticed that some birds performed a kind of dance movement over the ground. When she had mentioned this observation to her mum, she had been told that it was apparently done to trick worms into thinking it was raining and that in fear of drowning, they would pop up near the surface of the ground where the wily little birds would gobble them up. Even the green woodpecker it seemed performed this tactical ritual. As she cocked her head to one side to catch the far away but unmistakable notes of a lone cuckoo, the little blackbird was up and off the garden, lost to sight in the blink of an eyelid.

She paused for a split second before moving swiftly away from the window, sucking the remnants of the Gibb's Dentifrice toothpaste noisily from around her teeth as she did so. Chop, chop. This won't get the poe's emptied, she mouthed silently to herself as she moved towards the scullery to pick up the freshly scrubbed containers for the milk. At least when that cow arrived she would not have to collect the milk from Battle Barn Farm, she thought to herself, forgetting for the moment that she was in line to be one of the milk-maids with arguably more incursion into her spare time that that addition to the family would make. It was all down to Uncle Fred Sansom now, this finding and purchasing of a suitable animal. Although comparatively new to the area, having recently moved himself and his family into Wayside with their gran, he already knew his way around the local cattle markets and could haggle and bargain with the best of them. Anyway, that was as maybe and for the future, she thought. For now though, there were chores to be done before she could even think about that planned trip into Hastings this morning with Hazel, Pat and Hilary. Luckily the tank in the loft had not yet announced its desire for a refill, with that characteristic low, ominous, boom, which always reminded her of some mythological monster baying for human flesh, and she held her breath as she crept past the pump housing and out through the scullery door.

As she hurried along the farm track to collect the milk, she glanced towards the perimeter of the wood where the old caravan, now camouflaged by lush early summer growth, still nestled harmoniously within the protecting trees. Immediately a little ditty came to mind and she began to recite it silently to herself:

> '*I wish I lived in a caravan, with a horse to ride like a peddler man.*
> *Where he comes from nobody knows, or where he goes to, but on he goes.*'

The old caravan and its occupant were now clearly here to stay, but who knew what adventures they had had or what far away and interesting places they had visited in their long association. Her imagination took her away from her immediate surroundings, and she was transported back to her infant days when Mrs Vallor had read them instalments from the magical books entitled, 'The Lands of far beyond.' and she found herself in a world of magic and make believe. She knew without even looking, that the clattering and clanging coming from one of the large farm buildings on her right hand side was the sound of Miss Collins preparing feed for the animals, feathered and furred, this tall angular lady working as hard as any man and in all weathers. Sally knew the routine of this old farm off by heart.

Before she knew it, she was in the kitchen of the farmhouse chatting comfortably with Mrs Collins, while her imagination continued to transport her across deserts and oceans to lands mysterious and far away. She was conscious of and quite disturbed by the wheezing of this thin, asthmatic and kindly old lady however, and her mind returned to this as she made her way carefully back across the stile on her way home with the milk. As she retraced her steps back across the field, she began to take breaths of fresh air deep into her lungs then exhaled them out again noisily, grateful for the ease with which her lungs responded to the task that seemed to be beyond the scope of the lady she had just left and who had spoken to her with such difficulty. Suddenly, she became aware of the two containers with their contents, swinging precariously from side to side and immediately moderated her pace and exaggerated breathing. It would never do to arrive home having spilled even a portion of this precious liquid.

As she rounded the corner of the house towards the scullery, the unmistakable sound of water being pumped from the underground tank up into the header one reached her ears, and she muttered a rude word under her breath. When however, she moved closer, and could make out Hazel's clear and measured tone counting out the tally, she breathed a sigh of relief. "Seven hundred and sixty two, seven hundred and sixty three," she was up to, and the counting continued. By the time she had deposited the milk and had rubbed the stiffness away from her arms, the old tank would have been well and truly satisfied, she reckoned. Once again her sister had saved her bacon.

By the time Hilary arrived on the scene, the chores were done, the sandwiches cut and placed in Hazels bag and there was still time for the three girls to call for Patty Winchester, who with a bit of luck and time permitting, would be joining them on their trip into Hastings. Hazel, who was in the process of changing her frock, said she would join them at the bus stop. They hammered on the front door of Brookside, the little cottage in Crazy Lane, which was opened almost immediately by a flustered Patty, hair brush in one hand, and it was clear from her general demeanour that she was running out of time.

"You'll have to go without me. I've still got things to do," she shouted, having to make herself heard above the overall chatter and noise coming from within the house. "Mum's working this afternoon, so I've got to look after the little one's anyway," she added clearly disappointed at this lost opportunity to peruse the big shops in Hastings. As the girls stood just inside the open doorway, commiserating with their friend, Sally could see Mr Winchester's old Army jacket and kit bag, still hanging up behind the lavatory door, where they had been deposited and where they had stayed from the time he had been demobbed until now. A packet of Oxydol soap powder stood on the floor nearby, as though it had been used recently then placed there by hands that had hastened off to 'do' the next chore.

By the time the three girls made their way towards the bus stop, Hazel was already standing beside Lavender Cottage, looking down the road to where the bus was due to appear at any moment and then back towards the girls who were now hurrying towards her.

"How's that for timing then," said Hilary pointing towards Paygate Corner where the bus, slow and lumbering was making its way around the sharp bend in the road. "I just hope we can get seats together and so forth. We'll just have to get the boys to move about a bit if we can't, that's all," she added and grinned as she stepped up on to the bus, mounting the steps up onto the top deck two at a time.

As the bus passed Wayside, Sally glanced instinctively over the hedge and into the front garden. The first thing she noticed were the delphiniums standing tall and willowy within the borders, the dark blue of their foliage a contrast to the paler blue of the sky. She was vaguely disappointed that gran was not to be seen, pottering about amongst her beloved flowers, nor was any other member of the family to be seen either, if it came to that. But as she was bound to be visiting Wayside in the not too distant future, she was not too put out.

Further along the way, Hazel pointed in the direction of a shop with faded lettering on the wooden shuttering over its large plate glass window. She began to reminisce about the days when mum had walked Freda, Betty and herself all the way to this shoe shop, owned and operated by the kind and portly and competent Mr Apps, and the best shoe shop for miles around as far as she was concerned. Well, mum walked all the way, she said, pushing one or other of them to and from Silverhill in the pram. The only exception was up the steep and endless Ebden's Hill. There were always stories on the journey home, most of which remembered even now, she added and sighed nostalgically.

A few people left the bus en route, but the vehicle was stuck with most of its human cargo until it reached Wellington Square, where with a sigh of relief it disgorged them into and onto the sloping by-way. Many of the chattering children made their way towards Woolworths to spend a few coppers on cheap sweets and nick-nacks. The girls were not far behind, and finding the aroma of hot salted peanuts irresistible, followed their noses towards the kiosk, where Hazel parted with a shiny sixpence in exchange for a massive greaseproof cone filled to the gunnels with the crunchy delights. By the time she turned away from the kiosk, the other girls had lined up behind her and were standing, cupped hands at the ready waiting for a share

Still munching away, they made their way slowly through the store and out through the back entrance towards the public toilets. They paused at the top of the concrete steps for just long enough to lick the residual bits of nut and salt from around their fingers, then after wiping their hands quickly down their frocks, descended into the damp gloomy depths of the lavatory. This place, a facsimile of the one at Silverhill, reminded Sally of the chamber of horrors at Madame Tousauds. It also brought Rupert and his mates to mind and their grim association with deep dark dungeons, and she shivered as she sat down warily on the edge of the lavvy seat. She could not get out of this dark place quick enough she thought as she pulled up her knickers with undue haste, and beat a hasty retreat towards the stairway. Her first action on resurfacing was to gulp fresh air deep down into her lungs.

After leaving this place of musty odours and residual whiffs of Jeyes fluid, they made their way towards Mastin's, and after perusing the display in its window for a while, they went inside. The first thing they saw amongst the notices just inside the doorway of this multi-purpose store, was one advertising a service for the repair of ladders in stockings. 6d per ladder was the charge for this service, presumably regardless of the length of the offending snag, a fair price they reckoned. Sally however, was more interested in looking for a pair of navy blue knickers with pockets in the legs. The ones she had inherited from Hazel all those years ago were threadbare and as her sister now preferred something lighter and more feminine, that source of procurement was no longer available. She made their way towards and up to the lingerie department, and after searching through the underwear without success, examined the pink, long legged flock ones, tastefully displayed at one side of the plate glass counter. They were old granny ones, for likes of Granny Cotton and also old Mrs Blundell, who allegedly, wore hers when she attended one of the cricket matches in the grounds close by. She would not be seen dead in them. Nor did she fancy those Cami-knicker things, which were displayed at the other end of the counter. They were far too flimsy. They'd be useless for storing apples when they went scrumping, and not much good when they went tree climbing either. What did take her eye as they walked around the store though was a multi-coloured shirred-elastic swim suit, which clung flatteringly to the figure of the alabaster white dummy on which it was displayed. Now this was something she really could do with she told herself. Dad might even lend her the money to buy one and she could pay him back when her hop picking money came through. Her old navy blue one, second or even third hand by the time she got it, was far too small for her now anyway.

As they wandered back through the store, they stopped to watch the strange method of cash transaction, operated within this store and which never ceased to fascinate them. At the press of a button, the cylinder shaped contraption into which the shop assistant placed the money given to her by a customer, cranked swiftly and noisily across the room above their heads then disappeared from sight. After a short interval, it reappeared with the change and receipt, which was retrieved by the assistant and handed to the customer for inspection. It was several minutes before the girls dragged themselves reluctantly away from contemplation of this noisy but effective method of cash transaction. As Hazel reminded them, they would get another chance to see similar machines in operation when they got to the Plummer Roddis Store.

After leaving Mastin's, they made their way towards the Arcade, their sights set on Queen's road and Wilshin's, the next store on their list. Hazel and Hilary were looking for frocks and as they hurried along, were talking about the white linen one Freda had bought there recently. Embroidered on and around its full skirt was crinoline lady along with birds and flowers and other ornamentation. It had a tight bodice with a nipped in waist and looked so good on her that Joy Phillips had bought its twin, having first persuaded her dad to part with the exorbitant sum of six ponds to pay for it. Once into Wilshin's, they made their way towards the stairway and up to the first floor, where they picked their way carefully and slowly through the displays of frocks and skirts. There were one or two Mannequins dotted around the place, all tastefully decked out in various garb, and some with arms raised as though in silent prayer. For the most part however, the frocks and skirts hung limply from hangers hooked over the long silver coloured rails. Pat and Sally moved on, hesitating briefly beside a counter, with cubby holes behind it into which had been neatly stacked an assortment of blouses, folded neatly and packed in cellophane wrappers. They were not particularly interested in them or in any other item of clothing on display around here though they decided, preferring the familiarity of the clothes they already possessed. Now if Sally had been able to replicate that old yellow top of hers that had disappeared so mysteriously all that time ago, she told her sister, then that would be a different matter. She still missed the thing, even after all this time.

"You ready then?" asked Pat as she and Sally walked back over to where the other girls were still searching for a bargain from amongst the various garments that hung shapelessly from the silvered rails. The reply came with a nod after a further rapid search for a bargain, missed first time around, proved unsuccessful.

"Ok then, we'll just go and have a quick look in Posner's before we go to Plummer's to look for your knickers, Sal, shall we," said Hilary, looking back over her shoulder one last time as she moved towards the stairway. "Talking about knickers, do you remember the last time we came down to Hastings and had a look round Alston's the Corsetry shop?" she continued. "That poster about Aertex Corsetry they had in there was good wasn't it. 'Let your body breathe.' 'Achieve bosom grace and perfect health,' it said. And there was a picture of this slim woman with her arms up in the air in it, wearing some contraption or other. I love posters like that, don't you?"

"They don't do much for me I must admit," said Pat. "Maybe when I have to wear a brassiere and things to keep my stockings up I'll be more interested, but I doubt it. So it's Posner's next is it then, to see what their frocks and things are like, then on to Plummer's to look for your knickers Sal. Come on then." And she moved purposely off, the others following in her wake.

After browsing around the area of skirts and dresses in Posner's store for a short while, Hazel and Hilary decided that there was nothing here within their budget that also took their fancy, and they left the store empty handed. They made their way towards the Albert Memorial, and paused for a few moments alongside the antiquated building as they always did when visiting this part of town. This monument, with its Gothic style turrets, always evoked a solemn reaction from them, which was not surprising really. It had been erected in memory of Prince Albert, whose premature death had left his wife Queen Victoria bereft, grief stricken. It was said that even though she had lived on into a ripe old age, she had never got over the death of her Consort, her soul mate. A memorial to this illustrious lady had been erected at Warrior Square, where her image, upright and dignified, now stood on its pedestal looking across and out to sea. The war memorial or memorials to commemorate allied forces killed in those dreadful wars, had been erected elsewhere, one near the Pier the other in Alexandra Park, the latter where most of the ceremonies took place. Both were prominent structures, situated where they would be a constant and daily reminder of ultimate sacrifice. Many folk in Sedlescombe would have preferred a similar memorial in respect of the sacrifice of their own dear ones to have been erected on the village green, where it would be a daily reminder of sacrifice, rather than the plaque, inscribed with their names that was tucked away on the wall of the Church.

"Do you mind if we look in Jepson's before we go to Plummer's," asked Hilary as they moved slowly away from the Memorial. "Someone told me I might be able to get one of those new Biro pens in there. He reckoned they were invented for the Pilots to use in the war. Well, that'd make sense I suppose. He said they'd gone down in price now. I think he said they'd been as much as fifty five shillings or something when they first came out in the shops. No, he might have said ten and six, I can't quite remember. Anyway, whatever, I couldn't afford to buy one at either price."

Jepson's, with its beautiful ornate stairway sold what was referred to as 'fancy goods,' and within this remit were to be found just a small selection of pens, paper, rubbers and such like. The girls, studiously ignoring the fine displays of wool, material, cottons and silks etc., which dominated the lower area of the store, made their way to the rather more unobtrusive stationary section, where their eyes immediately alighted on a shelf, decorated with a small but neat display of the magic Biro pens with their seemingly endless supply of ink. They were tantalizingly close but just out of reach of inquisitive fingers, and as Hilary leaned over the counter to study the shape and price of these curious pens, her eyes lit up.

"That's better, that's a price I can afford," she said as she swivelled back round towards them, her face wreathed in smiles. "I don't expect I'll be allowed to use one at School though do you, but that doesn't matter. At least I'll be able to write all my letters and so forth with it without getting ink all over the place, and you girls can borrow it as well if you want to. Come to thin k of it, I could afford to buy you one as well Sal"

"What about me buying one for all of us," said Hazel, having summed up the cost of the pens and set that against the money in her purse. "I can afford it. We use them at work now, apart from Mr Thomas that is. He still uses his fountain pen. It's a Parker pen, just like the one I remember Jumbo James using when I was at School. I expect he's still using it. And I expect he's still got the little box it came in. They last for ever they do." Then she grinned as the girls, at first lost for words, began to talk and thank her all at the same time.

As they made their way back across the store towards the exit having purchased the precious pens, Hazel pointed towards a poster, which had been fixed to the wall alongside the ornate stairway, and the other girls paused to study the picture. It was a scene of quiet enchantment, with two little figures in pinafores, working away patiently and happily at the task of painting flowers. They were colouring them in, in the most delicate pastel shades, their little faces wearing an expression of complete absorption in their task. One of the little elfin like figures was standing on a milking stool, stretching up to decorate the top most blooms, while the other contented itself with decorating the lower daisy like flowers. Sally grinned to herself. These little figures looked just like the ones that according to mum, snuck into the house at night and tidied away the accumulation of the day's activities, casually left behind when she and her sisters went to bed. They cleaned and polished the house while the children slept soundly in their beds, using little fairy dusters rather than the paint brushes being held daintily by the fairy folk in this picture. After close scrutiny of this enchanting picture, they moved slowly away towards the doorway and back out into Robertson Street.

As they made their way towards the Plummer Roddis store, the aroma of freshly baked scones, toasted tea cakes and other mouth-watering delicacies wafted along the street. Then the smell of fresh fish assailed their nostrils, telling them that that both the Creamery tea rooms and Mac-fishery's the fish shop just along the street were open for business.

"Plummer's is busy today," said Pat as a buzz of activity met them as they passed through the doorway and into the large interior. "Mind you, they sell just about anything and everything, don't they, so you're bound to get your knickers here Sal. We just need to find the underwear section, that's all and it could be anywhere.

"Follow me, I know where it is. I used to come here quite often when Freda worked here," said Hazel. And she made her way through a maze of aisle's, passing counters displaying various items of clothing, cosmetics and other sundries, with the other girls following closely in her footsteps. In no time at all, they were standing in the lingerie department, examining the items on display here. Sally spotted the navy blue interlock knickers straight away, and her eyes lit up when on close scrutiny, she discovered not one but two pockets neatly sown onto the legs of this utilitarian garment. And, she could afford to purchase two pairs, how about that she remarked as she read the price tag. This store she knew used the same method of cash transaction as Mastin's, the first store they had visited, and as she passed her money over to the assistant, she watched as the cylinder was loaded with her money and then cranked its way high above her head before disappearing from sight. She kept her eyes glued to the spot watching for the canister to reappear, and in spite of her anticipation of this event, jumped as it was propelled suddenly from its housing, arriving at its destination with a shake and a shiver. This contraption was called a Lamson Vacuum Cash Transfer System she had discovered, a worthy name for a grand machine she reckoned. After a swift examination, the assistant handed the contents of the cylinder and the brown bag containing the knickers, over to Sally, with a smile that turned up the corners of her mouth ever so slightly but did not quite reach her eyes.

Leaving Plummer Roddis behind them, they made their way towards the seafront along Robertson Street, looking in all the shop windows as they went.

They sniffed appreciatively as the smell of freshly milled and percolated coffee reached their nostrils, following its delicious aroma to the frontage of Caves Café. The peeling façade of this tall impressive building was echoed in the other buildings in this parade, adding to the gentle charm of this substantial terrace of sea facing buildings, which were 'indicative' of an earlier era. They spent several minutes looking through the large plate glass windows, admiring its green and gold Décor, its wicker chairs and glass topped tables.

Had they not seen the place, they would have known all about its décor. Mum had worked in this genteel Café years ago when she was young, and had told them about Sir Henry Rider Haggard, who when he dined there, always asked that she should serve him. He had been a very elderly man even then, and had lived in a part of Hastings called Maze Hill. The coffee here was always served in heavy earthenware pots, and evidence of this sat on the sideboard in the front room at home. This squat, green and beige coloured receptacle had been given to mum by Miss Yates who had been manageress and part owner of this establishment and for whom mum had worked. They had remained friends until the old lady died having spent her last few weeks living at Sylvian and being cared for by mum.

Just a few paces further along the way, they paused outside another building, and stood in silent contemplation of the roundels, filled to the gunnels with postcards. There was a comprehensive display of local scenes here, but the girls were more interested in the ones on display inside. Although of equal age and design as Caves café, this building somehow lacked the old world charm of the building they had just been admiring.

They passed through the large open doorway of the shop and into a world brimming with postcards and 'kiss me quick' hats, paper and string and lots more, where they joined a group of noisy youngsters, obviously lured into this shop by the titillation of its huge array of saucy postcards. The girls stood for a while in silent contemplation of the capers of the youngsters as they jostled one another, vying for the best view of naked flesh and overt innuendo. After a while most of this noisy group of youngsters moved away, chuckling as they shared the best jokes and recounted the most risqué captions, their language enough to singe the hairs off a dogs back, as Hilary whispered in Sally's ear. Once the bodies had thinned out and there was enough space to accommodate them all, the girls moved forward to take a peek at the luridly colourful and smutty postcards that decorated such a large area of this shop.

There were paintings of smiling fat ladies with their bottoms and bosoms spilling out of totally inadequate swimsuits, and ones of equally fat men, bending over to expose bums that were grotesque - to say the least. There was one that showed a group of boys performing a two fingered whistle towards a shapely young woman who, passing on the opposite side of the road, had turned and was looking provocatively back over her shoulder at them. Another showed a young lady sitting at a typewriter, her long shapely legs being ogled by a man with a silly grin on his face. Yet another showed a man, belt fastened precariously beneath a fat belly scratching his head as he asked, 'has anyone seen my little Willie?' while in the background, a scruffy haired boy, an impish grin on his face, is peeping over a hedge right behind him. Some of the illustrations and captions on these cards were explicit with very little left to the imagination. Others however, were more suggestive, the puzzled frowns on the faces of the girls, a clear indication that most of them went right over their heads. The card that really caught their attention and drew a few 'ahs' from the girls, was the one in which a cheeky terrier, bum and tail in the air, front paws parallel to the ground, was tugging away furiously at the pants of a small boy, revealing his very rosy bottom. The expression of comic consternation on the face of this child was so funny that in spite of themselves, the girls began to giggle.

After a while, they drifted slowly away from these depictions of mirth and merriment, their eyes drawn towards an amusing but rather different set of postcards. These cards were overflowing with scenes of a rustic nature, with stylised farmer Giles characters, and farm animals in various and mostly improbable stances and guises. Amongst these cards, was a picture of a milkmaid, wearing a long white pinafore over a blue and white check dress as she sat on a three legged stool pulling on the teets of a short fat cow. The animal, happily munching away on fresh hay as the girl performed this ritual, had its head turned sideways, a quizzical look on its face as it surveyed its audience. The card that particularly took their eye however, was one with the caption, 'All the day as oi makes the 'ay. Oi be thinkin' of ee. That's 'ow oi be.' Standing in the foreground and grinning out at them, was a little man wearing a smock and a floppy green hat, his feet clad in cut down gum boots that seemed to be several sizes too big for his diminutive size. He carried a pitchfork as he stood proudly to attention, its sharp prongs angled ever so slightly towards the untidy heap of hay behind him, which was clearly awaiting his attention.

"It's no good, we'll have to go," said Sally after a while. "What time is it anyhow?"

"Three 'airs past a freckle," said Pat quick as a flash and Sally grinned before turning towards Hazel who rewarded her with a proper answer.

As they were leaving the shop, they glanced back just once more towards the stacks of cards, which were still surrounded by a considerable, and by the sound of it, appreciative audience.

A strong smell of mothballs assailed the girl's nostrils as they entered The Misses Cook and Pipers shop a few doors away from the card shop, and they wrinkled their noses in distaste. As they moved further into the shop, they realised that the pong was coming from an old lady who was looking through the fine displays of embroideries for which this shop was famous. They held their breath as they hurried passed her, making their way towards the section, which housed the materials needed to create these works of art, and stopped beside a tall, segmented unit. The long shallow drawers slid smoothly and silently along the casters as they slid them carefully one by one from their housing to examine the assorted embroidery silks inside, each hank held neatly together with its black girdle. Sally was short of green. In fact she was right out of that colour and had already 'borrowed' some from Freda. She also needed one or two other colours and along with the other girls, began to examine each tray with a critical eye, removing the silks one by one after carefully selecting the right shade. Before they made their way to the cash register to pay for their silks, they began to make their customary tour of this extraordinary shop. The whiff of mothballs was still in the air, but the old lady herself was nowhere to be seen and the girls moved freely around the displays of needlework, commenting on the patience and expertise that had gone into the making of these exquisitely embroidered pieces.

After a while, they moved reluctantly away from these works of art towards a tall impressive looking cash machine and the grey haired lady who stood beside it, half turned away from them as she sorted through a pile of various gage cross-stitch material on the counter beside her. (They had never been able to work out who was the Miss Cook and who the Miss Piper, but that had never seemed to matter). The bun tied neatly at the back of her neck disappeared as she turned to face them and she smiled as the girls placed their collection of assorted silks on the counter in front of her. She talked to them about this and that as she totted up the sum of their individual purchases, then placed the silks carefully into crisp white paper bags. The cash register clanked and squeaked as she opened it, and the coins chinked as she placed them into the individual compartments within this ancient receptacle.

After stowing their purchases carefully away in the Rexine bag, they moved towards and through the open doorway of the shop, then crossed the road and the promenade and stood in silence, resting their arms on the iron railings in front of them, as they looked out to sea. The tide was out with a few individuals digging in the sand or splashing about on the outer edges of the waves. A few clouds drifted slowly across the sky as though awaiting the arrival of the hot summer days, when the beach would be heaving with bodies, transforming the area in front of their eyes into one colourful animated entity.

Having decided that this was as good a place as any to assuage their hunger, Hazel rummaged around in one of her bags for the packs of sandwiches, and as she handed them around to the girls, she grinned. In seconds the packages had been unwrapped, the contents being despatched with gusto. "You hungry?" she asked with seeming innocence. But the girls ignored the comment, continuing to chew away at their feast with obvious pleasure.

They contemplated the sea, sand, sea-gulls and paddling individuals as they ate their sandwiches, then after a while their attention was drawn inevitably towards the Pier, where the chatter of excited voices could be heard over and above the chunk and whine of the penny machines. They watched the constant flow of bodies around the popular attractions, most of which were decked out with flags and banners. Some of these decorations had been there since the end of war celebrations, but others had been added quite recently. If Sally remembered rightly, the captured German Field Marshall Goering's, Mercedes Benz motor car had been driven along the sea front recently and the new decorations had most likely been added to the buildings on the Pier to celebrate this event. It was not long before the girls began to talk about their own, individual experiences around the miserly machines housed in one or other of the Pier's ornate buildings.

"Blow me down, just when you get that grippy thing in the right place and you try to pick up what you're after, really carefully, the blooming thing lets it go and then whizzes off back to the top of the machine again and sits there like a praying mantis" said Hilary. "It happens every time, no matter how near you are to getting a prize. I reckon it's fixed. It's all done on purpose. It's not just me it happens to. I've seen lots of other kids get that close and then not get a prize. A swizzle I call it."

They all joined in, relating with ever increasing volume of voice and animated hand movements, similar tales of woe when trying to extract a prize from these mean machines. Just as the coveted prize came within a whisker of a grasping claw or was being urged towards the aperture at the side of the machine by its long metal bar, the whole mechanism would come to a shuddering halt, their precious coins gobbled up and disappearing into the bowels of the thing with a sickening clatter. Then the bar would withdraw and the claw would click back into the preying mantis position, ready for its next victim.

After a while, they began to discuss the techniques used in the building of this pier. They tried to guess how far down into the sand and rock the thick iron palings would have been driven in order to support this heavy, ornate construction, and how the task would have been carried out. At the far end, even allowing for the daily ebb and flow of the tide, the sand and rock would always be submerged beneath several feet of water. Excavating holes deep and wide enough to accommodate such massive iron supports would have been difficult enough under such conditions, but what about the cement, a crucial ingredient in holding these posts in place. It would have been nigh on impossible to get the stuff to set, wouldn't it? They could not find a solution to that one. What they did agree on however, was that the designers though clever, had, had the easier task. The labourers had certainly drawn the short straw.

As they moved away from the railings, Sally's eyes moved eastwards to where the old castle stood in ancient dignity on the skyline. Then she grinned as, squinting to counteract the brightness of the sky, another image hit her between the eyes. "Here what does that old Castle up there remind you of?" she asked, her finger now following the direction of her half closed eyes. In the silence that followed her question, she replied. "The gapped teeth of some old Medieval witch of course. What else."

"You and your imagination. I don't know where you get it from," replied Hilary, clicking her tongue against her teeth and immediately moving on to another more pressing issue. "I'm really thirsty. How about going to Demarco's to get a cold drink before we go to the Chemist's. You can't beat a glass of water when you're really thirsty, but we've drunk all the tapperline. It's not far from Demarco's to either Boot's or Timothy Whites, and I can get what I want from either place."

They crossed back over the road, and as Sally looked towards the tall buildings, which housed Caves Café and the cluster of shops housed within the lower storey's of this impressive terrace, an article she had seen in one of her uncle, Frank Johnson's, publications popped into her mind. She had noticed it while she had been staying with him and Aunty Cis in London, ages ago now but she could still picture it in her mind's eye. 'The peeling façade of some Edwardian sea front hotel,' was the caption beneath an illustration of a row of buildings that were remarkably similar to the ones right in front of her eyes. She had remembered the words for their rhythm rather than content, but she now began to look at these buildings in a different way, with an appreciation for their quiet dignity. Uncle Frank, she began to realise, had a wide collection of interesting, informative books. When she had shown an interest in one particular tome on 19th Century art, he had taken the illustrated book down from the shelf and had sat with her, examining these colourful reproductions. He had then discussed with her the difference styles represented within its many pages. Like her dad, he could be rather gruff at times, but he was also very articulate, his enthusiasm for a subject close to his heart, very contagious. He had certainly sparked an interest, an appreciation of art in its many different forms and representation in her at the time and for that she was grateful.

Once in Robertson Street, they quickened their pace and were very soon retracing their steps back towards then past the Memorial with the usual straggle of bodies milling around this illustrious land mark. They hurried passed Sainsbury's, sniffing appreciatively as the familiar mixture of smells coming through the open doorway hit their nostrils, the aroma of bacon predominating, followed closely by the creamy smell of butter and cheese. This food store always seemed to be jammed packed with women and children who after queuing at one counter, moved on to the next to purchase other items on their grocery list.

Very soon other familiar smells and sounds, coming from the open doorway of Demarco's Café, reached their ears. The aroma of coffee, different somehow from the freshly roasted variety to be sniffed at when passing Caves Café, was mixed up with the smell of freshly toasting tea-cakes and bacon sandwiches. The chink of cutlery on china and of cups being placed on saucers was accompanied by the characteristic hum of verbal intercourse, as folk indulged in a rare moment of relaxation before returning to the hum drum routine of everyday life.

"There's Jesus over there," whispered Sally, indicating with the merest movement of her head, the lone man sitting in his usual seat in the far corner of the Café. His name was Mr Boag as they well knew, but for obvious reasons he had acquired this exulted nickname sometime back in the dim and distant past. An air of dignity shone through the long unkempt hair and even longer beard worn by this tall angular man. Even the shabby overcoat he wore year on year, summer and winter added to an impression of genteel decay. As he sat in the corner supping his mug of tea, he looked for all the world like some character from a Hogarth painting, a bit like Deffy and Bill really Sally reckoned and she grinned to herself at the observation. No wonder Granpy had had such a rapport with this man. They had much in common!

"I wonder if he still lives in that little old sentry hut, up beside the railway line," Hazel whispered as they made their way to the counter to order their drinks. Before the others had a chance to reply however, Mr Demarco was in front of them, smiling broadly and asking, as he always did, after the health and wellbeing of their mum. He had known their mother from way back, from the time she had worked in Caves Café all those years ago in fact but they mostly communicated these days through the medium of the girls.

"All the men who work on the trains know him," Hazel continued, once they had made themselves comfortable around the only table unoccupied in this busy, popular café and had carefully stowed their shopping bags around their feet. Although she kept her eyes deliberately away from the figure sitting in his corner seat, quietly supping away at his drink, they knew to whom she was referring. "They, the men on the foot plate and such like, even chuck a bit of coal off to him now and again as they pass by, and I think generally keep an eye on him. At one time he lived in a bit of copse wood right near the railway line, in a shack thing he'd made himself. Granpy told me that, years ago. He also told us that he, Mr Boag, goes up to St Helen's Hospital now and again for a bath. Well, he did then and I expect he still does He'd still need to go somewhere for one, wouldn't he?"

They chatted for a while as they supped their drinks, their initial thirst having been assuaged in the first few urgent mouthfuls. From this vantage point near the large window of the cafe, they could see the comings and goings of the buses in Wellington Square, with passengers alighting from or stepping up into these lumbering transporters.

"Pity we won't have time to go along to the old town today," Hilary was saying. "Your cousin Eddie was telling us about all the twittens along there that were used by the smugglers in the olden days. He also mentioned something I'd never heard of before called cat creeps, but I forgot to ask him what they were. I expect he'll be down again in the summer again though, though won't he? We'll bring him down here and then he can show us where they are and what they all look like. Should be quite interesting."

"Yes, he'll be down again this summer, with Aunty Nellie and Uncle Tom and the rest of the family," replied Hazel. "Mum was talking about them the other day. She also said that her brother, the other Uncle Tom, and Aunty Annie would be coming down as well. Maybe they'll all come at the same time. Now that really would be a laugh. I like the way Uncle Tom, mum's brother, always refers to mum as 'our Doll' and to Aunty Nellie as 'our Nell,' don't you? Anyway, getting back to the old town and the passages and things that were used by the smugglers in the olden days. Well, they used twittens as Eddie said and we know all about them. There's plenty around where we live and we use them all the time. Cat creeps as far as I can remember, are narrow alleyways or walkways, just like twittens but with steps leading up and down them. I remember Jumbo James telling us something about them one time when the weather was too wet for us to play outside. That was years ago now but I'm sure that's what he said they were."

"He's very knowledgeable. I can't remember any of us kids asking him anything that he didn't know the answer to," said Pat. "Only the other day one of the boys asked him something about the Great War, and he gave him an answer straight away, and more besides. Not that a lot of us kids knew what he was on about most of the time but it did make me think. Some awful things happened in that war, didn't they? So many people were killed and injured, he told us that. At the end he said something about if people could get around a table and sort things out after a war, why couldn't they do the same before starting the thing and killing all those young men. Well why don't they? I don't know. Anyway, we'd best make a move I suppose. We've still got to go to the chemist's to get that cream you want Hilary. What's it called?"

"Snow-fire cream. It's the best thing there is for chapped hands and so forth," replied Hilary. "Well Vaseline's just as good I suppose, but it's a bit greasy. I use that, Vaseline I mean, on my face when I go to bed sometimes, especially when there's been a cold wind and my cheeks feel sore. Anyway, as you say, we'd best make a move or we'll be late home for our dinner and that wouldn't do. Sally's like a bear with a sore head when she's hungry," she added grinning as she looked towards her friend.

As they shuffled their way off the closely packed seats and stooped to gather up their bags, Sally cast one more surreptitious glance towards the old man sitting at the far end of the café, and to her consternation, found that he was looking her right in the eye. As though he realised her discomfiture, the corners of his mouth lifted ever so slightly, and in a split second, his slow, enigmatic smile, seemed to convey some secret message towards her, and she felt an instinctive empathy with the old fellow. There was more to this man than could be realised by his outward appearance of that she was sure. It was a pity she had not thought to ask Granpy more about him before he, her great uncle, had died and taken all his knowledge with him, but that was life as she'd heard her dad say more than once. So be it. No doubt in due course her imagination would supply her with a plausible though highly unlikely life history, experiences and identity of this scruffy but intriguing man.

Every shop seemed to have its own individual, characteristic smell. From old Mrs Floyd's shop in Kent Street where the overriding and most powerful smell was a mixture of paraffin and candle wax, right up to the delicately perfumed aroma of the Plummer Roddis store. Each was however, in its own way just as agreeable. Here in Timothy Whites and Taylor's, the sensation of talcum powder, the pungent smell of cough mixture and sundry balms, created an aromatic whole that was truly satisfying.

Sally's eyes flipped from one display to another as she contemplated the vast array of goods on show and readily available from this chemist shop. There seemed to be a cure or remedy for every ill or ailment here. 'Bile beans – for Radiant HEALTH and a lovely figure,' was the first display that caught her eye. The words on these bottles puzzled her a bit. How on earth could such a little bean or pill live up to that kind of exulted commendation?

Next to the Bile beans was a smaller display of Carter's little liver pills, with similar claims about its efficacy, the specific benefits to those who imbibed a course of this physic, spelled out clearly on the accompanying poster. Luckily, she did not recognise a need in herself for a course of these deadly looking pellets.

Her eyes moved inquisitively on to where, hanging up behind the counter, she could see a neat display of bottles labelled, 'Glycerine, Lemon and Ipecacuanha,' and 'Tincture of Ipecacuanha.' The bottles hung suspended from a rectangle of cardboard, each one isolated from its neighbour and held firmly in place by threads of thin, strong elastic. She had sampled these syrupy cough and cold remedies several times in the past and liked the taste and sensation of the stuff. In fact there was a half empty bottle of the former, in the white metal medicine cabinet in the scullery at home. She had noticed it there recently when she had been looking for the bottle of Witch Hazel she needed to take the itch out of a nasty horse fly bite.

There were small bottles of Friars Balsam here as well, also suspended on cardboard strung elastic. A few drops of the stuff steeped in hot water and inhaled deeply down into the lungs eased the effects of dry, rasping coughs. She knew that from past experience. Her favourite way of imbibing this stuff though, was the one drop on a sugar lump remedy, the sweetness of the sugar counteracting the bitter taste of the liquid.

As her eyes moved a fraction to the right of the Friars Balsam, she shuddered instinctively as her brain registered the word 'Liquafruita,' on a few bottles of deceptively innocuous looking brown liquid that sat on a nearby shelf. Whether their isolation from the other cough and cold remedies was by chance or deliberation, she had no idea. What she did know however, was that she would almost rather chew a wasp or swallow half a bottle of cod liver oil than suffer the consequences of taking this vile medicine, an insult to the palate if anything was. The effects lingered for days, with every hiccup or burp bringing tears to your eyes and producing an odorous reminder of the stuff. And yet, she had reluctantly to admit to herself, it did work, and better than any other remedy she knew of. Coughs in particular, melted away when faced with such opposition. Her dad swore by it, and on the rare occasion when a cough threatened, would dose himself up on the stuff without a murmur. She found that quite difficult to understand when just a smidgen of cod liver oil from a carelessly discarded spoon, stirred into his tea, sent him into a kind of frenzy. As if by alto suggestion, her eyes alighted on the bottles of Sloan's liniment, and she grinned to herself remembering his painful encounter with the stuff on one occasion. She could not remember the actual incident herself, but it had been recounted often enough for the scene to be firmly 'ingrained' planted in her imagination. It had happened when her mum's application of the liniment to his back had been administered not by a gentle, bit by bit application but by the hasty tipping of a goodly portion onto the top of his back, which because she was unable to control the stuff, had run swiftly and painfully down the pathway of his spine and into the crease of his backside. Her mum would never live that indiscretion down. The experience had not put him off however, and once in a while when through some extra strenuous activity his back gave him a bit of jip as he called it, he placed his back and nether regions in mum's hands once again for an application of the liniment.

By the time she spied the Doan's back ache pills and the Kaolin Poultice, Hilary had found and bought a tin of Snow-fire cream and was pondering over the purchase of a tin of Germolene, which she reckoned would come in very useful. While she was making up her mind, Sally picked up a jar of white Vaseline and decided that as the one in the medicine cabinet at home was almost empty, she would purchase a fresh supply. As she waited to be served, she examined the letters on the rim of one of the coins in the palm her hand. She was pretty sure that the IND IMP was something to do with the Indian Empire, but she could not for the life of her remember what the FID EF stood for. She would have to ask Hazel. She would know. Then she spotted the packets of Quaisha chips and couldn't resist a grin. She had lost count of the times she had bowed her head over a bowl for an application of this foul smelling stuff to her hair, a cure for nits if there ever was one. Though used for a different purpose, this remedy had much in common with that other necessary evil, Liquafruita. All she needed to see now was brimstone and treacle but that was unlikely. Syrup of figs and Ex-lax had supplanted that evil remedy for constipation. She was so grateful to her mum for not insisting on dosing them up with purgatives every Friday evening as a lot of mothers did to their children. Just imagine having to hover in or around the lavatory all Saturday morning. That was cruel that was, and such a waste of precious time.

"Well, I think I've got just about everything I need now. I'm really pleased with all the stuff I've bought," said Hilary as she and the other girls made their way back out into the street. "Did you smell the T C P in there? I don't mind the smell mind you but it does catch in your throat a bit after a while. I always know when my dad's got a cold. He gargles with the stuff, and reckons it works better than any other remedy. I'd rather suck one of those soft orange and lemon things when I've got a sore throat, but mum doesn't buy them very often. She says they're too dear. Anyway, there's plenty of time before we can get a bus home. Anyone want to go any place else?"

"No not really," said Hazel. "What about an ice cream though? I'll treat you. Lyon's tea-rooms are only just along the road from here, and we can get a decent cornet for tuppence ha'ppenny in there. I like taking off that circle of cream colour paper myself and being able to lick it before I put the ice cream into the cone. Well, it always seems a pity to waste that bit. It just gets thrown away when they, the people who serve you do it."

The other girls were more than happy with this suggestion, licking their lips in anticipation of the cold, creamy treat to come. Hazel was so generous, so like their mum, Sally thought. She had to pay one and thru pence for her return bus fare to Hasting and back now, but she still always managed to save enough to treat her younger sisters to little treats.

The girls stood beside the Memorial, shopping bags around their feet, slowly licking around the circle of ice cream. As they nibbled away at the bits of cone, they pushed the residual ice cream carefully down into the crispy, diminishing, receptacle, their tongues and teeth in complete control of this delicate operation. After licking their lips, they stooped to retrieve their shopping bags and beginning to talk once again, made their way towards Wellington Square to await the arrival of the bus, which would take them home again. On the way, Sally glanced towards Demarco's and noticed that the café was still chocker block. She could not see into the far corner of the café however, to ascertain whether the old recluse was still there, but she doubted that he would be. He would most likely be on his way to who knew where, with just his own thoughts for company.

As the girls walked towards the straggly queue waiting for the number 12 bus, which would deposit them at various destinations on its way through to Tenterden, they saw a few familiar faces amongst the 'crowd,' which was not surprising really. Saturday was the one day, when a lot of youngsters managed to scrape up the bus fare into Hastings plus a little extra for a ticket to the cinema, the swimming baths or a quick session on or around the penny machines on the Pier. While awaiting the arrival of the bus, the girls listened to the general chit, chat around them, taking with a pinch of salt the obviously exaggerated stories being bandied about by some of the younger boys. They were well able these days to be able to tell fact from fiction, recognising the degree of exaggeration and embellishment within these tales – or so they thought. As they listened to the tale that was just unfolding though, they were not quite so sure. The name Freddie Fowler, accompanied by snickers was ominous in itself, and when the tale came from the mouth of a boy not prone to exaggeration, they pricked up their ears, their curiosity well and truly aroused. The girls listened with a mixture of horror and amusement as the boy, who lived at Staple Cross, recounted the tale of the cat.

"Well it was like this, see? I saw him lob something out of the top window of their house, and his is a tall house I can tell you. Tall as the Castle Hotel over there I reckon," he began, pointing in the direction of a large building in Wellington Square. "It bounced a bit as it hit the ground, sort of, but I didn't think no more about it until later. Well you don't, do you? He's well into his experiments is Freddie and you never know what the Dickens he's up to half the time. Well it were 'is poor old cat that hit the ground, weren't it, though I didn't know it at the time. He'd tied the thing into some sort of contraption he'd made before lobbing it out of window. Called it a parachute he did, but something made out of old rag and bits of elastic don't seem much like a parachute to me. More like a death trap, I reckon. He told me all about it when I saw him a couple of days later, and he sounded quite pleased with himself. He did say though that the idea needed working on before he tried it on again. I don't think he's got another cat. I bloody well hope not for its sake. He ain't human, he ain't." By this time all the boys were laughing so much that the girls could not find out whether the cat had survived or not. They certainly had their doubts.

Freddie Fowler was a strange youth who lived at Staple Cross with his mother and sister. They were like three peas in a pod, tall, angular and swarthy looking. While his mother and sister kept low profiles however, Freddie always managed to be around and in the forefront when there was trouble. In fact, he was more often than not, either the instigator or at least an accomplice when acts of a dubious nature occurred. It was not that he was cruel, far from it. He just seemed to take a perverse interest in the 'cause and effect' within a certain set of circumstances.

"Ere, what about Spud Taylor then," piped up Spiky, trying to upstage the other lad. "Well he were coming down the village on his bike alongside Pucker and Len and Bill Boxall, and they were all going like bats out of hell. Well, Spud didn't quite make the turn in towards the Brook's. By the Blacksmith's there, his dad's place, you know where I mean, and he just went arse over bulldozer onto the road there. Well in seconds a lump as big as a duck egg came up on his forehead and we thought 'e was gonna snuff it. 'Is dad came out though and just bunged a bit of wet rag on it and sorted out 'is knee and elbow, which were bleedin' somethin' terrible. 'E just went home after that. 'E's alright now and jest as bloody clever on that bike of 'is, course it had to be mended. Rides it jest like a bloody 'orse 'e does."

"When did that happen then Spiky?" asked one of the other boys. "I never heard about that."

"Can't exactly remember quite," replied Spiky. "A month, two months, or maybe even three, I don't know."

"I thought you meant it just happened, like yesterday or something, not ages ago you daft article," replied the lad.

Before Spiky had a chance to reply, the number 12 turned into Wellington Square, diverting the attention of most of the youngsters away from anecdotes and idle chit, chat, and onto the bus, now turning slowly and carefully around the square, and making its way to where they were standing.

Once the lumbering vehicle had ground to a halt beside them, there was the usual confusion around the foot-plate, which the Conductor did his best to control, followed by the inevitable scrabble up the steep stairs as a bunch of youngsters sought to secure one of the coveted front seats on the top deck of the bus. The girls followed them onto the bus at a more leisurely pace, deciding that they and their parcels would be safer on the lower deck, and where they were lucky enough to secure two side by side seats. Once seated, and with their parcels carefully stowed around them, they began talking

"Some of the boys are going to make a speedway track, somewhere round East View Terrace way," Hilary was saying. "Pucker told me and Sal about it the other day, in fact he said they'd already made a start on it. He mentioned Len Larkin, Spud Taylor and Brian Martin and one or two others I think, who were doing it. I told him me and Sal would give a hand with it and so forth, isn't that right Sal? Willy and Roy said they would help as well. They were with us at the time."

"The sooner they get themselves and their bikes off the roads and onto the track the better, by the sound of it," replied Hazel and grinned. "Didn't I hear something about Peter and Ian, putting a track in at Wayside, around where the old piggeries used to be? Yes, you told me about it Sal. Didn't you say they were going to call their team the Baldslow Boomerangs or something?" Their cousins, Peter and Ian Sansom had got their way with Granny Sansom, as Sally knew they would and were already well on the way with the construction of a cycle track at Wayside – with a lot of help from fellow enthusiasts like Peter Sellens, Bob Hunt and others. Sally had seen and been impressed with the result of their labours the last time she had visited Wayside. They certainly seemed to know what they were doing.

As Sally replied, she wriggled further onto her seat conscious of the conductor's slow progress along the aisle, the difficulty he was experiencing with access through gaggles of youngsters who, having failed to secure a seat within this crowded bus, were getting in his way. By the time the muddle had sorted itself out, the conversation had moved on and Pat and Sally were talking excitedly about the 'The Wizard of Oz,' a film starring Judy Garland. From the window of the bus they had seen an old poster advertising this film, fixed to the railings along the sea front, and although a bit weather beaten and tatty around the edges, still held the 'promise' of an enchanted world with its yellow brick road. They had not seen the film yet but had heard that it was to be shown at the cinema in Battle shortly. They could not wait to watch the exciting adventures of the girl with shiny red shoes, who with her little dog Toto, had been transported into a world of magical improbabilities.

As the bus turned into London Road, Sally had glanced towards ruins of the old St Leonard's, or Palace Pier, and thinking about it now, felt a little twinge of regret at its sad demise. It had been a hive of activity in its heyday, according to mum, with a constant flow of people, old and young alike milling around the peep shows and shops or just parading up and down, taking the sea air. An Orchestra had also performed there on a regular basis. She could see it all now through her mum's eyes, from the Pierrot with his sad eyes, white face and mechanical movements, to the Punch and Judy show, with its depiction of violent humour. She could imagine the cottual of youths who on hot summer days would be lounging around, leaning on the balustrade as they eyed up the deceptively prim and proper young ladies passing by. There had even been a roller skating rink at the far end of the pier, and for a short time after the Great War, an Orchestra, the Municipal she thought mum called it, had provided a musical diversion. And bathing huts a-plenty had lined the beach on either side of this unique structure.

Sally came to as the conversation moved on to Princess Elizabeth and the baby she was expecting - in the autumn they thought. Her marriage to Philip Mountbatten in the November of last year had been a very grand affair and a topic of conversation amongst old and young alike for months and months beforehand. Now the question on the lips of many folk and what the girls were repeating was, 'will it be a girl or a boy?

"Talking about babies, I thought it was really clever of Sir Alan Moore to be able to tell that you had been born feet first Hazel, just by touching the top of your head," said Hilary. "He called you a breach baby, didn't he? I wonder how he could tell, just like that. Just by feeling your head. Clever I call it." Sir Alan Moore, tall angular and very distinguished looking, was the school doctor and although kindly in his own way, scared Sally half to death. She answered his questions with a shaky yes or no, unable through some unaccountable fear, to articulate any other words. Luckily, his visits were few and far between, his examinations, followed by an entry into an impressive looking compendium, expedited dispassionately and with an almost imperceptible sigh of relief. Efficient and sufficient, as Hilary had uttered on one occasion when Sally's nervousness had almost got the better of her.

Before long, the girls attention was drawn inevitably towards the noisy exchanges taking place between a group of youngsters who were milling around and mucking about in the aisle, taking advantage while the conductor was busy on the upper deck. After a couple of games of pat the dog, they began to recite tongue twisters, their efforts becoming increasingly muddled and outrageous as they lost coordination between tongue and brain in their haste to outdo one another. They were oblivious to the stopping of the bus with its extra intake of passengers.

The girls began to giggle as the boys, having given up on 'red leather, yellow leather,' started on 'she sells sea shells on the sea shore,' their efforts with this set of tongue tripping words quickly becoming even more muddled and unrecognisable. By the time this was replaced by, 'how much wood could a wood chuck chuck, if a wood chuck could chuck wood,' many of the passengers on the lower deck, young and old alike, were laughing outright.

They were admonished once by the conductor who ran down the stairs to tell them they were making too much noise. They were overstepping the mark, he told them and distracting the driver. Before he made his way back up onto the upper deck again, he looked around at the youngsters, his expression stern. "Cor, that look was enough to turn a milk pudding sour," called out one of the boys, causing amusement amongst the perpetrators of the blathering nonsense, and before long they were off again.

They really made an effort with the next piece of tongue tripping doggerel, articulating each word with admirable precision – to start with. 'I said he was mad, he said mad? I said yes. He said, who? I said you. He said me? I said yes, he said oh.' It was not long however, before the whole thing degenerated into a free for all, the verse unrecognisable, without form or structure.

Sally's whispered suggestion, getting up close to her sister's ear to make herself heard, that she get them to recite, 'I rattled my bottles in Rollacky's yard, we rattled bottles and all,' was met with a definite and definitive, NO by Hazel. The place would be in uproar and they'd all be put off the bus if she did, she said.

At Christ Church bus stop in London Road, enough people alighted - some vacating their seats with a visible sigh of relief – making room for most of the bodies that had been cluttering up the gangway. After this, the noise dwindled, going down by several decibels as if by magic, and once again they could hear themselves talk.

"'Ere look at this. Rare as rocking 'orse shit it is," came a voice from the seat behind, recently vacated and now occupied by two of the gangway passengers. "Old Cokey gave it us. Said it come from some battle or other, back in the olden days." Sally skewed around in her seat to find out who was doing the talking, also curious about and eager to examine the object he was discussing with such enthusiasm. She had seen the lad before and knew that he came from Cripps Corner or Staple-cross, but that was all. The object he was holding aloft was the size and shape of a small plum, with a few deep indentations on its pitted surface, and gun metal grey in colour.

"It's a bit of cast iron shot see, from the gun of some old soldier back in the olden day when we used to fight each other," he continued. "It were given to Cokey by a bloke he was working with up in the woods, who told him it'd been dug it up from on an old battle field up country somewhere. Anyway, that's neither here nor there. Thing is I've got me something special here, it's mine and I don't care a tinkers cuss about who gave it to Cokey."

By this time Sally had turned back round in her seat, but she could hear the rustle of paper as he wrapped up the precious object before returning it to his jacket pocket. So old Cokey was more than just an old gas bag, she thought to herself. There was definitely another more appealing even generous side to his nature. Why else would he have parted with such a gem?

"Ere, talking about the olden days, here's something else Cokey told me," he continued once he had made doubly sure his precious piece of metal was safely stowed away. "He said that Roman soldiers and such like used to put garlic in their boots when they were marching." Sally's curiosity was immediately aroused never having heard that old chestnut before and she pricked up her ears, awaiting a logical explanation. The opening gambit was not too helpful but she continued to listen anyway.

"Garlic, what's garlic then? I've never heard of the stuff," commented the lad in the next seat. "You sure you got that right?"

"Course I have. It's that smelly stuff that grows along hedges and ditches. You must have run through it thousands of times," he replied. "It's all down along the ditch, Cripps Corner way, where we get the tadpoles from. You know? It's the stuff that smells like cats piddle. Anyway, Cokey reckons they stuck it in their boots to keep their feet from going mouldy. He called it an antiseptic or some such thing. Well, I think it was their secret weapon I told him. A combination of that stuff and stinky feet would frighten their enemies witless I said, and he had to agree. Well sort of. You know what he's like."

Sally knew what he was talking about now. It was the herb that Old Mrs Brooman collected, and used in her stews and things and it didn't half honk. She said it warded off coughs and colds and was a cure for many other ailments. Suddenly, she got a flash back to the winter and a memory of the odorous medicine that she had forced, coughing and spluttering down her throat. All at once she was sure that the secret and unpalatable ingredient in Liquafruita, was this smelly herb and a satisfied grin spread across her face with the certainty of her discovery. The mystery was solved, not that it would do her that much good, she realised.

The bus continued on its journey with only the occasional raised voice, accompanied by the whirr of the Conductor's machine as he churned out tickets and jingled coins around in his pouch, now disturbing the peace.

By the time the bus reached the top of Whydown Hill, the girls had already gathered their bags of shopping together and as they stood up and moved into the aisle ready to make their exit, a movement caught Sally's eye. Old Mr Weller was making his way slowly and carefully up the long flight of steps leading to his cottage, holding on to the iron railing that ran alongside as he did so. She grinned to herself remembering the times she and who ever happened to be around at the time, used this thick, hollow tube to despatch messages from top to bottom. One person simply whispered into the tube at one end, and the message would be conveyed into the ear of the person at the other end. And it really worked. Now and again however, a word, distorted by the angle of mouth on transmitter, would be misinterpreted, the result causing exaggerated mirth amongst the youngsters.

As they walked away from the bus and along the lane, Sally noticed blobs of cuckoo spit decorating the lush vegetation growing alongside the ditch, where some effluent from the cottage sewers still accumulated. What always puzzled her was how a creature hardly bigger than the head of a pin, a frog hopper they called it, could produce and then surround itself by so much spittle, but so far no one had been able to give her a satisfactory answer to this strange phenomenon. And spiders were other creatures that defied the laws of nature. How did their little bodies produce such copious amounts of thin, tough web with which to entangle their prey? And she knew how tough that web was. She had discovered its comparative strength years ago, after becoming entangled in the stuff while playing in the garden. Her attention was suddenly and instantly diverted away from contemplation of the miracles of Mother Nature to the plaintive call of a cuckoo. The monosyllabic notes of the bird were drifting over towards them from the direction of the big wood beyond Sylvian, and she could picture in her mind's eye, this aberration of the bird world proclaiming its territorial rights from an outstretched branch of one of the large trees over there. Pat had clearly heard the unmelodic but compelling sound and was the first to utter the words of the little ditty associated with this iconic bird.

> *"The cuckoo comes in April, it sings its song in May.*
> *In June it changes its tune. In July it flies away.*
> *In August go it must."*

"I've actually seen a cuckoo you know," she said as she finished her recitation. "Mum and me saw one the old oak tree, when we were taking some scraps to the chickens in the field over there. We got quite close before it saw us but then it took off just like a dart. In fact mum was saying that the cuckoo's flight pattern and shape are a bit similar to the green woodpeckers. It's just the colour that's different. The cuckoo's a bit dingy really."

Once they had outtalked all the virtues and otherwise of this harbinger of spring the conversation turned towards the cow and its arrival – imminent if recent conversations between dad and Uncle Fred Sansom were to be believed. They wondered what effect would it have on the chickens, and then decided, probably very little if the relationship between sheep, a similar creature and chickens were anything to go by. Mr Collins' sheep took not the slightest notice of the chickens or they of them, and they could see very little difference between a cow and a sheep when it came down to habit and attitude. Now when Plucky the cockerel had been around, things had been different. That little creature had been fearless and aggressive when the mood took him, and would square up to anything he considered to be a threat to his authority. The sheep though had either ignored his aggressive behaviour or had shrugged him off without even raising their heads from the all-consuming and satisfying business of grazing. He was long gone however, and with him that dubious threat to all creatures great and small. Anyway, all would be revealed very shortly, and their feelings about the advent of this 'ere cow spanned curiosity and excitement with a bit of apprehension thrown in.

As they walked wearily into the Kitchen, depositing their shopping bags onto the table, mum was rubbing vinegar into the Sunday joint to stop it going off over night, and Dorothy and Jacky were sitting up at the table beside her, scraping the remnants of the sponge mixture from around her large mixing bowl. The expression of single minded concentration and enjoyment of their feast, quickly changed and the satisfied grin that spread across their faces as the older girls entered the room, told its own story, as did the mess of raw mixture that, apart from the area within licking distance, had accumulated around their chops. In spite of her fatigue, Sally smiled, remembering her own extraordinary enjoyment of this sweet, sticky mixture, not so very long ago.

While they sorted through and examined their purchases, mum prised the scoured mixing bowl from reluctant hands, mopped up sticky fingers and faces with an old flannel, then made a pot of tea. As they girls sat, elbows on table and supped the sweet, milky beverage, their natural exuberance returned. Now rejuvenated, they began to recount the day's activities with a bit of poetic licence here and there. The acrid smell of raw vinegar was still in the air even though mum had removed the anointed joint from kitchen table to scullery and had covered the dish on which it sat with a mesh canopy, in readiness for the Sunday roast.

Dad preferred to eat his dinner at mid-day. Occasionally however, like today, their main meal would be eaten later when all family members were likely to be in the same place at the same time. Sausages with mashed potatoes, cabbage and blue peas were on the menu today it seemed and Sally's mouth watered as she anticipated the feast. Before that however, there was food to be gathered for the rabbits. Mum supplied the creatures with the outer leaves of cabbages and a carrot or two when she could spare them, also pea husks and a bit of lettuce when available. For the most part however, their diet consisted of what could be harvested from the countryside, and at this time of year that was no problem. Rabbits were particularly partial to the succulent leaves of dandelion, milk thistle and hog weed, all of which grew around the field and were particularly abundant at this time of year. The wild parsley, which acted as a sort of medicine for the creatures, was administered in small doses. Too much at one time, as mum told them, would scour them and that would never do.

Pat Hilary and Sally rose from the table, abandoning their empty cups where they stood. They were on a mission to gather enough green stuff from around the field to last the rabbits a day or two - at least. Dorothy and Jacky who were coming with them, scrambled off their chairs and hurried over to the shoe cupboard, which as usual was brimming over with footwear of all shapes and sizes. After a short while, and a bit of help from the older girls suitable footwear was found for them and they were on their way. The two little ones would have to be supervised, their contribution to the pile of green stuff sorted through carefully before it was fed to the rabbits. These creatures could safely eat most of the wild vegetation provided by Mother Nature in such abundance, but there were one or two plants that would poison, or at least make them very sick, and while the older girls were very much aware of these, the little ones had much to learn about such things. As they left the house, Jacky was reciting her favourite nursery rhyme:

> *Ride a cock horse to Banbury cross.*
> *To see a fine lady on a white horse.*
> *With rings on her fingers and bells on her toes.*
> *She shall have music wherever she goes.*

Then as Sally glanced back, she saw Hazel gathering together the cups and saucers on the kitchen table and beginning to tidy up the mess they had left behind. Like mum, she just seemed to get on with what needed to be done, without any fuss or bother. Sally tried not to grumble about chores, she really did, but somehow her resolve crumpled when she was faced with a task that seemed less important than what she happened to be doing at that particular moment. Perhaps one of these days she would change and be more like her sister, you never knew. However the chore they were just about to carry out was right up her street, and she led the way through the back gate and began running towards the far end of the field. There, with unerring accuracy she found and quickly stooped to gather up her first fistfuls of milky thistle and dandelion. She looked forward to providing the rabbits with a fresh dose of this greenery, even though she had been told that it should be allowed to wilt for a while before they got their chops on to it. She loved to watch as they chomped away on the fresh green leaves with obvious enjoyment, and with that curious side to side movement of their jaws, their eyes unblinking and almost unfocussed as they concentrated on the job in hand.

Dora and Jacky, though gathering bits of vegetation here and there, were easily distracted and kept trying to follow the movements of the hedge sparrow or creeping Jenny, its colloquial name, as it flew in and out of the hedge further down the field. They enjoyed forays in and around the countryside just as much as their older sisters, particularly if it included a trip to the big wood to call on Deffy and Bill in that old shack of theirs.

It had been a good day so far Sally reckoned, and with a fair wind and a following sea behind her, as the saying went, it would continue so. She was looking forward to staying overnight at Hilary's house, and if Willy Monk and Roy Chapman came along for the evening as planned, then that would suit her fine. They were good company those two, and always good for a laugh. But before then, there was sausage and mash to look forward to, followed by steamed sponge pudding and thick custard. She was already peckish and her mouth began to water in anticipation of this feast. .

Later that day, over-night bag in hand, she stood on the underground tank and watched as the sun slipped towards the horizon. Soon the darkening sky would be covered in stars and before Willie and Roy made their way back to the village, the four of them would almost certainly be stargazing. Roy had always shown a particular interest in the Heavens, and could identify more individual stars and constellations, than any one she knew. Except perhaps for Jumbo James, who like Roy had tried to explain to the youngsters, the vastness of space and what caused the stars to twinkle. In Sally's case as with most of the youngsters she reckoned, it went right over her head, literally. Her particular favourite group of stars was called Ursa Major and from the time the first star appeared in the sky on a bright moonlit night, her eyes would be scouring the heavens to observe the gradual emergence of this magical spectacle. In Roy's case she knew, it would be the Warrior that would be getting the lion's share of his attention.

'Moonlight, starlight bogey won't come out tonight,' she recited silently to herself as she jumped off the slab of concrete, and ran back into the kitchen to say her farewells. Then she and Hilary made their way towards the top gate and arm in arm walked briskly down the field, their conversation now wholly taken up with plans for the evening ahead.

Chapter 3

As Pat, Hilary and Sally walked up Crazy Lane on their way to the village on Saturday morning, they were talking about a teacher who had returned to the school after an absence of a couple of years or so. In that time her name had changed from Miss Facer to Mrs Bedlington, and it was not just her name that had changed, but her whole appearance and personality. Gone was the bright lipstick laden spittle that shot from her open mouth as she admonished some child for the slightest misdemeanour, and with it the tight permanent wave which had been tortured into her short dark hair. Gone also was the threat of being turned to stone by the bolt eyed glare from maniacal eyes turned on some hapless and terrified pupil, from whom she now gently coaxed an answer. And the volume of her voice had decreased by several decibels. She used to scare Pat half to death. She said she nearly used to wet herself if this teacher asked her a question, even when she knew the answer, which she nearly always did. She was so scared of saying the wrong thing and getting a mouthful that she could not get the words out properly. They were all inordinately grateful to and also curious about this faceless Mr Bedlington, and if perchance they were ever to meet him, they would thank this benefactor from the bottom of their hearts for his considerable part in the metamorphosis.

Dorothy, who had been at school for a couple of years now, had never experienced the unreasoned behaviour of Miss Facer, and for that mercy the other girls were thankful. She had found the transition from home to school quite difficult enough anyway. She had missed the one to one companionship of her younger sister, and had missed even more acutely, the comforting presence of her mum. Luckily, Miss Kirby a recent addition to the staff at the school, possessed a rare and instinctive rapport with young children, and Dorothy adored her. Mum referred to her as a gentle soul. She lived in Westfield, cycling through to Sedlescombe every day, no matter what the weather was like. Sally got the impression that she had replaced Miss Hall, a teacher who had survived for only a couple of terms at the school. This lady, though gentle and very articulate, had been more interested in warding off evil spirits than actually instructing her pupils with their studies. Sally had been sorry in a way, to see her go. This teacher, when on form, had held the interest of her pupils with her knowledge and her ability to share that knowledge with her pupils. And she had alerted the youngsters to the wonders of nature, with the spectacular displays of starlings as they prepared to settle down for the night, being a particular favourite of hers. Unfortunately, her behaviour became increasingly erratic with structured lessons fewer and further between, her obsession with all things evil taking precedence over all else. When she started blocking ventilation grills with pieces of paper to prevent an intrusion by these supernatural spooks, her classroom more often than not in uproar, the Headmaster was forced to take action. Her departure had been met with a mixture of relief and regret by many of her pupils, also in Sally's case, feelings of guilt. She had taken part in the rowdy exchanges, the general disorderly behaviour amongst the pupils when this teacher had tried in vain to quell the racket within the classroom. And yet she had shown Sally many acts of kindness and understanding, seeming to recognise the acute self-consciousness behind her outwardly brash behaviour. It was too late now however, and even the ripples created by this kind but ineffectual lady had all but gone away.

The girls paused at the top of Crazy Lane to get their breath back, and leaned against the gate leading into the Farrows' top field. A light breeze rippled over the grass, drawing their eye across the meadow towards the old farmhouse with its chimney puffing out plumes of lazy smoke, and on to the village nestling comfortably in the valley below, protected by fields and pockets of woodland. Sally was not deceived by the tranquil image that distance bestowed upon the landscape however. She knew that in and around the farmhouse, the daily routine on this busy mixed farm, would be grinding relentlessly on, and on closer inspection the village would be alive, with a steady procession of human and animal bodies with here and there, the occasional chuff, chuff of a motorised vehicle. At this very moment, Sally could picture old Fred emerging from the track at the side of Barrack Cottage with half his allotment on his boots, the other half on that dirty bit of rag, which he used to wipe his nose. This was definitely one of Sally's favourite views, both for its pleasing aspect and also for the memories associated with this place. She grinned as she thought about one of these incidents, their encounter long ago now with Mrs Moon and her daughter. She remembered with sudden clarity, the speed and accuracy with which Basil Winchester had fired his soggy missile at the ladies and the startled cry from Mrs Moon as the shot caught her fairly and squarely on the cheek. That lady had never as far as she knew, ever worked out where the missile had come from or who had fired the thing, even though the girls had been beside themselves with spluttering laughter. Another pleasing thought that crossed her mind as she stood admiring the view, was the times they spent sitting and chatting in the roughly dug trench that lay within a spits throw of where they were standing. What practical purpose the crude dug out would have served in times of war, she had no idea. She was not complaining however. With the excavation of a bit of soil from the far end of the trench, this had provided them with shelter on several occasions when the weather had suddenly turned against them.

As they turned away from the gate and made their way down Chapel Hill, they began to recite 'Cargoes,' a poem introduced to them recently by Jumbo James:

> "Qinquireme of Nineveh, from distant Ophir. Rowing home to Haven in Sunny Palestine.
> With a cargo of Ivory and Apes and Peacocks. Sandalwood cedar wood and sweet white wine.
>
> Stately Spanish Galleon, coming from the Isthmus. Dipping through the tropics by the palm green shore.
> With a cargo of diamonds emeralds amethysts, topaz cinnamon and gold moyadors.
>
> Dirty British coaster, with a short cake smoke stack.
> Butting through the channel in the mad march days.
> With a cargo of Tyne coal, road rails, pig-lead, fire wood, iron ware and cheap tin trays."

Having delivered the poem in the usual way, first two verses measured, methodical, the last belted out with gusto, they linked arms and continued on down Chapel Hill towards Cow Shit Corner and beyond. As they crossed the river bridge and were walking towards the bottom shop, they saw Henry Maplesden riding towards them on his sit up and beg bicycle. They came to a halt as he approached them, moving instinctively into single file as he passed by with that familiar faraway look about him and still sucking away on his old clay pipe. Sally reckoned he took that old pipe to bed with him, but sensibly kept that thought to herself. Their usual greeting, 'hello Henry, what you up to then,' was met with silence. He was once again in his own little world and totally indifferent to men and mouses, the expression they always used to explain the behaviour of this strange youth. They guessed he was on his way to Luff's Farm where, with Mr or Mrs Farrow keeping an eye on him, would occupy himself with doing a few odd jobs in and around the farm buildings. He was in his element on the farm. At the end of the day, it took a bit of gentle persuasion to get him on to his beloved bicycle, and then to point him and it in the general direction of home.

As they walked through doorway of the Post Office come General Store, Freda looked up from the well-thumbed ledger into which she was making entries. They moved up to the counter and passed the list and shopping bags over to her, knowing full well that by the time they returned, the bags would be filled and ready for them to carry back home. As they turned to leave, Sally glanced towards the Post Office counter where Mr Phillips was officiating some document for a customer who stood in front of him, She noted the well-practised rhythm with which he performed the task, his ancient relic of an old stamper, moving from ink filled pad to document like greased lightning. He was a genuinely kindly man, who as Freda said often allowed hard up customers food items on tick, seldom harassing them for payment. In fact she went as far as to say that he would write off the debt when he knew that payment would cause them real hardship.

Once outside, they set their sights on the old pump, noting that Amy Powell, Eileen Lawrence and Joan Jarvis were already there. They were seated on one of the hard wooden benches connected to this vernacular building, which as far as the youngsters were concerned, was just as important a feature of this place as the pump housing itself. Sally was always a bit wary of Joan. She was good for a laugh that was for sure, but it did not do to upset her, as Marlene Mc Cann had learned to her cost. After an altercation between the two girls Joan, with the reluctant assistance of friends of hers, had marched Marlene to Hurst wood and had tied her firmly to a tree, and just left her there. To Marlene's relief Ada Smizzen, one of Joan's reluctant accomplices had crept back later and had released her from her bonds, and since then the two girls had become firm friends. Marlene was quite feisty, a girl with a ready smile and a rare wit, who was well able to hold her own with the best of them most of the time. In this instance however, she had not stood a chance against the strength and determination of the older girl. And when Joan told her that she would never see her Grandma with whom she lived, or her mother and older sister who lived in London, ever again, Marlene said she had really believed her.

As Pat Hilary and Sally came towards the pump house, the trio shuffled up on the wooden bench to make room for them, and Sally used the time it took to arrange her skirt beneath her bottom as she sat down, to cast a brief, sidelong glance at Joan. The girl was clearly in a good mood, greeting the newcomers with her usual light-hearted banter, and yet Sally was on her guard. Once bitten twice shy was her motto, and even though in this particular case she had not been the recipient of the bite, she could empathise with Marlene's experience.

Almost immediately, the topic of Autograph books came up, and tomes of different hues were soon being held proudly aloft. Sally's was green, Pat and

Hilary's red and blue respectively, and each one was edged with a silver trim. Hazel, aware of this new and interesting hobby of theirs had bought and presented the precious and colourful books to them. Then began a general toing and froing of books, with entries made either from memory, from existing entries in one or other tome, or with reference to scraps of paper on which verses had been hastily written. Sally grabbed Eileen's volume from her wrote the following:

'The lightening flashed the thunder roared and all the world was shaken. A little pig curled up his tail and ran to save his bacon.'

This, courtesy of mum, was the first ever entry that had been made into her book, and was a particular favourite with both of them. Then she listened as other verses were read out and commented on before being entered into one or other book. Joan, who suddenly commandeered Sally's book, made a couple of entries and before handing it back, read them out aloud: "Never make love in a cornfield, remember the corn has ears," followed by, "Here is a man who never does a thing that is not right. His wife can find just where he is, at morning, noon and night. HE'S DEAD" And they all chuckled. Others followed, thick and fast:

'I wish you health, I wish you wealth. I wish you golden store. I wish you heaven after death, what can I wish you more.' and 'Love is like a mutton chop, sometimes cold and sometimes hot. Sometimes weak, and sometimes strong, so is mutton kept too long.' soon occupied a couple of pages in Amy's book.

'A slip on the pavement is better than a slip of the tongue.' and 'Life is mostly froth and bubble, two things stand alone. Kindness in another's trouble, courage in your own.' were read out and entered into Pat's.

'Patience is a virtue, possess it if you can. Seldom found in women, never found in man.' Sally wrote in Joan's book, albeit with a little trepidation. Then she paused for a few seconds, sucking the end of her pencil, before adding the following:

'It's easy enough to be pleasant, when life goes along like a song. But the man worthwhile, is the one who can smile, when everything goes wrong '

As she handed it back, Eileen waved her own book about hopefully. "Don't forget me then, I've only got one thing in mine." Soon remedy that then," said Joan setting her own book aside and taking it from her. Then she recited and entered a couple of bits of nonsense into the book.

"There was an old man from St Paul's, who used to do tricks in the hall's. His favourite trick was to sit on his stick, and wave at the girls in the stalls.'

'There was an old man from Bosham, who took out his false teeth to wash 'em. His wife said now Mack, if you don't put 'em back, I'll tread on the bugger's and squash 'em.' Then just for good measure and while the others were still giggling, she added another:

"Mother's meeting, Father's invited. Children can come if they don't get excited. Admission is free, and you pay at the door. You bring your own seat and you sit on the floor.

"One more, one more," she insisted as Eileen was about to retrieve her book. Then turning to the very edge of the back cover, wrote: 'By hook or by crook, I'll be last in this book.' Sally breathed a sigh of relief. For a minute there she'd been worried it might have been the one about the man from Australia and his dahlia, which was rather rude.

"There, now you can write this one in mine," Joan told Eileen, reading out some words written on a tatty bit of paper, before handing it over.

"Steal not this book for fear of shame, for in it is the person's name. When the last day comes, the Lord will say, where is that book you stole away? If you say, 'I do not know,' the Lord will say, 'get down below.'

Sally had a piece of paper in her frock pocket. Written on it, in Hazel's characteristic neat backward sloping writing was a meaningful quotation:

'True friendship has a soothing power, keening the treasures of each hour. Giving ease where pain would be, this your friendship is to me.' She knew whose book this one would go into.

"Don't look now but here comes Alan Turner," said Pat, then tut-tutted as the others looked up instinctively, unwittingly ignoring her advice. "He's wearing plimsolls not wellies for a change," she whispered as she sneaked another look at this youth from Cripps Corner, who was now cycling past. With him was a fellow called Phil, who the girls reckoned must be related in some way. Both were thin and wiry with the same lank dark hair, and they'd often wondered why he did not attend Sedlescombe School along with Alan. They waved as they passed by, but carried on towards the river bridge, anxious the girls supposed to make the most of this rare taste of freedom. For Alan, they knew, spent most of his spare time working on some farm or other.

Soon after they had ridden over the bridge and out of sight, Willie and Roy cycled around the side of the Pump House. Once they had abandoned their bikes, they shuffled the girls along the seat then squeezed themselves in beside them. "What have we got here then," asked Roy, leaning over and examining the albums on the girls' laps. As if he didn't know, thought Sally, as she reluctantly relinquished her precious book up and into his hands. After reading one or two of the entries, he decided to add one of his own:

'If this book should chance to roam, smack its bum and send it home.' he wrote. Then he passed the book over to Willie, who after a moment's thought made the following short sharp contribution:

'More haste less speed.'

"Is that all we get," asked Amy, as the book was handed back to Sally. "Okay, one more then. I've just thought of this one," said Roy and taking her book from her, wrote the following:

'I went round a straight crooked corner, and saw a dead donkey die. I got out my pistol to stab it, and it hit me one in the eye.' "There that'll have to do," he said as he handed the book back to her. "Now let's tell 'em about old Sniff and Spit then, shall we Willie?" Sally pricked up her ears at the mention of this strange character. She was hoping there might be a few cigarette cards hidden away somewhere within this tale, and her optimism was soon justified.

"Well, me and Roy went round to his place this morning, to get some cards he'd promised us. He'd only just got up and he didn't half look a mess. We reckon he needs to shoot those old socks of his before he puts them on in the morning. Stiff as a board they are. Thought of offering a bit of that Vinola powder of yours Hilary, but it'd only make him sneeze and then there'd be snot all over the place," and he grinned as Sally gagged. "Anyway, we followed him through to the kitchen, and there was his budgie crawling around at the bottom of its cage, trying to cover its head with its wings. 'Bloody thing's still alive then. 'E were on his back, looked dead as a duck when I went to bed last night, thought I were coming down to a bloody corpse this morning, Bloody hangover, that's all e's got, and serve the bugger right. E's a mite too fond of me tipple if the truth be known. Ere take these ere cards and leave me in peace' he told us and practically shoved us out through the door, because we'd seen the funny side of it and started laughing. Still we've got all these cards to sort out and share with you lot, that's something I suppose." The magic words for once however, were lost on the girls. In spite of Eileen's cautionary, 'poor little thing.' the minds and imaginations of the other girls were away with the drunken budgie, and her compassionate sentiment fell on deaf ears.

After a while, they began to sort through the stack of Turf cigarette cards, provided by old Sniff and Spit, searching anxiously and hopefully for the ones that were needed to enhance or in some cases, complete their set. In no time at all, the stack of cards had been reduced down to a mere handful, which Willie put away in his pocket in readiness for more deals with other youngsters.

This important business now dealt with, they turned their attention to other things and in particular, the past and current happenings within the village. Roy was re telling the tale about the time some of the older boys had turned over and released a round concrete bollard from its war time resting place, from just above where they were sitting, and down into the lower reaches of the village. What they had not taken into consideration was the speed with which it had careered down through the village, and it was a miracle that neither pedestrian nor motor car had been in its path at the time. Neither would have stood any chance against the menace of this thundering giant. Their act of bravado they admitted had turned into utter chaos, with what had seemed a bit of harmless fun with a chunk of concrete, turning into a hopeless battle with something over which they had absolutely no control.

The boys of course had been taken to task over their behaviour, with the dire consequences of what could have occurred as a result of this act of crass stupidity, drummed into them time and time again. Suitably chastened, they had kept a low profile for a while. Within the younger element however, a cult of hero worship had resulted, which did not appear to be echoed in the discussions of some old villagers who, at every opportunity, resurrected the incident, their faces animated as they discussed in morbid detail, what might have happened as a result of this crass behaviour.

There was always this spectre of bloody mangled bodies in their discussions, often punctuated with short ecumenical quotes like 'their but the grace of God go I,' and some even going as far as to cross themselves. However, if the sparkle in their eyes was anything to go by, there was a conflict here between memories of their own youthful indiscretions, and their present subsequent grown up common sense; an almost nostalgic connection with the past. Sally reckoned that given half a chance, they would have dropped the mantle of old age for a taste of youthful freedom, any old day.

As they chatted, Sally was watching the progression of people up, down and through the village. She had identified Mr Hill or the Rooster as they called him, as he had emerged from the footpath to the Waterfall; had noted the confidence of his stride and the upward tilt of his chin as he took his habitual constitutional. As the owner of a factory, which had manufactured munitions during the war, plus a spacious house at the top end of Balcombe Green, he was clearly a man of substance and fully conscious of his social standing within the hierarchy of the village. As he walked past them, she grinned, comparing this well dressed dapper man with those down to earth characters in the village, like Bangy and old Fred for instance, and the expression 'Chalk and cheese,' came immediately to mind. It took all sorts to make a world, she told herself, though knew exactly where her preference lay.

Her mind clicked back into sharp focus when Hilary mentioned the name Leonard Masters. The death of this lad had shocked the whole village in its sudden, horrific and totally unexpected consequence. Unknown to most people, he had walked in his sleep. On this particular occasion, he had missed his footing at the top of the stairs and had plunged to the bottom, dislodging and breaking a large glass vase, a shard of which had severed his jugular vein. Within minutes he was dead. They all still missed this kind, gentle boy, with his ability to identify and calm a difficult situation before it got out of hand, and also his keen sense of humour. He'd had them in stitches on many occasions. 'A sunny natured lad,' mum had called him. To imagine someone so full of life and goodness, dying in such an unbelievably horrific way, was a thing of nightmares. And Sally knew that she was not the only one who was still haunted by the image of him lying at the bottom of the stairs in that pool of blood.

For a moment or two there was silence, each one busy with their own individual thoughts. Then the expression 'Heaven sent,' popped into Sally's mind as she spotted Miss Dengate coming out of the track beside Blacksmith's

Bovey, and she gave an audible sigh of relief. Never had she been more grateful to see the old lady. With her sunny smile and her seeming ability to take everything in her stride, she was just what they needed right now to lift their melancholy, introspective mood.

"Here's Miss Dengate," Pat piped up just as Sally was taking a breath to announce the same thing, and suddenly eyes and attention were focussed on the unmistakable figure of this kindly lady as she began to walk slowly up the road towards them, pushing her old bicycle. When she reached the Butcher's shop, they got up and walked towards her, and as she came up alongside and smiled at them, Sally knew without a shadow of doubt, that this lady was aware in that wise old way of hers, their need for a bit of light relief and reassurance.

After a few preliminaries, she began to regale them with tales of her frisky old Billy goat. They listened with amusement as the tales unfolded, with one incident in particular, appealing to their sense of humour. For some time, she told them a group of youths, had been causing a bit of trouble around the farm. Amongst other things, they had rearranged a stack of hay, spreading the precious harvest far and wide, and they had also made off with some of the stakes she had prepared, ready to repair gaps in the hedges around the fields. It was when they had moved closer to the farmhouse, bombarding the windows with clods of earth and driving her old dog mad, that she'd decided enough was enough. She bided her time, and the next time she saw them messing about in the hedge at the back of the Farmhouse, she approached them, her old goat haltered and walking alongside her. She tried to reason with them, but they just laughed and threw sticks at her, and told her to bugger off, and just continued to wreak havoc in and around the hedgerow.

"Well, me blood were up be then, 'en I released owld Billy. 'En e dent need no biddin,' e were after 'em quicker'n a bolt 'o lightning. 'Em boys were up and off, screechin, en pushin en shovin through thet scratchy owld hedge, with Billy given 'em a bit 'o assistance 'ere en thar. En that's the larst oi seen of em, so fer," she said grinning widely.

After a while and a few more tales, she paused, and turned her attention from group engagement to the study of individual faces, and what a wealth of understanding there was in those old eyes Sally thought as they rested briefly upon her. As far as she knew, this outwardly simple soul, had never ventured more than a few miles from home and yet she possessed some sort of second sense, an understanding somehow linked to the human psyche. Miss Dengate however, would have been sorely puzzled by any reference to such things. Having satisfied herself that their mood of natural geniality had been restored, she bade them farewell. Then she moved her long skirt to one side, mounted her bicycle and rode slowly away, looking back just the once with her reassuring smile.

"Now don't you worry about old Mercy, she's well able to take care of herself," said Roy as the girls expressed their indignation at the behaviour of those miscreants. "Her and Old Billy are more than a match for them. She's only got to say the word, and that old goat'll be off and'll have the pants off them and at the end of his horns in no time, and they know it. They're not that stupid. The expression, trying to ride with the devil springs to mind," he added and grinned.

"You heard about Tony Taylor's accident then I suppose, he continued after a moment's hesitation, deliberately changing the subject Sally reckoned. "Well, I can tell you exactly what happened, just in case you don't know the details," he added after a pause in which no one uttered a yay or nay. "He just goes too bloody fast on that bike of his, that's the trouble, and he mostly gets away with it. He didn't this time though. He took that turn off the main road and into the track by the Brooks, just a bit too fast, and didn't half come a cropper. Pucker, Len Larkin and Bill Boxall were with him, and it shook 'em up a bit when they saw the state of him. He was grazed and bleeding, and there was a lump as big as a duck's egg on his forehead. Luckily his dad was working at the Smithy at the time and managed to clean him up a bit before he took him home. His mum would have had fifty fits if she'd seen him like that. Anyway, he didn't break any bones luckily, but he didn't half have some colourful bruises."

Sally had heard about the accident of course, Spiky had told the girls about it. She also knew that Tony, unfazed by the accident, had been back on his bike again as soon as his dad had put the thing together again. In fact he was also already back working alongside Derek Bishop, Pucker, Len, and other cycle enthusiasts, constructing a cycle speedway track on a spare bit of ground around Brede Lane. When up and running, their team would be called 'The Sedlescombe Saints,' they had decided. She and Hilary were also helping out on this venture from time to time, as unskilled labourers, leaving the planning process to those who had the skill, and a vested interest in getting the thing right. For all these lads, their bicycles were not just a means of getting from place to place, but also objects of pride.

As far as Sally knew, the speedway track at Wayside was now up and running. Her cousins, Peter and Ian Sansom had had plenty of help from their mates with this venture. Their team were called 'The Baldslow Boomerangs.' She thought about the piggery's that used to occupy this space, The high pitched squeals and snuffles of its former occupants, now resounding with the sound of protesting tyres as a rider took a corner at break neck speed. She had a strong feeling that the former occupants of this territory, along with Granpy, would be turning in their graves at the effrontery of these youths with their new-fangled ideas, and she grinned as a weird and wonderful apparition popped up at the back of her eyes. How long ago and far away that all seemed to her now.

"Isn't it about time we made a move," asked Eileen, getting to her feet. "Look, me skirts stuck to me legs I've been sitting here so long." The others were quick to follow, the girls pulling damp skirts from legs, the boys retrieving bikes, then bidding farewell and riding off towards Brede Lane. "Are you going home Chapel Hill way? If so me and Joan'll wait while you pick up your shopping and walk as far as the top there with you," said Eileen. Having all settled for the Chapel Hill route, they picked up and stored away their autograph books, then set off across the Green towards the shop to pick up their bags of groceries. As they walked through the door, they saw Mrs Northeast standing beside the counter talking to Freda and Joy. Sally had seen her walking down the road just a short while ago, and had been reminded yet again of the poster in Alston's corset shop in Hastings. 'Let your body breath. Achieve bosom grace and perfect health,' it said and she wondered if that characteristic glide of hers was due in no small part to one of those contraptions.

As they walked up towards the counter, she turned her turbaned head towards them and smiled. Sally thought not for the first time, that while most women she knew wore a turban to disguise untidy hair or curlers, this lady with just those few curls falling carelessly over her forehead, made a fashion statement with this most casual of head gear. She moved aside, and waited while they picked up the shopping, then as they left the shop, moved back to continue what the girls had interrupted. Sally would love to have been a fly on the wall, and privy to the conversation between Freda and Joy and this most impressive lady, with her very interesting lifestyle.

"You've got rabbit for dinner today," said Eileen as they walked towards the bridge. "I know because dad was on his way to your place with them when I left home."

"Goody, goody it's my turn for the brains and your turn for the tongue Pat," said Sally and grinned, knowing that unless she and their mum kept a strict rota on these delicacies, they would be argued over. Also, Uncle Alf and Uncle Fred were here for the weekend, and rabbit pie, especially the way mum cooked it it, was one of their favourite dinners. Uncle Alf reckoned that now that he and Aunty Lil were working so hard in the small guest house they had bought down in Devon, he would go into a decline if he were not able to recharge his batteries at Sylvian from time to time. That important issue taken care of she turned to this evening's entertainment, and the Lawrence family's part in it. 'Tippit' was the name of the game they'd be playing and with her uncles here, also Aunty Nin of course, and with Mr Lawrence as Master of Ceremonies, it promised to be an interesting and entertaining evening. It would also be the first time Dorothy and Jacky had been part of a team and if or when that sixpence dropped into their hand, they would almost certainly give the game away with that sparkle in their eyes. The older girls had been asked not to pick on them straight away, but for the time being, just to give them a bit of a chance. It would only dishearten them, and after all, they would learn the finer points of the game all in their own good time.

As they walked towards cow shit corner, Sally noticed a cyclist speeding along the main road towards them, and for a split second thought it was Denis

Crow When she realised it was Brian Martin, she breathed a sigh of relief. He was on his way to do a bit of maintenance on the speedway track he said as he paused briefly beside them. Then as he pushed down on his peddles and cycled off towards the village, Sally thoughts, triggered by that experience of mistaken identity, turned to her last encounter with her nemesis. She had been on the way to the village and on her own, which was unusual, when he had pulled up in front of her, halting her in her tracks. He had stared at her for a moment with his ratty eyes, and had then pretended to pull a bogey from his nose and eat it, the thought of which even now turned her stomach. Then satisfying himself that she'd been suitably shocked, he had cycled off, lifting his bum in the air and moving it slowly side to side as a final gesture. The whole incident had taken seconds, with not a word spoken, and yet she'd felt quite shaky for a few minutes afterwards. Still she refused to allow the memory of this experience to cloud her day, and brought her attention determinedly back onto what was going on around her. She spotted Gilbert Carter straight away, moving about in the field just below Luffs Farmhouse. This smiling young man had a natural flair for vernacular procedures, and could sew a drill, harvest a crop and follow a horse with the best of them. Thatching however, was his speciality, and Mr Farrow had the neatest, most well protected hay stacks for miles around. Mr Budgen was another such countryman. From the tip of his booted toes to the top of his cloth capped head, and every bit in between, he was a true old Rustic, albeit, deaf as a post. Even now, with his eyes rheumy and blood shot, he still managed to guide his beloved shire horses through country lanes, into farm entrances and onto fields where he could still plough a long straight furrow with consummate skill. It was rumoured though that just recently, he had stumbled over one of Mr Farrow's cud chewing Friesian heifers, so she began to wonder who had been leading who, through those narrow county lanes.

They paused at the top of Chapel Hill for just long enough to finalise arrangements for this evening and the rest of the weekend, then parted company; Eileen and Joan turning into Cottage Lane, and the others heading off down crazy Lane. Eileen's 'see you later,' was acknowledged with a wave of the arm, and then they were on their way.

They did have rabbit for dinner, casseroled with plenty of onion and accompanied by fluffy mashed potatoes, blue peas and cabbage. Mum was definitely the best cook in the world with Mrs Bishop, who cooked the school dinners, not that far behind, Sally reckoned. And she did not complain about missing out on the brains this time. Mum had dished her up a thick chunky middle portion, and it was delicious. It was jam tart for pudding, accompanied by a creamy rice pudding

Later, as they were sitting around the kitchen table, waiting for the team captain and family to arrive, Sally listened to dad and her Uncles discussing the 'will he or won't he' issues around this proposal for a National Health Service and Welfare State. She knew a bit about all this having listened to previous discussions and also from newspaper and wireless reports. She also knew who the 'He' was, Aneurin Bevan or 'The man from the Welsh Valleys, as some people called him.' These proposals for radical change, were she'd read, based on reports and recommendations made by various committees, and chaired by an economist called William Beveridge. It was entitled, not surprisingly, 'The Beveridge Report.' Most of the people calling for these changes it seemed were Liberals and Socialists.

"He'll do it. It'll be an uphill struggle, but it'll happen, mark my words," Uncle Alf was saying. "Old Bevan's not a man to give up easily and he's pretty passionate about this. He's seen a similar thing at work in the Welsh Valley's, on a much smaller scale mind you, but working well. I know he's up against some tough opposition from the Tories, and of course most of the Consultants and Doctors, with notable exceptions, are against it. But don't forget, old Bevan's now got an important ally in Lord Moran: Churchill's personal physician, and he's got a bit of clout. I wouldn't say he, Bevan, and Labour are within a whisker exactly, but they're getting there. Reminds me, what did Churchill call Bevan once? 'a squalid nuisance,' that's what. That was something to do with Russia if I remember rightly. I wonder what he's calling him now?" And he chuckled. "But anyway, I would say that a Welfare state embodies the whole spirit of the Christian ethic, wouldn't you? And what's wrong with that. What's wrong with trying to find ways for 'the elimination of the scourges of want, disease, ignorance, squalor and idleness,' as these reports put it."

"I just wish I were more of a believer," said dad. If I were I'd picture Brother George up there somewhere. And I know whose side he'd be on. It's all very well for folks to say, 'poor old Churchill, he did so much for us during the war.' And of course he did, don't know how we'd have managed without him. But the fact remains that he doesn't have to share a doctor with umpteen other people, like those in some of the London Boroughs do, where they've the devil's own job to pay for food let alone health care."

"You're speaking to the converted Pop," said Uncle Fred, and grinned. "I like your image of George though. I'd like to think about him up there and wagging his finger at one or two crooked officials he came into contact with down here. Do you remember the one he reduced to a stutter over some housing dispute? It didn't do much good though. The old bugger got away with it in the end. Upset our George that did. He hated what he saw as injustice. He'd fight anyone's corner if he thought they were being victimised. On the other hand, there was that lady who gave mum a florin when she was walking the streets with us as little kids. Mum hated charity as you know, but we'd been sold up by the bums, and it put some food in our bellies. Can't say I remember it but George did. He was that much older than us of course. Anyway, it'd give him the chance to thank her."

"I'd get him to have a word with old Solomon, or enemy number one as we called him," said Uncle Alf. A right old rogue he was. Then there was old

Crooke, or Mr Rent book. You remember him, don't you? He was another old rogue, though he did have a sense of humour. He always stopped for a chat if George was around. They got on quite well really. I remember he was always after one of George's pencil sketches, reckoned they were as good as any done by these so called 'artists.' He never got one though, as far as I know."

"Now I think he was the one who said that George was clever enough to make a sports coat for an elephant, or a bathing costume for a winkle, or something like that. Tickled our George pink, it did," said dad.

They all jumped as the scullery door opened suddenly and Bruce Lawrence popped his head inside. "Are we late?" he asked, as he took in the scene, the expectant faces turned towards him, and the kitchen table free of its normal debris. "What you making then Nin?" He asked, as his eye moved from the table towards the far window, where Queen Victoria's double was sitting on a straight backed, kitchen chair, crocheting away at a blanket she was making. "A dry stone wall," she replied without hesitation and without looking up. "Well that's me told," he said and grinned as he moved aside to let Mrs Lawrence and Eileen into the room. There was a brief discussion in which it was decided that Mr Lawrence and Uncle Alf were to be team leaders, then after a counting of heads, Nin was told in no uncertain terms, that she was needed to make up the numbers.

After the tricky manoeuvre of getting the right bum onto the right seat, the two teams sat facing one another across the table. Then dad stood up, tossed the silver sixpence into the air, deftly caught it with his right hand and smacked it on to the back of his left one. "Heads or tails," he called out and in no time at all the call had been made and the shiny coin was placed into Bruce Lawrence's open palm. Then the team leaders gave the signal for the game to begin.

A hush descended on the kitchen as Mr Lawrence held the coin aloft between thumb and fore-finger for the ritual inspection. Then he lowered the coin and began to tip tap it backward and forward over the row of passive, upward facing palms of his starter team, which were now resting on laps beneath the table awaiting the sensation of a light touch of cool metal. Then with a, "Are you ready then team? All together now, hands on table," the fists were raised and plopped onto the surface of the table like a team of synchronised swimmers.

The opposing team, who had watched the whole procedure with beady eyes, now concentrated on the facial expressions of their opponents as well as the slight give away bulge of a clenched fist. The young people around the table groaned as Nin, the first detective in this guessing game began the process of elimination. She was hopeless at this game. The subtle signs of possession of coin amongst the experienced players it seemed went way above her head and not only that, but she even seemed incapable of interpreting the dead giveaway sparkle in the eyes of the younger players.

She tapped and tut-tutted her way along the neatly lined up fists, which were springing open with no sign of the little sixpence inside. Then when just three fists remained on the table in self-conscious isolation, she sat back and for the first time, scrutinised the faces of their owners. Then after a couple of seconds, she bent forward, tapped Dorothy's fist and the coin tinkled down onto the table top. There were cheers all round, followed closely by comparative silence as the game continued.

Sally, who was sitting next to Uncle Alf, was in a position to watch the tip tap performance of her team leader closely. Like a cow with a musket and definitely lacking the flair and expertise of his opposite number, she thought to herself as he took his turn. He was whistling the tune to, 'hey little hen when, when, when will you lay me an egg for my tea,' softly, absentmindedly to himself, and she grinned. Then she came to with a shock as the sacred coin was dropped into her open hand, and in the split second it took to compose herself, she looked across the table and realised that Pat the scrutineer, had sussed her out. Serve me right, she thought to herself. I should have known better.

The game continued, until at a natural break in proceedings, Mr Lawrence sat up, and after flexing his shoulder muscles, withdrew his silver chained hob watch from his pocket. "Time for a cup of tea then is it Bruce," said mum as she watched him consult then replace the precious oracle back into his pocket. "I think that'll do us for tonight, don't you?" Nin was up on her feet in an instant, a look of relief accompanied by a rare smile on her face, as she and mum moved towards the stove and the kettle that was simmering on its surface.

Mrs Lawrence took the hint and followed and in no time at all, a rejuvenating brew had been made and set aside to infuse while the accompanying refreshment was prepared. After removing the mesh covers from two fruit cakes, Mrs Lawrence began to slice them up into thick chunks, and as Nin handed them round, the accompanying delicious aroma made Sally's mouth water, and she was not the only one. As Uncle Fred took his portion, he licked his lips, grinned and uttered a short prayer: "For what we are about to receive, may the Lord make us truly grateful." The 'Amen' however, was lost in the first sizable bite.

As they were eating, the tea was handed round, the cups rattling in their saucers as it was passed from hand to hand. "Pass me the runcible spoon will you Pop," said Uncle Fred pointing to the spoons in a tray at dad's elbow. "Say please then," said Jacky seriously. "You're right little 'un. I stand corrected. Please pass me the runcible spoon Pop," he added, with the emphasis very much on the 'please.'

"Can you tell us 'Brahn Boots' again please Uncle? I know some of it but it's taking me ages to learn the whole lot," said Sally, as Uncle Fred sat sipping his tea.

"Anything to oblige," he replied, then once he'd replaced his cup in its saucer, he began to recite the ditty:

"Our Aunt Hanna's passed away, we 'ad 'er funeral today. And it was a posh affair, We 'ad to 'av two policemen there.
The 'earse was lov'ly, all plate glass. And wot a coffin, oak and brass. We'd fah-sands weepin,' flahers galore. But Jim our cousin.......Wot do'yer fink 'e wore.
Why brahn boots, I ask yer, brahn boots. Fancy comin' to a funeral in brahn boots.
I will admit 'e ad a nice black tie, black finger nails, and an old black eye.
But yer can't see people orf when they die....In brahn boots

And aunt 'ad bin so good to 'im. Dun all that any muvver could fer 'im.
And Jim 'er son, to show 'is class, rolls up ter make it all a farse
In brahn boots, I ask yer, brahn boots. While all the rest wore decent black and mourning suits.

I'll own 'e didn't seem so gay, in fact 'e cried most part the way. But straight 'e reg'lar spoilt our day.
Wiv 'is brahn boots.

In the graveyard we left Jim. None of us said much to 'im. Yes we all gave 'im the bird, and then by accident we 'eard...
E'd gived 'is black boots to Jim Small, a bloke wot 'ad no boots at all
So p'raps Aunt Hanna doesn't mind, she did like people who was good and kind.
But brahn boots, I ask yer, brahn boots. Fancy comin' to a funeral in brahn boots.

And we could 'ear the neighbours all remark 'What 'im chief mourner, what a bloomin' lark.'
'Why 'e looks more like a bookmakers clerk....In 'is brahn boots.'

That's why we 'ad to be so rude to 'im. That's why we never said 'ow do' to 'im.'
We didn't know, 'e didn't say, 'e'd gived 'is other boots away.
But brahn boots, I ask yer, brahn boots. While all the rest wore decent black and mourning suits.

But someday, up at Heaven's Gate, poor Jim all nerves will stand and wait.
Till an Angel whispers, 'come in mate.....' Where's yer brahn boots?

"Well done Fred. That was even better that Stanley Holloway's rendition, and that's saying something," said dad.

"Thanks Pop. It's a favourite of mine, and Sally's as well I reckon. Better get it written down for her I suppose," Uncle Fred replied.

"Why does everyone call you Pop?" asked Sally, addressing her dad across a kitchen table that was beginning to assume its usual chaotic and muddled mess.

"Ah, I can answer that one," replied Uncle Alf, setting his cup down onto its saucer and looking across the table towards her. "He was always the serious one your dad, and somehow from quite an early age, felt responsible for us lot and for a time there, even kept old Soloman the rent man, off our backs. He was always in work of course right from the time he left school, and before then if you think about the odd jobs he did before and after school. He was good with his money, and often got the old lady out of trouble when the old man spent pretty near all his wages in the pub on his way home from work. He earned good money, your dad, when he worked as an upholsterer for Rolls Royce. He got the reputation for being the neatest turner of the corners on those large, cumbersome cushions they were decked out with, and that was a tricky bit of work I can tell you. And he got some of us started in the business as well. Then of course, me and Fred got married long before he did, and when our youngsters came along and we were hard up, he'd always help us out with a bob or two. When you moved down here, you never pressed us for us for your share of that house we'd all bought together in London, did you Pop," he continued looking directly across at his brother. "We've paid you back now, of course. We know you've had your lean times, since you've been down here, and I sometimes wonder how Doll manages to feed you all the way she does. And not just feed, but just think of all the washing gets through, and all those other chores, and I've never heard her moan. One in a million is Dolly," and he paused here for a few seconds before continuing. "And another thing, do you remember coming up to us in London and helping with all the fixtures, the shelves and such like, when me and Lil started up our cobbling business all those years ago, Pop? That was a job and an arf, that was. You brought one of the girls with you if I remember rightly." Dad sniffed and cleared his throat before replying.

"Hang on a bit. Anything I did for you lot, you've more than made up for by what you've done here. I'd had the devil's own job keeping up with all the maintenance on the sheds and chicken coops without you lot; that shed you creosoted for me this morning for instance. One of the girls would have got round to it eventually, but not with the same enthusiasm as you boys. And I've got plenty more jobs lined up for you, don't worry. For a start, there'll be a bonfire for you to take care of in the autumn Fred, as long as you promise to watch your eyebrows this time." and he grinned. "And those walks we do, come rain or shine or whatever, do me a power of good. It's not just the exercise is it, there's always something different to see and talk about, and we always, always meet up with someone round the country lanes who wants to stop and chat.

Anyway, we seem to have expanded the thing a bit, but as for this 'Pop' business, it started off as a bit of a joke as far as I can remember. And looks like I'm stuck with it."

Now that this bit of family hierarchy had been sorted, the conversation moved on, mostly now of an agrarian nature. Mr Lawrence was talking, and once he'd got around to explaining the secret of his success with growing peaches, Sally's interest was aroused. It was down to one or two basic rules really, he said. Position was important, and as he pointed out, having the run of Mr and Mrs Stafford's huge garden, gave him plenty of scope. He had chosen the south facing wall of a large building in the grounds, and had trained the branches along wires, which he'd nailed to the brickwork. Cordoning he called it. Some of these exotic fruits came their way from time to time, and they were sweet and juicy and unlike any other fruit she had ever tasted.

More tea was brewed, and as dad stood up for a re-fill, Sally noticed that he was wearing one of the sleeveless pullovers Dolly Pilbeam had knitted for him. She'd kept him well supplied with these homely woollies over the years, same style, differing only in the varying shades of green, brown and fawn wool with which she made them, and they were always a perfect fit. This kindly lady regarded by many of the village folk as 'simple,' adored mum and dad, who treated her kindly and with respect. She was aware of and seemed to accept that some people found her a bit strange so avoided or were off hand with her at times. Sally, to her shame had bobbed down behind a hedge once when she had seen her approaching. But she knew better now. As mum said, there was not one trace of malice in this kindly lady. This sentiment had been endorsed by the Smith family, now in residence at the Manse on Chapel Hill. They had also taken Ellen Brown, another simple soul under their wing. Ellen now insisted on supplying them with milk from her old cow, 'the good stuff for the grownups and the paltry 'orrible stuff for the littlens,' were her words. Sally would never forget the scolding she had received from her mum all those years ago, for teasing this gentle lady. As mum rarely raised her voice to them, this uncharacteristic reprimand from her had made an instant and lasting impact.

After finishing her second cup of tea, Nin went back to her crocheting again, clearly more at ease with this familiar task than with the perplexing game of Tippit. Her steel grey hair, rolled tightly and neatly into its characteristic roll around her head, barely moved as the hooked implement in her hand moved rhythmically in and out of the multi coloured blanket she was making. She was sitting squarely on her seat, back straight as a ramrod, and even though her legs were slightly apart, she still managed somehow to look majestic. Sally reckoned she could last forever, old Nin, just like Granny Cotton really who was taking a short break with Aunty Lylie at the moment: a bit different from poor old Solomon Grundy whose life had been foreshortened in verse, she remembered. Just those few words of prose had seemingly condemned the poor man to an early demise.

Her gaze went from table to a higher perspective as she contemplated the picture above the fireplace, 'mum's boy,' they called it. The tousled headed youth in the picture, clad in short trousers and casual, open necked shirt, was lying amongst raggedy tufts of dune grass, one bare knee cocked upwards, his eyes shaded from above by a sunburned hand. There was a rapt, faraway look in his eyes as he contemplated the Heavens. Within the fluffy cloud formations above his head, and clearly the object of his single-minded attention, was a visionary ship in full sail, dipping and gliding away towards imaginary horizons. So familiar with this painting was she, that if it were ever to be removed from its resting place, she would be singularly upset, bereaved even she reckoned. After all, this boy was part of their life now.

Her gaze and attention went suddenly from contemplation of the abstract to the here and now. Hilary had decided to amuse the little ones with a game of 'two little dickybirds sitting on a wall,' and had moved with them to the far side of the room. Having decorated the nails of her forefingers with bits of saliva soaked paper, she was now reciting the little ditty, her hands flicking back and forth across her shoulders as she did so. Dorothy and Jacky chuckled excitedly to begin with as they studied her every move. Then the predictable puzzled frown began to crease their foreheads as once again they had failed to solve the mystery of those contrary birds. Sally grinned. For her the swapping over of the two fingers was so obvious now, but it had not always been so. She remembered having got so upset and angry with herself for not being able to solve the puzzle that in the end, Hazel had taken pity on her and had divulged its simple secret.

"I knew I shouldn't have had that second cup of tea Dolly. I need to visit the little house now, just when I've got myself all nice and comfortable." Uncle Alf was saying and Sally turned and watched as he rose from his chair and made his way towards the scullery door, knowing that before long she too would be making that short but necessary journey.

"Do one for me while you're out there, will you," said Mr Lawrence as he took his precious time-piece from his pocket once again and carefully consulted the oracle.

"We'll soon have to be on our way, more's the pity," he announced, stretching then wriggling his bum around on the chair as he sought to prepare his body for the will to follow the instructions of his words. "That moon out there'll, hardly have enough strength in it to light us through the lane, let alone the short cut along the stream, the way that daughter of mine wants to go." Before he got any further, Uncle Alf burst back through the door.

"Quick, lock the door Pop, or Dolly'll be out there bowing and scraping to that old moon," he announced. "There's only the sliver of an eye-brow out there but you know what she's like. She'll be out there bowing and scraping and rattling those pennies around in her apron before you can say Jack Robinson, and she's not exactly got rich on it."

71

"Too late," mum replied a satisfied grin on her face. "I've already been out there and paid my respects to the little lady. You don't measure wealth just in pennies. I've got all these lovely daughters and a lot else to be thankful for, and who knows what would have been my lot if I'd not done my duty by her all these years. That reminds me, Betty will be down next weekend. Bless her." As she paused, Sally looked at her, and for a moment detected that fleeting, wistful look in her eyes, as though she was remembering those two little girls she had lost, and she experienced a pang of conscience. Mum always said nice things about her and her sisters, even though there were times when, she in particular, moaned and groaned when asked to perform the simplest of chores. Her mum also appreciated their individual culinary likes and dislikes and knowing dad's intolerance of waste of any kind, dished up food that she knew would not bring forth grunts and groans of disapproval. She always put the fatty stuff, the bits that made Sally's stomach heave if she tried to eat them, on to her own plate along with any vegetables that might have been a bit on the tough side. She would try, she really would try, to be a bit more helpful in the future.

"Well, better be off then," said Mr Lawrence as he rose to his feet. "That cake of yours has just reached me feet now Dolly, it'll get me home and up the wooden stairway to me bed, that's for sure. Thanks, it's been a splendid evening. Just let us know when you're down again, you boys, and we'll arrange another game or two. It's about time you got those chickens of yours shut up for the night, as well Pop. Else that wily old fox'll be there sorting out one or two for his supper. I can see he's still a regular visitor by the track he's made across the field. It's been there since kingdom come. Right, follow me then you lot," he added as after a general shuffling of chairs, a mass exodus seemed about to take place. "Well follow me then, I'm just behind you," he added as he headed towards the scullery door.

"See you Monday then Dolly," said Mrs Lawrence as she followed the others through the doorway. "Perhaps we'll have a go at the bedrooms if we've got time."

Mrs Lawrence spent Monday morning at Battle Barn Farm, helping Mrs Collins with washing and housework. At lunchtime she walked down to Sylvian, and after a spot of dinner, she and mum set to, to tackle various household chores. She was a dab hand at housework, her own cosy home reflecting this. Dust and dirt shrank away in terror when they saw her approaching with duster and floor cloth, and a room visited by this industrious lady seemed to shiver as it sought to hide its nakedness from prying eyes. It did not stay that way for long however. The speed with which the girls reversed this unnatural state of things was legendary. They would descend on a tidy room like a whirlwind, and in no time at all the girls along with the very room itself, would breathe a sigh of relief. But Mrs Lawrence never gave up.

This evening the little ones had been on their best behaviour, Sally reflected. Not once had they slunk under the table to take a look at Mrs

Lawrence's long knickers, the colour of which seemed to fascinate them. They had done the same thing to Granny Cotton and Aunty Nin at one time, but seemed fixated on this particular lady at the moment.

Not long after the departure of the Lawrence's, Hilary and Sally decided to make a move. Not that they were in too much of a hurry to reach Hilary's place. Ronald was staying with friends and as no arrangement had been made for Willie and Roy to join them at Windy Ridge this evening, they could just sit and chat to their hearts content. But definitely no more games. They'd had a surfeit of Tippit this evening, and if they succumbed to the excitement of a game of snakes and ladders, they would never sleep.

"Moonlight starlight, Bogey won't come out tonight," said Sally, and paused as she opened the top gate for Hilary to pass through. They both stood for a moment looking up into the infinity of the starry Heaven's, their eyes lingering for a

moment on the pale yellow crescent of the new moon, which seemed to hang suspended in the eastern Sky. The magical mystery of celestial space struck Sally anew, and she shivered with the wonder of it all. As they continued on their way, the sound of muffled voices reached their ears, and as they looked right across the darkening field, could just make out the shapes of the men as moved around the chicken coops. The old birds would be safe from the clutches of the old fox for another night, Sally thought to herself. As dad said, that old fox was wily enough without actually inviting him in for a meal.

Once indoors, the girls spotted the thick chunks of buttered bread on a plate beneath a mesh cover, also the cheese dish and a tin of syrup to one side, left there by Mrs Elkins. They were hungry they decided. The lump of fruit cake they'd eaten earlier on was gone and almost forgotten about as they studied the food in front of them.

"Yum, yum, I'm having syrup on my bit of bread," said Hilary, then grinned as she saw Sally's face contort. "I know, I know, syrup makes your teeth itch, well you can have the cheese then," she added moving the dish over to where Sally would be sitting. They, like everyone else in the country, were looking forward to the 25th of July when bread rationing was due to come to an end. 'Christmas day in July,' as this momentous event was referred to by many folk. It was not that they, personally, had gone without, but the sooner the old ration books could be done away with the better.

Once they had eaten and cleared the plates away, they decided that a few games of noughts and crosses would not be too taxing for their little brains, and Hilary soon found and brought paper and pencils to the table. While they played this simple game, they chatted away, and to start with the chatter was frivolous. After a while however, the conversation became more serious, their expressions solemn as Hilary began to speculate on the fate of that Spitfire pilot, who had been so badly burned when his plane had been shot down during the war. He had spent many months in the village, being cared for by Miss Mc Kean at Asselton House, and travelling to and from East Grinstead for treatment. His injuries had been a grim and visible reminder of the horrors of war, and the sacrifices made by this brave and dedicated band of men. He had been treated by a man called, Sir Archibald Mc Indoe, the name imprinted on Sally's mind by the very nature of the work he did, the near miracles he performed. This Doctor, or Surgeon, was a pioneer in the practice of skin grafting, and the Pilots who entered his special Burns Unit, were referred to as guinea pigs. She remembered her first glimpse of this young man as he had stood silhouetted against the window of Asselton House, soon after his arrival in the village. The image of that fire ravaged face, had caused her to recoil for just a split second, but it was long enough for him to register her reaction. The memory of the haunted expression in his eyes as he had turned away from the window, still filled her with shame. Indeed, the image and her reaction to it still had an effect on her even now. However, by the time he had left the village, although many scar's still remained, the contours of his face had been restored, the look of disfigurement had gone. And with it, and best of all, that haunted look had left his eyes.

After a while, they put pencil and paper aside. It was Ovaltine time Hilary decided, and as she got up to prepare the beverage, Sally noticed Mr Elkins' Brownie Camera sitting on the edge of the side board, and she wondered what on earth it was doing there. He was usually so careful with the thing. It had not even been replaced in its box, which stood beside it, still adorned with the picture of a little man with a fat belly and impossibly thin legs, and still wearing that ridiculous cap. Perhaps this blip in Mr Elkins's normal behaviour was something to do with the tension between himself and Mrs Elkins, which was becoming more and more noticeable as time went on. Hilary was very worried about the situation, especially its effect on her younger brother for whom she felt somehow responsible. She had spoken to Mum Cotton at length about it, and had derived a measure of comfort from mum's support with this difficult and tricky situation. It wasn't fair, Sally thought. Her friend was one of the kindest, most generous people she had ever met. She did not know what she would have done without her friendship over the years. She felt so inadequate. She appreciated the seriousness of the situation, and yet was unable to help her friend in any way. Why did grown up fallings out seem so much more serious than childish ones, she asked herself. Then she relaxed. As Hilary placed the steaming mugs of Ovaltine on the table, she noticed a cheeky grin on her friends face.

"I've just been thinking about what Willie was talking about the other day," she said as she sat down and cupped her hands around her mug. "I know it happened ages ago and we'd heard it all before, several times, but it's still funny. It was after I'd mentioned old Mr Soan and his allotment, wasn't it. We've pinched one or two of his carrots and so forth from time to time, haven't we?" Sally grinned, remembering the flavour of those hastily pulled carrots they'd munched on after they had given them a quick rub on their sleeve, and she continued to grin, knowing what was coming next. Hilary was about to recount what had happened when Albert tried to get his own back, for what he considered unjust punishments from his dad over the years. She was more than willing to listen to a rehash, especially when Hilary was in charge.

"Looks like old Charlie was a bit of a tyrant in the old days, and Albert seems to have got more than his fair share of hidings when he was little, didn't he," she began. "Mind you, he was a bit of a tearaway, but then what his dad saw as mischief, he reckoned was a bit of harmless fun. The things Willie mentioned, that Albert was supposed to have got up to as a kid and got hidings for, didn't seem that bad to us really, did they. But there you go. Anyway, it was when Albert realised he could run faster than his dad that the gun thing happened. I can't make out if he planned his revenge or just got lucky. Whatever, the outcome was the same. Fancy using your dad's bum for target practice! Trouble is we've got too much imagination," she said, pausing for a few seconds to compose herself as the absurdity of the whole thing hit her. "I can just picture it, can't you? I can just see Old Charlie coming out of the lavvy, down the garden there, his thoughts miles away, and that pellet hitting him right on his backside. I think it was with his gun, too. As Albert told some of the boys later, he hadn't hung around once the deed had been done. His dad had let out an almighty howl and that was it. He'd just legged it. Can't say I blame him. His dad'd soon clocked him. Anyway, you know as well as I do that he had to keep well out of the way of his dad for ages after that. As Charlie came in one door, Albert shot out of the other, Mrs Soan said. These days Albert treats the whole thing as a joke, but he's still adamant that his actions were justified. His old man, he says dished out some right old hidings to him when he was a little kid."

They both knew this incident would continue to crop up in conversations from time to time. They reckoned it would probably join other notable and humorous tales, passed down from one generation to the next, by people like Bangy Smith and old Fred. It was certainly on a par with old Phillie Brooman and the stinging of her bum with that bunch of nettles, and that tale would certainly enter into village annals, folk law, or whatever you chose to call it.

After a while Hilary moved over to the sink to rinse out the mugs, and when she returned, rubbing her hands together to rid them of their dampness, she began talking about the fete at Westfield Place. "Pity Betty's going to miss the fete this year, she always tries to get down for it, doesn't she. It'll be good to see her next weekend though. I remember her telling us about the Sunday club she Freda and Hazel used to go to at Westfield Place when they were little. Lady Newton organised it of course as she does the fete and so forth. She said that it wasn't religious exactly, just a prayer at the start and another at the end of the thing. When it was fine she said, they had games and nature walks, that sort of thing. But when it was cold and wet, they had needlework and cookery lessons.

Well the girls did. Don't know what the boys got up to. I remember her telling us about the vase Doris Saunters won for a piece of needlework she did. Betty said it was ever so pretty, the vase, and had cost one and sixpence from Woolworth's. Don't know how she found that one out. She told us Lady Newton was quite generous, she always awarded prizes for good work."

"Talking of sewing, have you seen the table-cloth Betty made for mum?" asked Sally. "She brought it down last time she was here. She's embroidered flowers all around the outside, and a cluster of roses in the centre. It's got something called filigree work on it as well. I've never seen anything like it, it's lovely. I don't know how she does it. One thing's for sure, mum won't dare put it anywhere near us lot, it'd get ruined in no time. She'll keep it for the front room table I expect." Then she paused for a moment. "Do you know what Betty's favourite poem is?" She asked. "It's 'The Lady of Shallot.' She knows it pretty well off by heart, like I do Greys Elegy. And she's just taught me the froggies poem. Do you want to hear it?" Before waiting for a yes or no, she began to recite the little ditty:

> *"Twenty froggies went to school. Down beside a rushy pool.*
> *Twenty little coats of green. Twenty vests all white and clean.*
> *We must be in time said they. First we study then we play.*
> *That is how we keep the rule. When we froggies go to school*
> *Master Bullfrog grave and stern. Called the classes in their turn.*
> *Taught them how to nobly strive. Also how to leap and dive.*
> *Taught them how to dodge a blow. From a stick that bad boys throw.*
> *Twenty froggies grew up fast. Bullfrogs they became at last.*
> *Polished to a high degree. As such froggies aught to be.*
> *Now they sit on other logs. Teaching other little frogs."*

"There I really like that one don't you? Bit different from Grey's Elegy, but just as good in its own way."

After a while they began to yawn. The day's activities had finally caught up with them. Before they made their way to bed however, they decided to take one more look outside. Once in the garden, Sally's gaze went immediately towards the Heavens, and she sighed with the magic of it all. The thin arc of the new moon had moved further across the darkened sky, and was floating on a seemingly endless Universe, pierced by a million stars.

Chapter 4

The thunder-storm that had rumbled around the Heavens a couple of evenings ago, had cleared away the hot, sticky humid air that had been hanging around, and Sally reckoned that if this early morning sunshine was anything to go by, today, Saturday would be hot, sunny and just about ideal for a day on the beach. She grinned as she remembered mum's words of comfort to Dorothy and Jacky as they had sat at the kitchen table, wide eyed and frightened, as the storm had rumbled and flashed around the Heavens. 'Listen, it's only God banging his drums,' she said, and after a while they had joined the other girls up at the kitchen window, gazing and exclaiming at the spectacle. Mums words of comfort had worked their magic as usual.

A day or two before the arrival of the storm, Sally had noticed clouds of flying ants emerging from the ground around the underground tank, many pecked up and devoured by cheeky sparrows. She had seen even more of these insects emerging from cracks in the pathways as she had made her way to school that day. This strange phenomenon, often the precursor to a summer thunder-storm she had noticed, never failed to intrigue and fascinate her. Somewhere in that tiny brain of theirs she reckoned, must be an ability or instinct to anticipate such things. She found it all quite fascinating.

Mum was baking bread and the aroma hit Sally's nostrils as she and Pat passed the copper-house on their way back from Battle Barn Farm with the milk. Sally loved helping with this chore, her favourite bit the mixing of the yeast and sugar together into a khaki coloured liquid She had done that job before she'd left home. Now there were sandwiches to prepare, some with meat paste and some with cheese and slices of dad's juicy tomatoes in them. They would probably be a bit soggy by the time they ate them, but who cared. She would also make a few from that jar of last year's blackcurrant jam mum had found at the back of her store cupboard. It had a bit of mould on the top, but that was easily scraped away. No trouble. Better than one of Desperate Dan's cow pies any old day.

She and Pat had also to search out bathing costumes for them all. The swimming costumes along with the girls' under wear, were stored away in the bottom drawer of the sideboard, where they proceeded to turn themselves into a jumble of androgynous miscellany, or a bunch of bastards as she usually called it, under her breath of course.

Hilary was making her way up the field as Pat and Sally put the finishing touches to the food and drink for their beach picnic, and the little ones, having seen her coming through the bottom gate, had rushed down to meet her. Now, It was almost time to depart. Just a last minute check of goods and chattels was needed, that was all.

Once Pat and Hilary had picked up bags and Sally had hoisted her dad's old rucksack on to her shoulder, they were on their way. When they reached the lane, Dorothy and Jacky paused for a moment to inspect a bumble-bee that was taking a well-earned rest amongst the tufts of course grass that grew in abundance along here. As they extended a tentative finger towards the little furry creature, Pat stooped down beside them and began to recite a little ditty, much loved by the little ones.

> "A swarm of bees in May is worth a load of hay.
> A swarm of bees in June is worth a silver spoon.
> A swarm of bees in July is not worth a fly."

They caught up with Hilary and Sally at the end of the track, and crossed over the main road with them. In just a few minutes, the bus was drawing up beside them, and once on board, they made their way to the top deck, where luckily, there were enough empty seats for them all to sit together.

As the bus passed Brown's place, Sally caught sight of little Mrs Edwards, and knew she would be on her way to Sylvian. She often popped in to see mum, and if there was washing up to be done, or clothes to be mangled and hung on lines, she would roll up her sleeves and just get on with it. Then the two of them would sit down and enjoy a chat and a cup or two of tea together. Sally winced as she remembered her last encounter with the old mangle. The monotony of feeding countless items of clothing through those rollers, had lulled her into a false sense of security, and suddenly there was an ominous crack, and her favourite cardigan emerged the other side, two of its buttons smashed to smithereens. It had taken her ages to find replacements from within that large biscuit tin of mum's with its assortment of buttons, press-studs and other odds and ends, and she'd vowed to be more careful in future.

Pat, she suddenly realised, was talking about Aunty Annie and Uncle Tom who were due to arrive at Sylvian by early to mid-afternoon. It was a long journey from Bicester where they lived and the first thing they looked for as they made their weary way up the field they said, was a glimpse of mum standing at the door, waving the tea pot at them. They reckoned the first sip of sweet, milky tea from her old brown tea-pot was a life saver. The girls had heard recently that Uncle Tom's nick-name was Spicker, but because he couldn't stand the name, they weren't to mention it. Sally thought she might just be tempted. After all he did have a very good sense of humour, and Spicker did have a nice ring to it. June, their one and only daughter would not be with them this time. She was out to work now, so of course had very little spare time. It was a pity really. She also had a keen sense of humour, and when her visit coincided with Aunty Nellie and her family, it was a laugh a minute.

The bus rumbled on, pulling into the side of the road at regular intervals to allow more passengers on board. The Conductor was up and down the stairs like a yo-yo. No wonder he looked like a skinned rabbit, Sally thought to herself as she listened to the chatter and clatter going on around her. She had a brief glimpse of Wayside as the bus passed by, that was all and in no time at all it seemed, they were passing the Briars, then on and into Silverhill. They began to gather their bags together once the bus reached the bottom of London Road, and when it reached the bus stop at White Rock Pavilion, they were organised and the first to alight there. Then once they had crossed the busy main road, they made their way down onto the beach, to the west side of the Pier.

The area alongside the pillars of this impressive structure was already alive with colour and movement, but they soon found a space big enough to accommodate them and their bags. After a bit of shuffling and general organisation, the older girls removed their outer clothing to reveal their shirred elastic swimming costumes, of which they were justly proud. The setting in place of those vexatious but necessary rubber bathing hats, took a little longer, and made them look like Mediaeval gargoyle's, but it had to be done. Then once this tricky manoeuvre had been taken care of, the little ones were helped with their own preparations.

The tide was on its way out and it was mostly the very young and the elderly who were sharing the shallow fringe of its gently lapping water. The men with trousers rolled up over bony knees, and the women with skirts hoisted up as they moved cautiously through the water, contrasted strongly with others, who were thrashing around enthusiastically in deeper water. The number of those in the latter category was soon to be doubled or even trebled if the number of costumed bodies now tramping through the shallow surf and out into deeper water was anything to go by, Sally reckoned. Then she paused for a moment, and allowed her mind and imagination to flip from the narrow to a wider perspective. With a sudden clarity of vision, the whole scene around her seemed to morph into one colourful, moving charade, and she held her breath, absorbing this multi-dimensional impressionistic image. Then she blinked, and immediately, individual shapes and colour came sharply back into focus, and she returned to the here and now.

The older girls divided their time between keeping an eye on the little ones and swimming in the deeper water, and it was when Sally was returning to the shallows for her turn to oversee the little ones, that she spotted two familiar figures.

"Well blow me down. That's Alan Turner and Phil what's his name over there. I'm sure it is Hilary," she said pointing in the direction of two skinny youngsters in baggy bathing trunks who were splashing about in the water, several yards west of them. Can't really mistake them, can you? Seen more fat on a chip," and she grinned. "Wonder where their bikes are? They must've brought them down here, they take their bikes everywhere with them. Anyway, they can't have seen us, or they'd have been over here. Off you go then. Don't waste precious time," she added.

After a while the swimmers returned to shallow water to join the others. It was time for a change they decided. So they made their way over to the rock pools, only to find that these havens for shrimps and crabs and other sea creatures, had clearly received more than a tidy bit of interference from nets and spades and inquisitive hands. The creatures that would have been there, had either been caught or were cowering somewhere in the depths of its cloudy waters. So it was the creation of a masterpiece in sand, or perhaps and more likely, the building of a couple of common or garden sand castles, they decided. Without further ado, Sally made her way up across the beach to search amongst the bags and baggage for digging and sculpting tools. She found the two large table spoons straight away. She had included them knowing from past experience how good these culinary objects were for digging in soft, damp sand. She looked again at one of them, and wondered, not for the first time what the letters and numbers, 5RGR 5188 inscribed into the handle stood for. It didn't matter really she told herself as she ferreted out the two spades. She also found a bucket for the moulding of turrets and the carrying of water for the moat, before carefully making her way back down to join the others.

They set to with hands and implements, and after several wobbly starts, an impressive castle began to take shape. After decorating the thing with pebbles and bits of bladdered seaweed, they started to build another one. This one however, was smaller, and a bit naïve. The need for sustenance, a drink in particular, was creeping up on them. Once the moat had been filled to their satisfaction, they rinsed the sand from their hands in its water, then stood back for just a moment to admire their handy work. Then Sally walked back up across the beach, followed closely by Pat and Hilary, who were carrying the two little ones. She quickly stretched towels over the stoney ground, and once they were all settled, began to sort out food and drink.

"There, you'll do," said Hilary as she turned to Jacky and rearranged the white sun hat over her blond curls before passing a sandwich into her outstretched hand. "Better see to yours as well," she said picking up Dorothy's hat that had made its way onto the ground beside her, and placed it back onto the top of her shiny, dark, straight hair. Then, quickly following Pat and Sally's example, she began to pull the rubber hat off her head. "There, I'd rather put up with a bit of water in my ears than struggle into that thing again," she said as she placed the tiresome thing firmly down onto the ground beside her.

As they chatted and munched away on their sandwiches, a sea gull suddenly swooped down, and if it had not been for the quick reaction from the older ones, would have made off with the contents of Jacky's clenched fist. They felt the air disturbance of its wings as it came to within a whisker of its prize, and for a split second saw its round beady eye fixed unblinkingly on its victim. And then it levelled out and rose up and away to seek an easier meal from the hand of a less vigilant individual.

"Whew, that was close," said Pat and grinned as she saw the startled expression on Jacky's face. "Not to worry. Let's do 'this little piggy went to market' first shall we? And then we can have a game of 'I spy."

The games that followed put the gull incident, if not completely from their minds, then far enough away to be of any significance. For a while, Sally fully participated in these simple games and chanted nursery rhymes, but gradually her

attention began wander. Not far from where they were sitting, she spied a man chewing absentmindedly on his moustache as he dried his hair vigorously on a small towel. She quickly averted her gaze as he paused, looked up and caught her eye.

Within another group close by, a harassed mother was doing her best to provide her noisy, squabbling youngsters with the sandwich of their choice. Sally grinned when she heard one child firmly reject the sandwich being offered to him. 'I ain't eating blo'er paste, no way. Give it to 'er,' he said pointing towards a little one, with a decidedly snotty face, and wriggling away on its mother's knee. She was able to study this family to her hearts content, so totally absorbed were they in each other. They were far too absorbed in their own petty disagreements and squabbling to care a tinker's cuss what was going on around them.

After a while, her attention drifted towards the Pier, with its and seemingly endless sources of entertainment. Although her view of this elevated place was limited from where she was sitting, her memory and imagination was well up to the task of filling in the detail. She cupped her ear with one hand, and could just make out the clanking sounds coming from the forest of machines, housed within one of the Pier's large, ornate buildings. Pennies would be rolling down narrow slotted grooves, most to be gobbled up by the greedy machine, without so much as a hiccup. There would be frenetic turning of wheels on other machines to control horses or to partake in a game of football, accompanied by shouts and the occasional expletive. On another piece of apparatus, rubber rings would be thrown in the direction of some coveted prize, usually without success.

And at this very moment, young, fashionable ladies would be clattering along the deck, coming to an abrupt halt as they caught their high heels in the spaces between the planks, their subsequent giggles betraying the fragility of their own perceived persona. Some would hesitate beside a certain kiosk, its doorway shrouded in thick, heavy curtains, where a fortune telling Gypsy would be ensconced, surrounded by the simple tools of her trade. Some would even venture inside, enticed by the beckoning finger of the exotic lady and the allure of its dark interior. For the bravest and most affluent, the crystal ball would be on offer, the aura of power and mystery surrounding this orb, enhanced by the deep penetrating expression in the Gypsy's dark eyes as she placed her hands ceremoniously over the ball without disturbing its perfect symmetry. Others would choose the packs of cards, which would be cut, their curious symbols interpreted by the lady in her low monotonous voice. Or, for a few coppers, the curious could just offer up the palm of their hand, nervously placing it into and entrusting it to, the scrutiny of this enigmatic lady. This Madam something or other.

There were always side-shows on the Pier, and the Punch and Judy show was one of these. On a day like this however, the puppeteer would almost certainly have set up his show somewhere on the beach, moving the display, lock, stock and barrel from time to time, as he sought a fresh audience to entertain - or terrify. She allowed her thoughts to dwell for a few moments on the time the little ones had been exposed to the rough humour and even rougher behaviour of this extended family group of puppets. They had been terrified. Mr Punch, the weird hooked nosed puppet resplendent in red and yellow costume and wearing a funny hat, was as usual, the main protagonist, with poor Judy bearing the brunt of his ill humour. The violence, so overt and realistic, was accompanied by the loud booing and hissing of an excited crowd, grouped closely together around the highly decorated puppeteer's kiosk. As Judy keeled over having taken several blows from a cosh wielded by her violent partner, a squat, red faced, helmeted policeman suddenly and fortuitously popped up. As he wobbled from side to side, repeating the phrase, 'allo, allo, what's goin' on 'ere,' he sounded more like a parrot than a policeman, A bright green crocodile had then burst on to the scene, and had begun to chomp away indiscriminately at the trio of fantastic puppets. By the time it had got the head of the terrified policeman in its jaws, squeaking and screeching, 'that's the way to do it, that's the way to do it,' it all became too much for the two little ones, and they had burst into tears. Sally had breathed a sigh of relief as she and the other girls had hurriedly whisked them away from this scene of violence and manic manipulation, having to force their way at times through the cheek by jowl audience. It was all so garish, nightmarish almost. She found the whole thing quite bizarre.

She looked across the beach, and having satisfied herself that Mr Punch and his entourage were not in the immediate vicinity, her gaze moved towards the receding tide, its lapping water now frothed and indistinct with human activity. Its timeless, relentless ebb and flow however, could never be interrupted nor even compromised by such disturbance. The old moon, she'd been told, was very much in charge of this puzzling phenomenon. Then she leaned back, narrowing her eyes to counteract the brightness of the day. After a while, the whole area in front of her began to shimmer with a florescent glow, the miscellaneous clusters of bags and bodies, water and sand merging until it resembled some gigantic abstract painting. The apparition lasted only seconds, and once gone, refused to replicate its magical self. In fact, her vision was now so keen that she was able to make out individual figures far away down the beach. And she was sure that two of them were the hairless pipe cleaners.

What a contrast to the cold winter days when often the only sign of life here were the hardy sea birds, silhouetted against the moody sky as they wheeled and dipped in and over its grey water. And maybe just a lone human being, head down as it battled determinedly across the beach, against the elements.

Between the general chit-chat, games were played and stories told. When it came to Sally's turn, she chose the tale of Little Red Riding hood. The little ones still found it a bit scary even though they knew the tale and its eventual outcome off by heart; but not too scary. Then she watched as Hilary having found her hankie, spit and polished the bits of food from around the faces of the two youngsters. "There that's better. You won't get the flies around you now," she said.

Eventually, they decided to pop down to the water's edge for a quick cooling off, and as Jacky seemed quite comfortable where she was, they decided to let her be. After clearing the large stones away from a small area, they gave her a bucket and one of the large spoons, and left her to play in the residual layer of small sandy stones and bits of shell.

"Don't worry. We won't be long. Then we'll have a bit of fruit cake when we get back, said Hilary, straightening Jacky's hat before following the others down across the beach.

The water was surprisingly cold but refreshing as they walked into it, and it was not long before they were up to their waist and then with a lunge, were in it up to their necks. While Pat and Dorothy splashed around in the shallows, Hilary and Sally decided to swim out for just a couple of minutes, just long enough they said for a bit of practice to the breast stroke. Their enthusiasm for this craft had come about as the result of a fib really. For a long while they had been content to half swim half doggy paddle, but having told Daniel Smith and John Hullock that they could really swim, they'd had to put in some serious practice; more so as the two boys had challenged them to a race to the end of the Pier. At the time it had given the girls just two weeks to get their act together, and they often recalled the frantic efforts they had made to master the basic stroke and then to get up a bit of speed. On the day of the race, the boys had given them a head start, which the girls had taken full advantage of. By the time the boys had realised their mistake it had been too late. The girls had won by a whisker.

As Hilary and Sally turned and began to swim back to shallow water, they saw Pat waving to them and realised by the urgency of her gesture, that something was wrong. "Jacky's gone, she's not there," she said as the girls moved up to her.

"Me and Dora went to look for her just now and she wasn't there. We've looked everywhere."

Sally's stomach did a triple summersault as she took in this unexpected and very worrying news, and she and Hilary rushed up across the beach, regardless of pain, to where Jacky had been sitting just a short while ago. Well had it been that short a time ago she was asking herself. They looked frantically from left to right and all around before setting off to scour the beach and rock pools. They looked everywhere they could think of, to no avail. It was just when raw panic really set in, and Dorothy and Pat began to cry, that they found her. Sally recognised the hat first and beneath that, she saw a bedraggled little girl, her little sister, hand in hand with a very worried looking young man with two children alongside. As they rushed towards him, gathering Jacky up into their arms and hugging her with palpable relief, his face lit up. He had found her wandering around the rock pools, crying her eyes out as she looked for, she had told him, 'my big sisters.' He had tidied her up as best he could he said, before beginning to search along the beach and sand trying to find and reunite her with her sisters. In reality it had taken minutes rather than hours, but to the girls it had seemed a lifetime.

After thanking him profusely, they stood back and held her at arm's length, then gasped as they saw the state she was in. Her little legs were scratched and bleeding and the palms of her hands were also grazed. She told them she had been scared on her own, and when they had not returned after what she thought had been ages, had gone to look for them. She had made her way across the beach to start with, and had then made her way to the rock pools where they had played earlier on. It was while she had been scrambling and slipping over the barnacle covered rock, that the man had found her, crying her eyes out.

Hilary gathered Jacky up in her arms and began to make her way back to their own unique and untidy pile of bags and bathing paraphernalia, and sat her carefully down on towels hastily folded and arranged over the pebbles by the other girls. They still could not believe what had happened, how abandoned she must have felt. She was very quiet now and allowed them to bathe her cuts and grazes with the edge of a towel moistened with the water from one of the bottles, without a murmur. Even the offer of another piece of mum's moist fruit-cake did not raise much enthusiasm in her. Once they had made her as comfortable as possible the girls, having rubbed the dry sand from arms and legs, began to dress beneath towels hastily but securely fixed around their bodies. Then once the little ones were tidied up and dressed, they gathered up the bags and made their way up towards the promenade.

The older girls, while in the process of dressing, had decided on the conscience easing strategy of purchasing a book or small toy for the little ones, and with this in mind, and taking turns to carry Jacky, they made their way towards the back end of Woolworth's. To their intense relief, once through its double doors, Jacky began to take an interest in the colourful nick-knacks displayed in and around this Store. She loved books of all kinds, but the thin volumes containing pictures of cut out paper dolls, costumes and all, which were stacked up on one counter, were of particular interest to her. While Hilary held her up to first peruse then select a couple of these coveted books, Sally lifted Dorothy and balanced her on one knee while she did the same. By the time the leg supporting Dorothy began to wobble, the little ones had made their choice, and the pennies with which to purchase them had been placed in their hands.

As they moved towards the front entrance of the store, the girls discussed then immediately dismissed the idea of walking the short distance along to the Old Town. Although Jacky seemed brighter now, they knew that those scratches and grazes on her legs and hands needed to be bathed, and then treated with mum's special ointment as soon as possible. So they walked across the road and into Wellington Square, and while they awaited the arrival of the number 12, talked about their last visit to this favourite bit of the town instead. Hazel had been there on this occasion and had treated Hilary, Pat and Sally to dishes of cockles and whelks, the thought of which made their mouths water even now, they said. Apart from Hilary, who was allergic to it, the portions had been doused in vinegar, then sprinkled with a goodly shake of pepper before being gobbled up hungrily. They had been fascinated as always by the variety of fish on the stalls around the area of tall, fishing net decorated sheds. The words, 'Wonders of the deep,' chalked up on a blackboard alongside one of the stalls, was no exaggeration, they thought. As Hazel had remarked at the time, some of the fish looked like they'd been designed by a group of youngsters, playing the 'fold the paper game.' They all listened as Hilary began to tell the tale about one chubby specimen that had been singled out for special treatment. Though off told, this tale never ceased to amuse the younger ones. This fat fish had been displayed on a slab at the front of the stall, a cigarette wedged firmly between thick lips that had been liberally smeared with lipstick. Once enough youngsters had gathered around to scrutinise this curious creature, a man had stepped forward, and lit the cigarette, which had glowed as he gently squeezed the belly in and out. As he had stood up and looked around to gauge the reaction of his audience, Sally, whilst appreciating and seeing the funny side of the curious demonstration along with the rest of the laughing crowd, also experienced a slight queasiness at the pit of her stomach. Did fish have souls, she had wondered for a split second, before the infectious laughter around her had taken her mind away from such serious speculation.

These idiosyncratic fisher folk, with their roots deep in old Anglo-Saxon, had their own unique and descriptive way with words. Names like 'squalliky' and 'switherin' were used to describe rough, stormy weather, while soomer it seemed, meant weather of a calmer, more gentle nature. 'After you, old young'un,' was an expression she had heard many times, usually when one person was obliged to back into a doorway to allow another access along one of the narrow pathways in the Old Town. And another, 'aye, that's a definite maybe,' had it seemed, become part of general conversation. And they were superstitious to the nth degree. Even Granny Sansom whose own wealth of wise saws and old wives tales was legendary, was impressed by these many and varied maxims that had been handed down through generations of like-minded and similarly employed people. A superstition of theirs that had always puzzled Sally however, was the one that suggested that women + fishing boats = bad luck, or some such thing, which she thought was rather absurd. Whether it stemmed from some desire to protect their women folk, or as had been suggested, was purely a ruse to keep a space where they'd be free to swear and fart to their hearts content, was anyone's guess.

What with its unique Characters, its myriad alleyways, twittens and cat-creeps, its narrow houses in even narrower streets that bent towards one another as though in conversation, it was indeed a very interesting and also, a rather quaint little place.

They breathed a sigh of relief as the bus turned into Wellington Square, and watched in temporary silence as the driver skilfully manoeuvred his vehicle around the circuit before coming to a halt beside them. In no time at all those on board had alighted, and the Conductor, once he had twiddled with his machine, allowed them on board. Sally waited for the girls and other passengers to alight, then swung her ruck-sack onto her back and followed. As she squeezed awkwardly passed the Conductor, she banged her elbow on one of the chromium uprights. Her funny bone responded instantly with a shooting pain throughout the length of her arm, followed by a temporary numbness. She paused for just a second, sucking in her breath, and through gritted teeth, uttered an involuntary, 'Ow.' and then she followed the other girls to their seats, muttering the usual platitude to any minor injury, 'don't worry, It'll be a pigs ear in the morning.'

Once settled in their seats, Dorothy and Jacky began talking about the Trolley-buses, which with their overhead rails, and strange method of propulsion, fascinated them. The older girls, who were equally interested in these delightful conveyances, were only too pleased to promise them a ride on one of them the next time they came into Hastings. They were discussing the sound and smell and special feel of these trams, when they became conscious of an increasing commotion from the top deck. In a very short time, four youths came clonking down the stairs and sat down in seats adjacent to the ones in which they were sitting.

"Whew, that's better. Some bloke up there's smoking fags that smell like camel shit," said one of the lads, clutching his hand to his throat in a mock theatrical gesture. "Nearly choked the living daylights out of me it did." Then having satisfied himself that he had captured their attention, he grinned. "'Ere, what's heavier, a ton of lead or a ton of feathers then?" he asked angling the question towards his mates, while at the same time, taking a furtive glance towards the girls to make sure they were still listening.

"Feathers. Everyone knows lead's heavier than feathers," replied a lad, clearly the youngest member of the group. There was spontaneous laughter and a slapping of backs as the other three fell about, clearly having anticipated this answer. "No, a ton's a ton, no matter what it's made up of idiot," came back the spluttering reply. Sally was not impressed, and was tempted to ask what their own answers had been the first time they'd been asked that question. Even if she'd been brave enough however, the lad was now up on his feet, delivering his next riddle: "I saw Esau sitting on a see-saw, how many s's in that? Answer me that one then," he said.

"I'm not answering any more of your daft questions. You'll only laugh at me if I get it wrong again," replied the youngster. Then clearly upset by the ridicule, he turned his back deliberately on his inquisitor, ran a hand through his hair, and sat on the edge of his seat with his arms folded, refusing stubbornly to be drawn into further discussion.

"Now just think about it. It's quite simple really," said one of the others, trying to coax a reply from the youngster. "The question really comes down to, how many s's in that, T-H-A-T, easy isn't it?" he said and grinned encouragement at the boy. He had to be a relative this lad, an older brother most likely, Sally reckoned. The similarity in features and colouring, was quite striking. After a few seconds, the youngster unfolded his arms, and as he turned around, a huge grin crept across his face.

"That's it, I've got it. 'None.' There's no s's in THAT, silly," he replied." You thought you were gonna catch me out again, didn't you. Well, hard luck, I'm just too smart for you," he added and stood up, making the mocking wobbly finger on forehead sign towards the quiz-master.

"Yep, you're too smart for me, I must admit," came back the reply, the young lad's rude gesture just dismissed with a casual wave of the hand. "Now just sit down will you. You look silly standing there like that, and you're rocking the bus," he added quite forgetting that just a short time ago he had been on his feet, gesticulating with both hands as he had delivered his nonsensical bit of verse. He paused for just a couple of seconds, then as he rose to his feet again to maximise the impact of his next bit of rhetoric, a smile crept across his face.

"Can I do yer now sir?" he said, and in spite of herself Sally chuckled out loud as the far from dulcet tones of Mrs Mopp, the office char lady from the programme, 'I.T.M.A' issued with surprising accuracy from the throat of this youngster. Instantly, the other lads, not to be out done, fell over themselves to mimic one or other of the exponents of comedy from this popular programme. They started off in unison with a harmonised rendition of Tommy Handley's 'It's that man again,' followed at once by the upper class accent of the alcoholic Colonel Chin Strap with his, 'I don't mind if I do.' The high pitched voice of old Tatty Macintosh and Sophie Tuck-shop's, posh winge, followed immediately, delivered with the same speed and accuracy as the original cast of characters in this popular BBC programme. After this though it began to degenerate into a free for all, with the voice of the Commercial Traveller pretty well drowned out by the Man from the Ministry and other voices in the mix that were even more difficult to differentiate between. The girls however, from the constant re-enactment of this programme by the boys at school, were well equipped to pick out the main characters.

The chatting and bantering continued, and it was only when the boys shot up and out of their seats, that Sally realised that the bus was passing beneath the bridge at the top of Ebden's Hill, the two little ones were spark out and that she had even failed to do her automatic check on Wayside.

She had no time to dwell on this oversight however. The boys were already making their way hastily and noisily down the aisle towards the exit. As they stepped down off the bus, one of the lads looked back over his shoulder and called out, "after you Cecil," to be answered immediately by the boy right behind him, "no after you Claude." Then as they stood on the narrow grass verge, they grinned and waved to the girls as the bus moved off on the next stage of its long journey.

Once the bus had passed Carpenter's Barn, the older girls began to rouse the little ones, and by the time it had reached the top of Whydown Hill, they were awake and ready to exit the bus on their own two feet. They quickly gathered their belongings together, and as they passed Brown's place, Hilary pressed the bell, and they lined up ready to alight once the bus had pulled up beside the entrance to the Garage. They walked along the lane, stopping for a moment to examine a cluster of comma butterflies that were jinking over the lush undergrowth alongside the hedge. The older girls were able to identify these particular ones simply because the boys, predictably, always referred to them as full stops. After a while they moved away, and once through the bottom gate, Dorothy and Jacky turned their attention towards thick clumps of clover that grew in abundance around here. Unable to resist the temptation, they stooped and plucked the miniature mauve trumpets from their hosts and sucked away at the sweet, bee favoured nectar.

As they walked into the kitchen, mum was busy making pastry, but spotted the grazes and bruises on Jacky's arms and legs straight away, which was inevitable. The older girls knew she would. They also realised how angry she would be when she found out the circumstances under which her baby had received these injuries. What made things even worse was that mum rarely raised her voice against them in anger. Exasperation, yes but that was something different.

"Whatever's happened to this child?" she asked, lifting her hands from her large brown and white crock, and hastily wiping the residue from the partially massaged ingredients, on to a piece of cloth. There was silence for a moment as she bent down beside Jacky and after carefully examining her wounds, gathered her up into her arms. Jacky's whole demeanour changed in an instant and she burst into tears, burying her head against mum's shoulder.

"Mum they left me on my own on the beach," and when I went to look for them, I fell on the rocks and it really hurt and I was so frightened and I was crying," she sobbed, now secure in her mum's arms.

"Now, now, just calm down. You're home safe and sound now," said mum, rocking her to and fro and patting her gently on the back until her sobs subsided. "Is this true what I'm hearing? Did you really leave this little one all alone on the beach?" Mum asked the girls, drawing a deep angry breath as she searched the faces of each one in turn. They nodded, and stood before her in silence unable to find an excuse for behaviour, which had seemed so reasonable at the time. She did not mince her words. She reminded them in no uncertain terms, of the dangers to which they had exposed their little sister. She did not need to raise her voice, however, she did not need to. She knew by their demeanour, that they realised the distress their irresponsible behaviour had caused. As she stood there in silence, Sally was reminded of another time mum had upbraided them in a similar way, though for a different kind of thoughtlessness. This time it was Ellen Brown she'd been defending, and rightly so she now realised. They had been teasing this inoffensive Lady on and off for a while before mum had become aware of it. When she did find out, she had been really upset, and had taken them to task for their thoughtlessness. Once she had made them aware of the impact their behaviour had had on Ellen, the teasing had ceased. Sally knew that neither she, nor any of the other girls, would taunt this Lady ever again, or anyone else if it came to that.

Acting on mum's instructions, the girls fetched TCP, Germolene and Dettol, also pieces of gauze from the white enamel medicine cabinet in the scullery. Then after scalding out the small china basin, kept for such purposes, they half filled it with fresh warm water, and stood back as mum began to bathe Jacky's wounds. Jacky whimpered to begin with, and the other girls held their breath in empathy with her. They had all experienced the horrid stinging sensation of medicated water and salve applied to fresh wounds, and added to their discomfort of course were acute feelings of guilt and responsibility. They would never, ever leave her on her own like that again, that was for sure.

Once mum had finished with the bowl, Sally carried it into the scullery and as she emptied its contents down the sink, realised how grateful she was that Aunty Annie and Uncle Tom had been out and about with dad somewhere, and not in the house to witness their shame.

Aunty Annie and Uncle Tom loved Sylvian, and uncle reckoned that every time he came here, he got a new lease of life. Therefore he was going to live forever, he said. She grinned as she remembered another thing he'd said, the last time he was here. 'Just as well I'm not a centipede. It'd take best part of a day to tie up laces on these ere type boots' he had exclaimed as he had squatted over the pair of dad's old boots he was borrowing.

As she turned away from the sink, her eyes strayed towards the sticky yellow fly trap, hanging from the ceiling by a thin cotton string. It was engorged with dead and dying flies, the iridescence of their wings and bodies accentuated by the light from the window. Though macabre, it was also astonishingly beautiful somehow, she thought to herself.

Chapter 5

Pat and Sally were up bright and early, and after collecting the milk from Battle Barn farm and pumping up a full tank of water, were hungry enough to eat a scabby donkey. Luckily, the rather more palatable boiled eggs with dunkers, was on the breakfast menu, and as usual, mum had managed to get them cooked just about right. The yolk was runny while the white of the eggs was nicely firmed and not the least bit snotty. Pat had got the white and yellow duck design egg cup this morning, and was holding egg and container carefully together as she dunked chunks of bread into the rich creamy yolks. Sally had chosen the chirpy cockerel, with its head up and its beak wide open. A bit like dad's cockerel, she reckoned though not as colourful and not nearly as noisy. The cup Dorothy was using and always chose, was a bit of a puzzle really. This creature, of indeterminate shape and appearance, had a bright orange beak and sported a tail that looked just like some Oriental fan. Jacky always chose the blue rabbit, which apart from its unnatural colour, was the most realistic representation of a creature within the whole motley group. The cup shaped into the image of a wily fox, the one the girls always insisted should be for the exclusive use of their dad, was the most defined caricature of the real thing. It sat on its haunches, brush curled around its front paws, its large limpid eyes at odds with the wicked grin on its face. This one had been fashioned by someone with a dodgy sense of humour, Sally reckoned. He, dad, would be in a bit later for his breakfast. He had mentioned something about these being 'dog days,' or something quite recently, and when she had asked him what he meant, he had told her that it just meant hot days in mid-summer when some star was in a certain position in the sky. He called the star something like, 'Sirius,' if she remembered rightly. Perhaps if she stayed up late one evening, he would point it out to her.

The air was hot and humid as Pat, Hilary and Sally made their way towards Stafford's wood, and as they crossed the road and into Crazy Lane,

Sally sucked in the acrid smell of hot tar and Tarmac from the recently resurfaced main road with deep satisfying breaths. She had been amongst the dozen or so youngsters who had stood at the roadside recently, watching the spectacle of that enormous, lumbering steam-roller flattening the freshly tarred and asphalted surface. Round, fat tar bubbles had popped up with the heat of the sun since then, and she along with the other youngsters, had been unable to resist the temptation of squashing one or two of the larger ones. It had to be done carefully. As one of the boys had pointed out, 'this stuff sticks to your boots like shit to a blanket.'

The smell of raw sewage that had assaulted their nostrils as they walked along the lane just now though, was something else and Sally had held her old hankie to her nose until the danger zone had been negotiated. What that smelly ditch needed in this hot weather was a good dose of old Mrs Wintergreen Edwards's Condy's crystals. No germs or smells got away from that stuff, no way. A similar thought struck her as they were walking beside Stafford's stream, which was a bit sluggish at the moment. This was a sure sign that the flushing of some of the lavatories in Blackbrooks would be a bit hit-and-miss today, another candidate for those crystals. At times like this, the Elsan lavvies at Sylvian, with that characteristic whiff of Jeyes fluid, did not seem half so bad.

The bread and cheese in the hedgerows was past its best now, its shoots dark green and tough, in contrast to the soft bright green of early spring, when a few would be plucked and munched away at, very slowly.. Very soon, bright red berries would decorate the bushes along here, and blackberries, rose hips and sloes would emerge to provide an abundant harvest for bird, beast and human alike. There would also be poisonous berries, like woody and deadly nightshade and briony, and the marginally less deadly but unpalatable ones like the spindle, Sally's particular favourite. The wood from this particular tree she understood and, as its name suggested, had been used for making spindles on which young girls processed wool fibres. Right now this particular tree was inconspicuous, blending in with the abundance of greenery along the way. In the autumn however, when its leaves suddenly changed from dull green summer plumage to a deep dark red, the temptation to pick and examine the bright orange four chambered clusters that accompanied this metamorphosis, was irresistible.

The girls all breathed a sigh of relief as they crossed the stream and into Stafford's wood, their appreciation of the shade afforded by the thick canopy of trees here, quite obvious. They had soon made their way to the area where the remains of a hastily extinguished fire was still in evidence. As Hilary nudged a curious mound with the toe of her plimsoll, the whole thing exploded into a mass of wriggling maggots and they all stepped back as though they had been shot. The suet pudding, abandoned all those weeks ago in that sudden burst of rain, had come to life in a quite unexpected form. After a couple of seconds they moved back towards the ashes to examine the gross spectacle more closely.

"Phew, smells just like bus drivers gloves," said Sally screwing up her face and covering her nose with the back of her hand as she leaned over to get a closer look. "Looks like this is the result of a blow fly that's stuck his bum here and laid thousands of eggs. It's a wonder they've not been gobbled up by robins and jenny wrens by now. Aren't you glad you're not a bird," she added after a short pause. "Makes you feel sick, doesn't it."

"Well stop looking at them then, move away from there. There's plenty of shade under the trees over here," said Pat, having turned her attention and person away from the pulsating mass. The others followed, and after shuffling around for a few moments, chose a likely resting place, then dropped to the ground like puppets suddenly released from the controls of some capricious puppeteer.

"It's like another world here. This stuff's grown a foot at least since we were here last," said Hilary fingering the foliage of the bracken that seemed suddenly to have closed in around and above them. "I don't mind though, it makes me feel safe somehow. It's comfortable too," she added, drawing her knees up to her chin and encircling them with her arms, her action followed immediately by the other two. "Tell you what, we haven't made any bows and arrows for ages, have we? Forget about catapults. We don't have much luck with them for some reason, do we," and she grinned. "Some of the boys do though. They use them to kill those poor little grey squirrels. I know they strip bark off trees and so forth, and they're not as pretty as red squirrels, but it does seem a bit mean. Mind you they get a tanner a tail, so that'd give them a good enough reason for doing it I reckon." She grimaced, and paused for a moment, before turning the conversation away from the rights and wrongs surrounding these cute creatures and on to other things.

"I can't get over how we hoodwinked Tony Powell that time, can you? We were only mucking about," she began. And Pat and Sally grinned, knowing immediately the incident to which she was referring. They had been gathering conkers from beneath the large horse chestnut trees across the Brooks last autumn, when they had discovered a tatty old lisle stocking. For a bit of fun, they had decided to fill the thing, and as Hilary held the top open, Pat and Sally had filled it, first from those already in pockets and then by gathering more and more from the surrounding area. By the time they'd finished, and had propped it up against a tree it really had looked like a leg, albeit with a nasty infestation of varicose veins.

As they were admiring their handiwork, they spotted Tony cycling down towards the footpath, and once he had lifted himself and his bike nimbly over the stile, they called out and beckoned him over. He had ridded to within a dozen or so yards, and had then stopped, a look of surprise, even horror on his face. Then he had turned and ridden off as though the devil were after him. To the girls it had been a huge joke, just that, until they saw him return, surrounded by half the boys in the village. They had been surprised even a little worried as the posse had descended upon them, obviously full of morbid curiosity, and had backed away from the tree displaying their work of art. The silence lasted mere seconds, immediately followed by loud guffaws. "That's not Philly Brooman's leg," spluttered one of the boys. Though blow me down if it ain't a carbon copy for it," he said moving closer to get a better look at the object.

As he did so, another boy stepped forward, and the others watched as he touched the thing gingerly with the toe of his shoe. It wobbled for a moment, then slow motioned sideways, its shape curiously realistic as it flopped to the ground. "Bloody 'ell, that scared the living daylights out of me," he said stepping smartly back onto the foot of his friend, almost losing his balance and giggling nervously. Almost immediately, one brave soul stepped forward and kicked it vigorously, dislodging many of the painstakingly stuffed conkers, and ruining the girls' work of art in an instant. Others joined in, and before they knew it, their creation had reverted back to scattered conkers and an old lisle stocking.

"It took Tony ages to live that one down," said Hilary, bringing the tale to an end. And then she giggled and the other two girls knew exactly what was coming. It was the latest village occurrence that was up for discussion and amusement, and for one girl in particular, something that was also going to take a bit of living down.

Only a couple of weeks or so ago, as Iris Baker had been participating in a particularly energetic dance in the Village Hall, her knickers had suddenly slipped down around her ankles. She had hastily retrieved them and stuffed them up her sleeve, hoping the incident would have gone unnoticed. No chance. Brief whispered messages were soon buzzing around the dance floor, and in no time at all, every ear had received the information, with varying degrees of mirth and, or, sympathy. This was not an isolated incident, as they well knew. After a few turns in an old copper, elastic soon lost its resilience, and some girls they knew even put their knickers underneath their suspender belts to hold them in place, just in case the elastic let them down. Another trick widely used, was the use of farthings, which were just about the right size to use as temporary replacements for the small white buttons on suspender belts, that were so often crushed between the jaws of the old mangles. Anyway it seemed that Iris was taking the whole thing in good part, which was just as well. She would have received a lot more teasing if she had not, they reckoned.

They continued to chat about this and that, and after a while, Freda's name popped up. "Don't you think she's taking her piano lessons just a bit too seriously," Sally asked. She spends ages on scales and things, and the other day she played 'Come see where golden hearted spring,' over and over again, for hours. I like that bit of music, or I used to, but you can have too much of a good thing." Then she grinned. "We got our own back though didn't we Pat," she added. "We went into the front room after her and played 'O Gander wash your dirty feet' several times over. We only stopped when mum said it was driving her round the bend." Sally did feel a bit guilty at times, as Freda practised her set pieces regularly and with dogged determination, and was becoming quite an accomplished pianist. Her feelings of guilt however, were never quite strong enough to deter her from this little bit of mischief.

"I couldn't half do with a cup of tea. Pity we didn't think to bring a bottle or two along with us," said Hilary after a while. "Not from that old black Billy-can of Basil Winchester's though. You'd need your brain half soled and healed, or at least be dying of thirst to drink that stuff. Even Patty reckons it tastes like it's been strained through one of Spit and sniff's old socks. The other girls nodded in agreement, knowing exactly what she meant. For Sally though it was just a slurp of water she needed, which she'd probably risk getting from the stream close by. Even in its sluggish state, she'd be more willing to partake of its waters than to insult her palate with that Billy-can stuff.

After a while, they roused themselves, and after skirting the maggot infested area, which did not look half so bad now anyway, walked towards and across the stream. As they made their way alongside, Hilary was talking about the three children, aged seven, four and eighteen months, that she had helped to look after last summer. They and their parents, Mr and Mrs Prowse, had been staying with Miss Mc keen at Asselton House at the time. Mrs Elkins who had volunteered Hilary's help with the children, had told her that both parents were having to work long hours, due to something called, 'straightened circumstances.' Hilary had not minded in the least, though getting three children up, washed and breakfasted before she herself went off to school, had been a bit of a rush. And more so when one or other bed was wet, with sheets needing to be washed and pegged out to dry, which often happened. The only anxious moments she'd had she reckoned, was while waiting for her replacement. If the Lady taking over from her had been late, then she would have been late for school and that was what she'd been worried about. Thankfully, she had always arrived on time, so Hilary had never had to deal with that scenario. Her thoughts often strayed to those little ones for whom she'd developed such a special bond, she said. They and their parents it seemed, had disappeared overnight, and she had never managed to find out what had happened to them. It was all a bit mysterious. All she really wanted to know was that they were happy.

Their first deed when they arrived home was to assuage their thirst, and having grabbed mugs down from the dresser in the scullery, they proceeded to fill them with drafts of water. After slurping this life saving elixir noisily down their parched throats, they stood back, agreeing that this water, with its unique flavour, tasted better than ever today. This moment of contemplation however, was short lived. Dorothy and Jacky were on to them, and from their endless chatter and boundless energy, it seemed that another outing was inevitable.

"Okay, okay, just give us a moment. We'll take you up to Beanford Farm, no further mind," said Pat. "No, we won't have time to go as far as Deffy and

Bill's place," she added as the youngsters jumped up and down excitedly, uttering the magic names. They could tell by mum's visible sigh of relief when they told her their plans, that she welcomed the opportunity for a bit respite from these two live wires. So they set off with their halos firmly in place.

Once through the back gate and into the field, the little ones took off, scattering chicken's that clucked indignantly as they ran in amongst them. Sally did her best to ignore them, allowing her eyes to make their customary scrutiny of the area instead. Most of the sheds in the field had been creosoted, some courtesy of her uncles. One however, stood out starkly against the rest. No matter how many good coats of 'looking at' it got from dad, it was still clearly in dire need of a bit of beauty treatment. Mind you there was nothing to stop her doing it she supposed, she did after all quite enjoy the sensation of brushing this runny, pleasantly odorous liquid across a thirsty surface. She just never seemed to have enough spare time these days that was all.

As soon as Dorothy and Jacky had been lifted over the stile at the bottom of the field, they ran off down the track, with the repeated request not to venture further than the farm, following them. The others followed at a more leisurely pace, chatting idly amongst themselves, at the same time noting the frequent pauses of the little ones, as they stooped to examine this or that flower or insect, along the way. The proliferation of wild flowers along here, reminded the older girls of the primroses they had gathered back in the Spring, not from around here but mostly from the primrose secret. These special flowers had been bunched up into neat, leaf encircled posies, which they had taken to the Buchanan Hospital, selling them for thru' pence a bunch to visitors and Nurses alike. They had then donated all the money they received, back to the Hospital itself.

Sally remembered the care and kindness she'd received within the walls of that special place, when she'd been scalded and taken along there for treatment. The Nurses in particular had done their best to make the youngsters who were there, as stress free as possible, even setting up a special ball game for those who for one reason or another, were confined to their beds. They simply tied one end of a long length of string to a ball, the other end to a bed so when an aimed throw fell short of its target, it could be easily retrieved and thrown again. It all seemed so very long ago now.

They all stopped for a moment to watch the erratic flight pattern of a magpie as it flew alongside the hedge. Though they appreciated the striking appearance of the bird, they were also conscious of its penchant for feeding its babies on the offspring of other birds, blackbirds and thrushes in particular it seemed. The green woodpecker was also guilty of this practice they had learned recently, much to Sally's dismay. As she'd been told, a newly hatched, squirming baby bird would be much the same to them as a fat juicy maggot. She found it hard to accept that one of her favourite birds would behave in such a brutal way. Anyway, most of these birds would have fledged by now, though they would still have stalking cats and other predators to deal with. Dad's expression,' red in tooth and claw,' or some such thing, came immediately to mind.

When they reached the bend in the lane, they paused beside the pond, and watched the ducks and moor-hens doing a bit of dignified posturing and quacking here and there as they swam across the water and in and out of the weed around its edges. In Spring all hell broke loose around here, all dignity was discarded, to be lost in a cacophony of territorial squabbles.

After a while, they looked into the shallow water for signs of smaller wildlife in the shape of newts, frogs and even the diving beetles, which they found quite fascinating. Sporadic stirrings in the mud caught their eye, an indication of the presence of some small creatures but there was nothing here that they could positively identify, and they turned their attention to the many winged insects, hovering above its surface. The bats would be having a feast here come nightfall. Dorothy was the first to spot the dragonflies, or skimmers as the boys called them, and pointed excitedly across the water, trying to follow the lightning flashes of iridescence with a wobbly finger as they darted hither and thither over the reeds. In movement and colour they were reminiscent of the elusive Kingfisher the youngsters had spotted across the Brooks on rare, magical moments, the girls reckoned. They could not help comparing this tranquil scene with how it would have been when Hazel had taken that unexpected dip in the water, one cold winter's day. Although Freda and Betty had dried her off as best they could, and had covered her with their own coats before taking her home, she had developed double pneumonia soon afterwards. It had been a really anxious time for mum and dad, they'd been told

After a while, they turned away from the pond and continued up the track towards the entrance to Beanford Farm.

The Partridge family who had owned the farm for ever it seemed, were no longer here, and although its present occupants, Mr and Mrs Clarke and their daughter Ann were okay, it was very different here now. Sally missed the comfortable hustle and bustle of the milking parlour and dairy, the ease and naturalness with which their presence had always been accepted around the farm by the Partridge family, if not always welcome; as when her older sisters had terrorised Porky, or George all those years ago. But that was another story. She still missed the presence of Mrs Partridge with her wispy hair and her yearly invitation to them to help themselves to those delicious pears in her orchard. It was only their old bull that she had not been sorry to see the back of, but had he been that bad really she asked herself? Then she shivered as her imagination kicked in once again. Yes it bloody had. With its mad, bloodshot eyes, it had terrified the living daylights out of her.

On the way back home, they stooped automatically to pick dandelion leaves, hog weed and the narrow and broad leaf plantain, which proliferated alongside the track, also milk thistle, a particular favourite of the rabbits. These creatures were in for a feast this afternoon, Sally thought to herself. She grinned as she remembered the way they looked at her with those unblinking, expressionless eyes of theirs as they munched away methodically through their greens, with that curious jaw movement of theirs. One of Dorothy and Jacky's favourite pastimes was to feed the rabbits leaf by leaf, holding on to the pieces until the last moment, then giggling excitedly when the stuff was jerked out of their fingers impatiently by hungry teeth.

They could smell the sausage casserole as they crossed back across the field, and hurried towards then through the back gate, depositing the rabbit food on to the top of the cages as they went. By the time they reached the scullery door, they had decided that it would be dished up with mounds of fluffy mashed potatoes, new carrots, peas and maybe a bit of cabbage. Then for pudding, it had to be apple pie with rice pudding, they would not settle for less. Even though the Bramley's were not ripe yet, there would surely be enough of those early drops to feed them. Yum, yum mum's cooking was the best in the world they told themselves, especially when they were this hungry.

When Hilary and Sally left the house en route to Windy Ridge, dad was just about to perform a sides-to-middle operation on some cotton sheets, which had worn to a dangerous degree of thinness in the middle. With the aid of his trusty treadle machine, of course. Mum had already split them down the middle lengthways, and had pinned the outer, unworn sides together to form what would now be the slept on part. Once that had been machined, all he had to do was to neaten off what had now become the outer edges of the sheets with a narrow seam, tie off the ends and the job would be done. They were still wearing the worthy mantle of virtuousness as they made their way down the field and into the lane. They had actually volunteered to do the washing up this evening, or rather Hilary had. Sally had not complained for once though, even when mum had crept up on them a couple of times with more crocks, when they had thought the job done.

This Saturday evening promised to be a quiet one for a change, they were telling themselves as they walked towards the house. Willy and Roy were helping with the setting up of the cycle speedway track in the village, and Ronald as far as they knew, was there as well, along with his mates Ray Winchester and Michael Soan. As they made their way towards the back door however, they got a bit of a surprise. Ronald's bike was propped up against the wall, its back tyre flat as a pancake. As they walked into the kitchen, he was in the process of filling a large bowl with water, and around him were assembled an assortment of table spoon, and other items suitable for prising tyre from rim to get to the punctured inner tube. Also alongside, was the long slim tin housing the puncture repair kit, his 'where with all' as he called it. He was a dab hand at this operation, and had helped Sally out on more than one occasion. It wasn't that she couldn't do the job. It was just that he was so much quicker at it than she was.

He looked up as they entered, and after explaining what had happened, made his way outside with the bowl of water, followed by the girls, carrying the rest of the paraphernalia. He worked away with enviable ease, and within a few minutes the job was done. As he tidied the tools away, he told the girls he had decided to stay put now. Ray and Michael had not been planning to stay that long in the village this evening anyway, he said and he had already made arrangements to meet up with them again tomorrow.

Once they were seated around the kitchen table he began to tell the girls about his plans for the next day. He and his mates, he said, were planning to renew their efforts to find that village in Battle Big Wood, abandoned at the time of the Black Death. They had a rough idea where it might be, and now that Mr James, the Head Master, had given them a few tips on what to look out for, they reckoned they were in with a chance of finding it this time.

"The first things to look out for, Jumbo told us, were clumps of stinging nettles, and other bushes and plants he described to us. He'll show us pictures of them sometime. Evidently, they're a sign that the ground around there has been disturbed at some time or other, not necessarily for a village, but you never know. It's then a question of digging around, to see if we can find a bit of evidence, a few bricks and bits of rubble and things. Trouble is, as he warned us was that a lot of their buildings would have been made of wood, and that would have rotted away by now. Mind you. If we're careful we might find the remains of old posts and things." The he paused for a just moment. "We reckon Mr Glyde knows where that old village would have been, but he's not saying," he continued. Well he lives in the wood, doesn't he? He knows that whole area like the back of his hand. It may even have somewhere near those clap board cottages where he lives, you never know, though we don't really think so. We think it's more likely to be somewhere up towards the top end of the wood, leastways that's where we're going to be looking tomorrow."

Sally was also of the opinion that Mr Glyde had discovered the site of that old village some time ago, and would, she knew, have his reasons for not broadcasting his find. He was a woodsman from the top of his head to the tips of his toes, and the last thing he'd want was a lot of youngster's causing havoc in his beloved wood. Still she wished the boys luck in an odd sort of way, at the same time knowing how difficult their task would be. She, Pat and Hilary had spent many hours looking for that mysterious old village up there, without success. They were now on the lookout for the remains of another, more substantial building in the wood; an old Manor House according to Pam Gay, who had told them about it recently. And yet that too seemed to have disappeared without trace. They were bound to come across it sometime, they told themselves, especially if as they suspected, it had been constructed like the old Manor Cottages and House in the village. A few bricks and the foundations would have survived even if the lathe and plaster had disintegrated over the years. It was all very mysterious and intriguing and addictive

They continued chatting for a while, moving seamlessly from one subject to another. Then as if by magic or more likely a mutual recognition of hunger, greed even, decided it was time to eat. Without more ado, Hilary stood up and moved over to the old larder, opening the zinc mesh door, and taking out cheese and butter dishes, which she placed on the table in front of them. A nice crusty loaf, taken from the enamel bread bin followed, and it was not long before they had grabbed a plate apiece, and were tucking in to their feast. There was nothing quite like a thick chunk of buttered bread with a nice lump of cheese they decided. As he munched, Ronald was re telling the tale about the fox hound that he and his mates had suddenly come across, up in the Big Wood, back in the winter. "It was all on its own poor thing. It kept wandering off and then a bit later, it'd turn up again. It didn't seem distressed or anything like that, just puzzled, as though he thought what should be there, just wasn't, that sort of thing. Anyway, we looked after it for a while, but in the end we took it along to Mr Collins who knew exactly who it belonged to. Luckily he's got a phone, and called someone up about it, there and then. Even before he told us though, we'd worked out that the little hound got left behind when the hunt went through. We'd heard it, the hunt. Well, you couldn't not hear it, could you, not with all that noise and 'Tally-ho' and what not going on. Do you know, we really missed the little fellow, even though we'd not had him long. He'd have come home with us I'm sure he would. Wondered what's happened to him now," he pondered. "I hope they don't treat fox hounds the same as they do homing pigeons when they get lost that's all. Those birds don't get a second chance, do they?"

For a short while, they contemplated the fate of the lost hound and its woodland adventure, but the mood of serious contemplation did not last for long. Hilary had only to mention Willie, Roy, Ray and Patty, and Ronald and Sally grinned in anticipation of an amusing rehash of recent events involving these friends of theirs. The incident Hilary was about to discuss was what they now referred to as, the day of the storm; a day of moody overcast skies that had culminated in one of the most spectacular storms they could remember.

"I don't know if we were really as safe down in our old cellar here that evening as we thought we were come to think of it," she began. "It wasn't half dark, even with those two torches we had. They were okay for giving us enough light to see where we were going, but as much use as a chocolate tea pot when it came to seeing the dots on the dice we were trying to use. I still wonder why we took snakes and ladders and so forth down with us. I think it was Roy who'd suggested it. I can still remember how loud that thunder was, even down there, and those flashes of lightening were dazzling even though we were over the far side. I sometimes wonder if we should have taken those bricks out of the wall down there to make our den with, but there you go. Not much we can do about it now. At least the house hasn't fallen down. Well not yet," she added with a wry grin. After a moment's contemplation, she continued. "Ray was the first one out. I remember that because he nearly knocked the torch out of my hand as he made for the entrance. A right old scramble that was. But I managed to hold on and followed him out, and was I glad to get indoors, well we all were come to that. Really, when you think about it, the only mistake we made was to play that game of packed sardines. If we'd stuck to 'Snakes and Ladder's,' and 'Beat your neighbours out of doors,' and so forth, that accident would never have happened. Or even if we'd just carried on hiding under beds and in cupboards and such like, we'd have been alright."

"Ah, but we got away with it, didn't we," said Ronald, a grin suddenly puckering up his cheeks. "If you think about it, that storm might have encouraged us do what we did, but it also saved our bacon. Mind you, I did think at the time, when we all piled up into the attic to hide from Patty like that, that we'd have to be a bit careful, but I didn't dream someone would be clumsy enough to put their blooming foot through the ceiling. I can still remember the shock of seeing the state the kitchen was in when we'd scrambled down to find out what damage we'd done. There was plaster and dust and stuff all over the place, wasn't there. We didn't know where to start or what to do to begin with, did we, and then Roy and Willie were all for clearing it up. I reckon it was my suggestion that we just leave it be that saved our bacon though. Because when mum got home and we were all tucked up in bed, she just thought the storm had brought it down. She never even asked us so we didn't need to lie. Whew," he exclaimed, the twinkle in his eye suggesting a measure of satisfaction with his part in the end result.

It still surprised Sally that Mrs Elkins had just assumed the damage was down to the storm, without even questioning them about the incident. She still remembered how she'd felt at the time. How sure she'd been that Mrs Elkins would have spotted the guilty flush that she knew had crept up across her cheeks. The hardest bit was when Mr Rudge had turned up with that trug of vegetables, just as they were finishing their breakfast. They had had to sit there while the grownups discussed the damage, concluding that Bill Thomas, the local builder, was obviously the man to contact to get the job done. They had not dared to look at one another, for fear of nervous giggles, and had later agreed that the experience had been, 'highly disagreeable.'

"I don't know about you, but I could do with a drink now," said Hilary after a while, and as Ronald and Sally nodded, she got up from the table taking the empty plates with her. In a short while, Sally's hands were cupped around her mug, and as she took her first sip of the liquid, reckoned it was just as delicious as the cocoa mum made. This was not surprising really, she thought. They both prepared it in the same way, always cooking the mixture gently over the heat for a few moments to get rid of that raw taste.

As they sat sipping their cocoa, the events of another Saturday evening became the focus of their attention. On this particular evening, the weather had been fine and warm, in complete contrast to the rough, stormy conditions of that earlier one. Michael and Peter Clements were amongst the group of youngsters assembled in and around Windy Ridge that evening, and Sally grinned as she recalled the stir these two handsome boys had caused, when they had first arrived in the village. Few girls had been immune to their good looks, herself included she admitted. At least these two raw recruits had not been subjected to the wire trick, the girls had seen to that. They remembered only too well their own painful experience with this innocuous looking piece of wire. It was just the tail end of some electrical fitting, protruding a mere few inches through the wall at the north side of Windy Ridge, and yet, when lightly touched, packed the best bit of a tidy poke, as the boys put it. Instantaneous shock and brief paralysis, was the way Sally would have described it.

She listened now as Hilary and Ronald chatted and enthused about that evening, chuckling now and again as they recalled the fun they'd all had.

After a slow start, with the larger than normal group of youngsters milling around the front steps for a while, they had gradually made their way to the rough bit of ground at the back of the house, and from then on they had never looked back. Jokes were told and giggled over, and games of 'I Spy' brought forth the usual questionable subjects to ponder and argue over. It was when they'd moved on to games of hide and seek however, that the fun had really begun. First the boundary was set, with the Twitten and Crazy Lane on one side, Lavender and Pay Gate Cottages on the other. Most of the youngsters knew the area like the back of their hand. For a few however, one or two mishaps were inevitable. Someone almost lost a shoe in the ditch beside Pay Gate Cottage, not realising as the locals youngsters did, that even in the driest of weather, a layer of questionable sludge lurked beneath its grassy camouflage. Yet another missed the sewage outflow from Windy Ridge by the skin of his teeth, plus and more importantly, the quick thinking of another youngster.

The game had continued with the usual noisy interaction from the seekers as they sought to be the first to expose the hiders, at the same time, managing somehow to keep a rough adherence to the rules. It was when they had stopped to get their breath back and to slake their thirst in a noisy gaggle around the tap in the kitchen, that they had realised Roy was missing. In fact no one had seen him for quite a while. So they set off, some individually and others in small groups to search for the miscreant. After a while, and with the mystery still unsolved, they came together at the front steps of the house, scratching their heads and imaginations, in bewilderment. Ronald was the first to spot the Constable. He was cycling down New Road towards them, waving his arm in the air as he came towards them. There was a guilty silence for a moment as they automatically searched memory and conscience for some misdeed or other. Then as he drew closer, they could see that his arm was waving not just at them, but was also pointing towards the roof, and as they looked upwards, there was Roy waving to them from his perch beside the chimney pot.

There was another silence, a stunned one this time. By the time they had got their speech back however, before they'd even had the chance to ask the miscreant how he'd got up there in the first place, the red faced Constable was beside them. He had told them off in no uncertain terms, explaining in great detail, how foolhardy it was to indulge in such dangerous behaviour. As if they didn't know, they'd thought, though at the time they had kept their mouths shut. He had waited for Roy to scramble back off the roof and make his way to and through an open window, and had then peddled off towards the village, muttering something like, 'I've got better things to do with my time.'

At this point, Hilary, Ronald and Sally began to chuckle, and more so as they recalled that worried look on Roy's face as he had appeared around the side of the house; how the expression of guilt on his face had changed immediately to one of satisfaction, once he realised the constable had disappeared. As they had gathered around him, he told them he'd been watching their antics for some time. He had in fact been on the verge of giving himself up, just as the old Constable had ridden along and done it for him.

"He was right when he reminded us that he'd remained undiscovered in a game of hide and seek for longer than any of us lot," said Hilary. And Willy was also right when he told him that all he deserved for scaring the living daylights out of us lot was a bloody putty medal. Still we did have fun that evening, even though after that we had to calm things down a bit after that.

In the break that occurred after these particular reflections, Hilary began to clear the mugs away from the table and when she returned, she began to talk about Mr Walder, or the Mad March Hare as they called him. They had had one or two confrontations with this tall, thin man who always seemed to have a dew drop wobbling on the end of his aquiline nose. He had moved into Lucks Ness, the bungalow just above Crazy Lane, when the Linch family had moved out, and he was as different from them as chalk was from cheese. Sally allowed her thoughts to linger briefly on Mr and Mrs Linch, who had been sorely missed when they had left the area. They had been such an important part of her childhood, and even now, many people in the area, really missed them. They did visit occasionally, which was better than nothing, she told herself, and she, Pat and Hilary had walked over to see them at Three Oaks, where they now lived, Mind you, it had taken them hours. Then she grinned as she suddenly realised what Hilary had just come out with. Talk about stating the bleedin' obvious, she thought as she listened to her friend's observations on the particularly awkward Mr Walder.

"He doesn't like children, does he," she'd said, and then she had she paused having registered Sally's look of amusement. "Well, he doesn't, does he? I'd even go as far as to say he takes a delight in scaring the living daylights out of us lot. Take the time we were just carefully leaning over the barbed wire fence at the bottom of his garden and he hollered at us. Loud enough to scare the old Beanford Bull, it was. And we were only looking at the fish in his pond down there. I remember we were rooted to the spot for a moment, and then we shot off across Jaybez's field and down to Stafford's stream without stopping. Mind you, what I was going to tell Ronald about was that other time, when Amy was with us." Sally grinned wryly, remembering only too well their close encounter with the man, and the way Amy had come to grief on that spiky wire fence of his.

"Grant you that time we had actually climbed over the fence, because someone who shall remain anonymous, reckoned she'd seen him leave the house; if he had though he'd soon doubled back again," she added. Anyway, we'd thought it was a chance to get a really good look in the pond and so forth, so over we go, only to be confronted by the old devil himself. Well, we just panicked and got over the fence as best we could, except Amy and Sal collided and Amy caught the top of her leg on the wire. We didn't dare stop until we'd got a safe distance away from the place, and by that time, her leg was a bloody mess, I can tell you. I mopped it up as best I could with Sal's old hankie, but there was nothing we could do about her knickers. They were split to smithereens. Anyway, once we'd looked at the wounds, there was more than one, and seen how deep one was, at least I did, that Sal's a bit squeamish, we decided she needed a bit of first aid. So went back to her place, knowing there'd be no one there to tell us off, and once we'd found the Dettol and a bit of muslin, I cleaned it all up properly. And not before time, that wound looked really angry. She did wince, but she never complained even though it must have really hurt while I was sponging it clean."

After a while, the girls noticed that Ronald was finding it increasingly difficult to disguise his yawns, and as they looked at one another, suddenly realised that the day's activities, plus and all this chattering, had suddenly caught up with them as well.

"Time for bed then, I reckon." said Hilary, stretching and yawning as she got up from the table, and Ronald and Sally followed, doing likewise. The washing and cleaning of teeth could wait till morning, they decided.

It did not take Hilary and Sally long to don their pyjamas and crawl into bed, and though tired, they whispered together for a while. Betty would be home next weekend, they reminded themselves, with a sense of satisfaction. She always brought a little ray of sunshine with her, as well as a few special treats. Sally grinned to herself in the darkness as for some reason a vision of her sister's first close encounter with a bad tempered Ram, suddenly popped up into her mind and imagination. Not that she'd witnessed it of course, it had happened many years ago, but she had heard the tale often enough. Betty had been a small child at the time, and the owner of a new coat with a matching hat, with which she'd been inordinately proud. She had been walking across the field hand in hand with mum, when the wretched thing had hurled itself at her and it had only been a quick reaction on mum's part that had prevented a more serious outcome. As it was, she had lost her footing along with her hat, and most distressing of all, had dirtied her brand new coat.

Poor Betty, Sally thought, she had not had much luck with Rams on the whole. There was that other one, with which she'd come into conflict a few years later. That psychotic beast had supposedly butted her up and onto one of the chicken hutches in the field, as she been on her way home from the farm with the milk. A slight exaggeration on her sisters part maybe, but she'd had to have made a good case for having lost the day's supply of milk. Sally could identify with her actions though, and how. She would have dropped the milk and run if she'd been faced with the spectre of that bloody creature coming towards her, head down and at the speed of knots. All Rams were mad she reckoned, and it was just as well they did not have the enormous bulk of the Beanford Bull, and also that they only grazed the field for a few terrifying weeks in the autumn.

Hilary was quiet now, her even breathing suggesting she was already asleep. So she turned on to her side, made herself comfy and prepared to join her friend in the land of nod.

Chapter 6

The field was still asleep beneath its misty blanket, the waning moon in the early morning sky casting an eerie glow over the whole shadowy autumnal landscape. Sally shrugged her old cardigan more closely around her shoulders as she stood at the bedroom window, shivering not with cold but with the sheer magic of the scene in front of her eyes. As she gazed upwards at the slowly diminishing orb, and into the vast and timeless mystery of the Heavens, her mind drifted away to recently discovered books of myth and legend, lent to her recently by her Headmaster, Jumbo James. Stored within the pages of these books were strange and fascinating tales inscribed here and there with black and white sketches, which added to the air of mystery and accentuated the antiquity of the stories. She had only had time just to skim through the books as yet but already the wanderings of Sir Gerwain and the Green Knight fascinated her, reminding her in a way of books like 'Lands of Legends and Heroes' and 'The Land of Far Beyond,' that had sparked her imagination as a small child. She could not wait to explore the tale of Beowulf with his epic battles against evil, depicted in both in human form and that of the most fearsome dragon. The adventures of Rupert the Bear, that had scared the living daylights out of her not so long ago, paled into insignificance against this Nordic legend from days of yore. The words, 'Longest epic poem in old English,' inscribed on one of its foremost pages, suggested a tale of endurance at the very least, but from what she had already gleaned from within its pages, it seemed to be more than just that. Within this multi layered, imaginative poem with its overall message of the power of good over evil was the very essence of the poet. Showing through the rust of antiquity, was a human being on his own personal journey, both of the heart and the spirit.

She shivered again with the cold this time, then as she cocked an ear towards the bedroom door, the quiet as a mouse silence that had met her first awakenings, had been replaced by familiar sounds of activity coming from the direction of the kitchen. The muted clicks and clunks she could hear meant that the first cup of tea of the day was being brewed. She quickly wriggled into the dirndl skirt that she had left on the bottom of the bed overnight, and made her way silently and unerringly across the bedroom floor towards the kitchen, and as she opened the door, breathed the comforting warmth from the re-kindled Rayburn and the aroma of freshly brewed tea up into her nostrils. Dad looked up as she entered, and without a word, added another cup, saucer and rich tea biscuits to the tray. She watched as he poured the tea, the amber liquid making its short journey from spout to cup in an instant as he performed this early morning ritual. She could not have timed her entry into the kitchen any better, she reckoned as she sat down at the table to enjoy the brew.

After collecting the milk and pumping up the water, Pat and Sally prepared themselves for the walk into Battle, to collect the cod liver oil and orange juice from the 'Ministry of food' shop, plus one or two sundry items from Till's the ironmongers in the High Street for dad. Hilary, who would be swapping school for full time employment at the end of the year, would not be with them today and they were really going to miss her company. She would be spending the day working in Mr Brann's grocery store in Cripps Corner, where she had been offered full time employment as soon as she left school in December. He was a good boss, she told them and Sally reckoned that he also recognised and appreciated the 'attributes' of her hardworking and conscientious friend.

The old wooden table on the grass verge near the Bee House, normally laden with eggs, honey and a selection of vegetables, was empty, its surface covered with the debris of recent hedge cutting. Curly shrivelled leaves mixed with a few ringlets of shaven wood, now adorned its ample surface. A brief glimpse through the gateway as they passed by also showed the result of recent pruning. Mrs Knight they reckoned had been at work here busy clipping back the dead foliage from several of the bigger shrubs in the borders of this large garden. This lady was a hive of information on wild flowers, berries, trees and birds, with a natural gift of imparting this knowledge, which the youngsters took full advantage. When they met her on one of their forays in and around the country lanes, or whilst seeking out the wild strawberries that grew in abundance on the bank near the Bee House, they knew that she would have some new and interesting wonders of nature to impart. And she was a dab hand at flower arranging, another gift she shared with the community. The Churches in Sedlescombe and Whatlington in particular, benefited from this natural talent of hers.

The smell of wood smoke hit their nostrils as they approached the brow of the hill, and as they topped the incline and looked out across the Brooks and wooded valley below, could see layers of lazy smoke drifting in the crisp clear air. The age old practice of charcoal burning was in process, the evidence of its distillation now drifting slowly across the valley towards the village. As they turned into Marley Lane, Sally sniffed the air appreciatively. The smell of wood smoke here, mixed with the acrid smell of decomposing leaves, was the very essence of autumn as far as she was concerned.

There were flocks of small birds swooping into the hedges along the way, alighting for a few moments at a time to gorge on the abundant red berries before taking off again to make their noisy chirping way towards the next feast.

The furtive movements of the little Jenny Wren, rooting delicately amongst the rotting vegetation at the base of the bushes, however, were more difficult to see. With its keen, beady eye constantly on the lookout for tasty grubs, the only indication of its whereabouts was the slight movement and rustle of a leaf as it went about its business, or if you were very lucky, the blink of an eye flash as it darted from one bush to the next. The dun colours of late autumn were the perfect camouflage for this delightful little bird.

As they walked along the lane, they were talking about this and that, moving with ease from one subject or reminiscence to the next. When their discussions were sad, like the untimely death of their school friend Len Masters and the death of Mr Upton who had lived with his family in Crazy Lane, their voices were low and serious. Death was a loathsome but unavoidable part of life they realised, something that lurked then struck, sometimes indiscriminately. They did not dwell for long on this particular subject however, and their gloomy mood lifted as quickly as it had descended upon them, as their thoughts and observations moved towards life and the living of.

They were soon giggling as they vied with one another to recount yet again the fun they had had with their cousins, Eddie and Peggy Doe earlier in autumn, whilst the family were here on one of their regular visits. One occurrence in particular, which was always good for a laugh and uppermost in their minds, was their encounter with an irate farmer, anxious to protect what was lawfully his, and what the youngsters had got up at the crack of dawn to gather on this particular day. They had made their way to a field close to the Brooks, which had been a hop garden at one time and on which there had been a particularly good flush of mushrooms. They had set too, swiftly and enthusiastically, and in no time at all, had parted a goodly amount of the white-capped fungi from the ground, chatting quietly as they sliced through the thick stems with an expertise borne of practice, before placing them stem side up in their baskets.

Eddie had been the first to spot the enemy as he appeared over the brow of the hill, not the girls who, totally absorbed by their enthusiastic gathering in of the harvest, had become a bit careless. In one swift, movement however, the half-filled baskets had been whisked from the ground and they were off across the field, their mission to put as much distance between themselves and the farmer now bearing down on them at a rate of knots. 'Run like hell,' were the only words uttered as they sped towards the Brooks, calculating with instinctive accuracy its narrowest crossing point. Eddie, the first to cross the stream, had leaned across the narrow gap, grabbed their baskets and had then pulled them one by one up the short steep incline on the safe side of the river. Unfortunately, his grip on Peggy's wrist had slipped and she had fallen back into the water and it had taken a supreme effort to drag her out, spluttering and giggling, before the old farmer reached them. Luckily he did not pursue them, probably calculating that they had left him with enough mushrooms to feed himself and his family for the next day or two.

By the time they considered they had put enough space between themselves and the farmer, Peggy was shivering uncontrollably and all the other girls could do was to divest her of her soggy coat and cardigan and to cover her shoulders as best they could with their own. Her bottom half had just had to wait. On the way home Eddie had tried his best to entertain them with his jokes, but they had mostly fallen on deaf ears. It was not that they were not interested. They just did not have a clue what he was on about. Even as Sally recited the one and only joke she could remember from that day, she had no idea what it meant. She only remembered it because the words had a certain kind of resonance about them. 'What's Titus Oates' cousins name then?' he'd asked. To which she had replied, 'Titus who? What? Who the hells he when he's at home. I don't know do I.' Titus-a-ducks-arse of course.' He had replied and although she had grinned she had not had a clue what he was on about – still had not if it came to that.

But the highlight of that visit as far as Pat and Sally were concerned was when Uncle Tom had taken them to Lewes on the train. On the coastal section of the journey, Peggy had pointed out a fox, slinking nervously along a hedge, belly almost to the ground as it tried to minimise its profile, and a heron being buzzed by several crows. Then as the train had made its lumbering way from Eastbourne, they had looked out over the Downs. They had gazed upon the chalked image of the old man of Wilmington with awe and admiration, and at the countryside spread out before them, breathtakingly beautiful and unfamiliar. There had been one short section on that journey however, not so very far from Lewes, that had affected Sally in some strange way. She had shuddered, her eyes and senses focussed unwaveringly on this space with its aura of grief and deep seated tragedy. Something quite awful had happened here, she was convinced of that, some sixth sense told her so. The sensation of creepy fascination was so strong it had lingered for several minutes, and she knew with certainty that this was something she would not forget about in a hurry.

They had toured the town of Lewes stopping frequently to examine the exterior of certain buildings, with Uncle Tom and Eddie looking up the history of the places in their much-thumbed guide-book, and they had actually entered and explored some of these ancient monuments, which were open to the public. It had taken a while to ascertain the site where the Battle of Lewes had taken place, followed by a comprehensive account of the defeat of Henry 111 by the victorious Simon de Montfort, all those centuries ago, but the running commentary from the two males with their natural flair for expounding on all things historical, plus their overt enthusiasm for the subject, had been infectious. As Pat was saying, she had enjoyed the whole thing a lot more than she had expected. Eventually, and by common consent, they found and then sank down onto a tract of grass to eat their sandwiches, and only then had they realised how weary they were. They had munched away in silence for a while, but as soon as their hunger had been assuaged and their aching limbs rested, the men were off on the verbal exploration of local history once again. The name Anne of Cleves, one of the wives of Henry V111, who must have lived around these parts at one time, was mentioned briefly and other names that somehow had a familiar ring to them. Sally shivered in silent horror as the listened to them discussing the fate of the Protestant Martyrs, ' The Marian Martyrs' she thought they had called them, and puzzled over the overt brutality of these people. The Tudors she reckoned had been a particularly bloodthirsty lot, though there were other regimes it seemed that had not been much better. Sadly as far as she could make out, religion had caused so much conflict. It had been used to justify the greed and covertness of certain peoples, and with it had come those unbelievable acts of cruelty. She wondered, not for the first time, what Jesus would have thought about it all. Her mood had changed instantly, she remembered at the mention of Thomas Paine, another name connected with this town. She had heard dad and her uncles discussing this man. 'A reformer,' they'd called him; 'a man who had railed against injustice, who had championed the cause of the poor,' or words to that effect. In fact there was a book in the front room called 'The Rights of Man,' which had been written by him now she thought about it. Perhaps she would read it one day. She liked the sound of this man.

Later that afternoon, as they had been on their way towards the station to await the arrival of the train, there had been just enough time to stop off for a glass of lemonade and a piece of cake, which Uncle Tom had treated them to, and it had gone down a treat. All in all Pat and Sally agreed, it had been a very special day, which had given them a lot to think about. They had thoroughly enjoyed exploring this town of Medieval Towers and Priory's – and so much more. .

As they continued to talk, Sally looked towards the swampy ground where in spring the Kingcups would be decorating the whole area in their 'decorous' yellow glory. A bit further along the way, her eyes strayed towards an old Gypsy caravan, once brightly painted but which now crouched in a state of sad neglect amongst tangled weeds and thorny briars. Even in this state of peeling paintwork and slowly rotting timbers however, it looked oddly majestic as it gradually metamorphosed. Sally knew somehow and instinctively that Mother Nature was in charge here. It was she who would be taking care of it in the same way as she did all other organic matter - but in her own good time.

Granny Kenward, Jessie's mother had lived in this caravan for many years, Sally had been told, but this fierce old lady was now long gone, had faded into the mists of time just like old Meg the Gypsy she thought. Most of the youngsters had left her well alone, many having been on the receiving end of that rough edged of her tongue of hers, for some slight misdemeanour on their part. Even her own grandchildren had been in awe of her, having learned the hard way as Tony had told them, that she did not suffer fools gladly and suffered youngsters even less. As he put it, one of her withering looks alone had been enough to freeze the balls off a brass monkey. 'Old Misery,' they called her. Not to her face of course. And she had always smelled of mothballs.

They passed Marley house, without so much as a glimpse of the Dutchman who now owned the place, not that that surprised them. He kept himself very much to himself, and the place had settled quietly back into its former closed mysterious self. Now the Pyke or Dodds farmhouse, Sally could not remember for the life of her, which family actually lived there now, was a different kettle of fish altogether. It was always a hive of activity and today was no exception. From way back down the lane, the girls had heard the unmistakable sounds of interaction between men, machines and animals and had breathed the stench of slurry into their lungs along with the cool autumnal air. In fact it stank so bad that as the boys would have said, you could'a sown a button on it.

They paused at the cross roads at the top Marley Lane, and before carrying on up the High Street, looked down towards the Cinema in which they had spent so many happy hours, briefly recalling some of the films they'd seen there. At the mention of Charley Chaplin, Sally grinned remembering the posters advertising his films, which had decorated the foyer and the façade of the old building. Then she sobered up again as she thought about the poverty that had dogged the childhood of this comic genius. Dad had told her a lot about this little man, including his incarceration in a workhouse at one stage along with the rest of his family. As she recalled what dad had told her, one poster in particular popped up into her mind and through some strange figment of her imagination, felt a psychic pathway through to the very essence of the man, expressed through those extraordinary eyes of his.

Another poster that had caught her eye and imagination was one advertising a film entitled, 'Lady from Shanghai.' It was colourful and exotic and totally different from those depicting her favourite comic actor. Provocative was the word Amy had used to describe it and even though she had not heard the word before, it did sound right somehow. The stars of this film, Rita Hayworth and Orson Welles, were glamorous there was no doubt about that. There was also a hint of wickedness about them somehow, if the poster was anything to go by. It was a film for grownups rather than children, she reckoned.

They stopped beside the Abbey, to refresh their memories on the content of the shopping list, and then moved forward again. 'Till's of Battle,' the shop that sold everything, would be the first port of call, they decided. What was not actually on show, would be stored somewhere down in the bowels of the place, they had learned. Today however, the small relatively light items dad wanted would, they were sure be on display at ground level.

Although they had shopped here on numerous occasions, this particular store never ceased to fascinate them. It was packed to the gunnels with this and that and the array of agricultural tools and farming equipment was overwhelming. There were many items in this area that defied the imagination and after a while the girls had given up on this particular guessing game. What for instance was this gadget, with its double row of wicked looking teeth, held together by that substantial spring, used for? While they were waiting to pass the list over to an assistant who would select the right size and number of nails, screws and washers dad wanted, they took a quick look around the hardware shelves here. Alongside the nails and hammers and string and wire, were pots and pans and dishes of every description, and butted up to all this were the packets of starch and spills, and boxes of matches, and white waxy candles by the hundred. 'Allworks' shop in Battle!

Once Sally had put the surprisingly heavy but neatly wrapped parcel of nails into dad's old rucksack, and shrugged it back onto her shoulder again, they made their way back into the street. Before they collected the other heavier items however, they decided, as usual to take a brief reconnoitre around the shops in this busy market town.

As they paused beside the sweet and tobacconist shop, Sally remembered those disgusting little things called Imps that she and Hilary had bought here, the only so called sweets they could find that were not on ration at the time. It had not been their intention to walk to Battle on this particular day, but rather a lapse of concentration on their part. They had been part of a large crowd of observers at a wedding in Sedlescombe Church, and had watched and cheered along with the rest, as the newly-wed couple had walked slowly through the impressive doorway, smiling happily around them. Once the photograph's had been taken and couple and the pathway liberally sprinkled with confetti, the girls had left the scene intending to make their way home back via Whatlington.

However, their minds were still very much on the spectacle they had just witnessed and still chatting away nineteen to the dozen had, without thinking passed right over the New Road at the top end of Stream Lane, instead of turning left as had been their intention. After an age, they had found themselves at the top of Battle High Street, hungry and thirsty, and with only a few coppers between them, had hoped to find salvation in the little sweet shop. They had purchased a small bottle of lemonade, which they had shared, had reclaimed the deposit on the bottle, and had had just enough money to purchase the innocuous looking but deadly, little black chips of poison. Sally grinned as she recalled the look of astonishment and disgust on Hilary's face as she had sucked on that bitter pill. Then she grimaced as she realised that a duplication of her friends distorted features, must have been mirrored in her own face.

Pat was the first to spot the pile of Picture Post magazines just inside the doorway, and led the way into the shop to buy a copy for mum. This was one periodical that she enjoyed browsing through when she got a few minutes to herself, which was not that often they had to admit. Still, it would not be wasted. It was a magazine that the whole family enjoyed reading and would be well thumbed through before being passed over to Granny Sansom for her to read and then to use to line one of her rabbit hutches.

An old poster caught Sally's eye as she stood in the shop. It had been there for ages and although faded and curling up at the edges, the writing was still legible. She cocked her head to one side as she read the caption once again. 'Craven 'A' it said at the top of the poster, followed by: 'no matter how many you smoke, Craven 'A' will never 'get your throat.' They've an extra touch of quality, which you'll take to right from the start – a smoothness and coolness which brings you greater smoking pleasure.' They were ten for sixpence she noticed or you could get forty for two shillings. Dad's thin roll ups did not resemble these tubes of sophistication in any which way, she thought to herself.

After tucking the magazine into the top of the rucksack, the girls made towards the Ministry of Food building to get their ration of the bottled cod liver oil and orange juice There was still an old war poster high up on the wall above the doorway in this place advertising War Bonds, Sally noticed but her favourite one with the chubby kneed children running happily through long wavy fields of wheat, was long gone. Gone also was Potato Pete – energy food, another favourite of hers. Even to this day, she missed that character with his basket, and faded green hat and the smile that spread right across his cheeky chops. However, other posters had taken their place, and as she stood in the queue, one in particular took her eye and she began to study it in detail.

There were little fairy like creatures here, their hair streaming out in the wind as they rode high above magical misty mountains on the backs of the most graceful swans in the whole wide world, while other mythological creatures, seated on equally fantastical mounts, rode alongside. Far, far below this strange enchanting convoy, ribbons of water snaked through the misty landscape, with an impressionistic image of wild mountain thyme on mossy banks and mountain ash and other wild and wonderful flora. This was truly enchanting. A magical fantasy if ever she'd seen one.

Then she grinned as another poster very different from the one she had just been studying caught her eye. The little fairy folk in this one, chubby legs and feet encased in rubber boots and gardening implements in hand, were smiling as they went about their work. The ground beneath their feet was covered in clumps of herbs, grasses and flowers, the latter daisy like and offering up smiling faces to the bright yellow sun, and presumably their pollen to a passing bee or two. She was still studying this one, when she suddenly realised that she and Pat had reached the head of the queue, and a woman behind the counter was waiting to serve them. They took their ration of cod liver oil and orange juice from her and once they had stored the bottles carefully away in their bags, made their way outside and prepared themselves for the walk home.

By the time they reached the Prefabs below Coronation Gardens, they were well into their stride. These curious looking buildings, hastily erected all over the country to house people made homeless by the bombing raids of the war, were deceptively small on the outside but quite spacious once you got inside. And they were cosy with all the basic amenities installed, and according to some folk were better equipped and more comfortable than the homes the Luftwaffe had deprived them of during the war.

As they continued on down the lane, Sally noticed with interest something that had escaped her attention on the outward journey, namely the curious shape of the crab apple trees along the way. Having shed their fruit and most of their faded leaves, the bare bones of the tree, with its tangle of lichen splashed branches, was revealed in all its craggy splendour. This tree was more interesting in its winter nakedness, than when decorated with the fresh green mantle of spring, she thought to herself. Not so pretty certainly but curiously pleasing in an odd, abstract kind of way.

The bindweed had lost its vigorous hold on the hedgerows along the way, but ivy continued to insinuate itself slowly and insidiously around every tree and bush it could get its surprisingly strong, tenacious suckers on to. This evergreen cleaver was however a source of food and cover for many insects and birds she'd been told, so even though it was slowly squeezing the life out of the old oak tree, that supported their beloved tree house at the bottom of the field, her single minded resentment was tempered somewhat by this recent information. There were two sides to every coin, as the saying went.

Pat was reminiscing now about a day trip back in the summer, in which they and just about every other child in the school had participated, plus a goodly amount of grownups. These summer outings, organised year on year by the school and various committees in the village, were funded in part by the proceeds from whist drives, dances, jumble sales, fete's etc. Mr Elkins, Hilary's dad had always taken a major part in the organisation of these school trips, right down to the monitoring of the day itself. He was also the person who made sure that every child was provided for. The rattle of coins that accompanied tickets in some of the envelopes Hilary and Sally delivered, were a sure sign that any short fall in this family's budget had been taken care of.

The coaches that ferried them to and from the various venues were always packed with excited youngsters and Sally grinned as she recalled the comment of one boy as he'd wrestled his way down the aisle. 'Gor, a money spider ad 'ave to get off your arm to get down 'ere.' He'd said.

The front seat on one of the coaches was always reserved for Johnny Gain, who with his wheel chair tucked in beside him, took in the scenery and the general chit chat going on around him with equal and obvious enjoyment. Although crippled for as far back as Sally could remember, he never grumbled, and his sense of humour and musical talents were legendry. He was quite special was Johnny. When he and Tony Powell were in the Coach and Horses it was always 'full house,' with a keen, anticipatory audience ready and waiting to be entertained by these two talented lads. And as far as she knew, they had never disappointed their audience.

Pat and Sally were now trying to decide a favourite amongst the many coach trips they had been on in the past. Southend-on-Sea, they decided straight away was their least favourite, possible because it had rained on and off on the day they had visited the town. The trips to the Zoos were provisional favourites, with the one in Chessington just having the edge over Regents Park London, possibly because of its rural setting and the extra facilities it provided. Mind you they reminded themselves, the London one did have a 'Pets Corner,' which was a bit of a winner. However, both Zoos were on a par when it came to their menagerie of diverse and exotic birds, beasts and reptiles, which were cared for, studied and admired. For many visitors, the reptile enclosure was viewed with an almost primeval repulsion and to be avoided at all costs, but that was not so for Pat and Sally. They were fascinated by the snakes with their glassy stare, their little round beady eyes unblinkingly focussed on the object of its scrutiny, their bodies seemingly controlled by a separate mechanism. They would watch the regular flick of their forked tongues as they tasted the air around them and marvel at the variety, the different coloured patterns and sizes of these creatures, who subjugated their prey either with poison or with muscle power.

Once they had exhausted the subject and objects of Zoos, they moved on to another favourite outing, the boat trip down the Thames to Hampton Court and Runnymede. For this trip they had been extraordinarily lucky with the weather, and had been able to see and appreciate the ever changing scenery and the occasional glimpse of wild life along the river. Best of all however, was an exploration of ancient buildings and monuments, with their heady atmosphere of power and influence, intrigue and life changing documents that they had only previously seen and read about in their history books.

115

Perhaps this particular outing had the edge over all the others after all, Sally reflected, her mind and imagination now filled with images from that day.

The closer to home they found themselves, the more they stepped it out, ready now for the mug of cocoa mum had promised them. Sally now insisted on using the mug Hilary had given her recently with the pleasing legend about Uncle Tom Cobley on it, and she began to recite the little ditty out loud now, in time with their marching feet:

> Tom Pearce, Tom Pearce, lend me your Grey Mare.
> "All along, down along, out along lee.
> For I want to go to Widecombe Fair.
> Wi' Bill Brewer, Jan Stewer, Peter Gurney,
> Peter Davey, Dan'l Whidden, Harry Hawk.
> Old Uncle Tom Cobley and all.
> Old Uncle Tom Cobley and all."

The sickly smell of freshly paunched and skinned rabbits assaulted their noses as they walked through the scullery door and into the kitchen, and Sally almost heaved. Chickens were stinky enough when they were being divested of their innards, singed of their residual feathers, but that smell did not turn your stomach the way the stench of raw rabbit did. As she looked towards the primus table where the naked corpses were lined up on strips of clean sheeting, she wondered not for the first time, how mum managed to turn these smelly, elongated strips of flesh and bone, into those tasty casseroles, stews and pies, the former disgusting, the latter bloody delicious. No matter, it was another of those things in life for which she was truly thankful.

The clouds were tramping across the sky as Hilary and Sally hurried down the field in the early evening, forming and reforming, and building up into what promised or threatened to be a very wet and windy night. A few drops of rain were already falling by the time they arrived at Windy Ridge, and they shivered as they made their way through the back door and into the warm kitchen. Ronald was sitting at the table, surrounded by string, sticks and lots of brown paper, and was well into the exacting task of kite making, at which he excelled. His ability to get the balance right was all down to accurate measurement he reckoned, and Sally believed him. While his works of art seemed to soar through the sky like graceful swans, the ones she made behaved just like crazy witches on broomsticks. Hilary had mastered the art. Her creations mostly stayed airborne and under control and did not plummet ignominiously back to the ground in seconds. She would just have to keep on trying, that was all Sally told herself. In the meantime it was quite therapeutic just to sit and watch Ronald working away with skill and determination.

Once the job had been done to Ronald's satisfaction, the accumulation of kite making paraphernalia was removed from the table and stacked neatly away on the sideboard for the time being, and replaced with a feast of bread, butter, cheese and a jar of fish paste. At first they ate in silence, but after a while the action of munching away on the grub triggered off some salutary tales associated with the recent visitation of the school dentist. The crop of horror stories related by each one in turn, almost brought tears to their eyes. It was not as though any of them had progressed beyond a cursory examination as yet, but the lurid tales from those who had faced the dreaded drill of the demon dentist as he prepared a cavity in a tooth for its steel grey amalgam filling were legendary. They had actually seen this instrument of torture with their own eyes while their examinations had taken place. They had also heard the high-pitched screech of the thing as they had sat on the edge of their seats in the next room, and imagined with fear and trepidation, the torment of the occupant in that dreaded dentist's chair. Facing a tooth extraction could not be as bad as this surely. At least you had the choice of laughing gas or Cocaine for this procedure and as Ronald pointed out, you could always ask for your tooth back if you had the nerve, then pop it under your pillow that night and hope for a tanner from the tooth fairy.

Being checked over by Sir Alan Moore, the School Doctor, was a doddle in comparison they all agreed, and even factoring in the embarrassment of the girls who had to strip down to vest and knickers for their examination, this was far from the fear shivering experience of that other procedure, and one to be tolerated rather than dreaded. He was tall and thin, and quite friendly in a remote, dignified sort of way, and yet Sally was always tongue tied and nervous in his presence. Somehow it was though he second sensed her discomfort, and once the procedures were over and done with, he always dismissed her with a kindly smile that quite transformed the severity of his features. Maybe, she was not the only youngster to exhibit this irrational behaviour, she hoped not. It was foolish really when she thought about it. Never the less, she was thankful that the frequent and very necessary task of checking heads for lice, nits and other vermin was left to the District Nurse.

From Dentists, Doctors and Nurses to face packs, was a natural progression as far as Sally was concerned, and she and Hilary began to embark on a discussion of this cosmetic preparation with glee. Freda swore by it. She reckoned that an application of this white chalky mixture onto her face once every two to three weeks, would stop spots and blackheads in their tracks, and so far this treatment did seem to be working. She carried out this treatment in her bedroom, but on one occasion had popped into the kitchen for her reading book, only to be confronted by the two little ones. The look of astonishment and terror on their faces as they witnessed this apparition for the first time, brought a guilty chuckle from the two girls. Dorothy in particular had shot across the room and up into mum's arms as though beset by seven devils, and Freda had been forced to remove the stuff and the scarf with which she had tied back her hair, to prove her identity. Since then however, Dorothy and Jacky, with a little help from the older girls, had managed to get their own back on Freda. These days no matter how secretive she tried to be, they often managed to catch her in the act, and when they did, they tried to make her laugh, thus cracking the crisp surface of the dried up application into a mess of flaky powdery stuff. And they nearly always succeeded.

This was as good a time as any for a game of tiddly-winks they decided. It would round off the evening nicely, and perhaps inspire them to come up with a subject on which to base this 'ere concert that Miss Smith seemed to be so keen on. They were sure she had a few ideas on the subject but would rather have the youngsters come up with one of their own. Certainly Sunday School or Bible Class as they now called it, was a lot more interesting these days, and had been ever since the Smith family had moved into the Manse. They were a truly Christian family that was for sure, but not the least bit pious like a lot of religious people seemed to be. A bit like Jesus really. They involved the youngsters in all sorts of projects, including the rescue of injured animals for which Mr Smith, aided by Daniel and John Hullock, had put together one very large cage and some smaller ones as well. The large cage now housed a squirrel, found injured and rescued by Hilary and Ronald, plus two or three others, all now tramping around the wire netting like clockwork springs. The contents of the smaller ones varied day by day. These cages often housed little creatures like mice and voles, many having been wrestled from the jaws of some predatory cat or other, and sometimes birds with broken wings and other injuries, found refuge here.

The game of tiddly-winks soon degenerated into a free for all, with the little coloured disks flying out of control and in all directions. Hilary and Sally were now far more interested in Sabbath's and Chapels and in particular the prospect of travelling all the way to the Methodist Chapel in Robertsbridge tomorrow in the back of Miss smith's little old motor car, which they had just remembered. That she managed to cram so many bodies into such a small space defied the laws of science, but they were not about to complain about that 'Jam packed' and 'full to the gunnels', were just a couple of descriptions that popped up into Sally's imagination as she anticipated the journey, which she admitted guiltily to herself was the highlight of the day, rather than the service itself. And no matter how restricted her movements might be in that old motor, she always managed somehow to crane her neck around far enough to catch a glimpse of a couple of pine trees that grew in the hedgerow along Whatlington way that, by a strange quirk of nature mimicked one another in every last uncanny detail. The thing that fascinated her most of all, were the identical branches that sprang from each   trunk and reached out and upwards in perfect symmetry like the beckoning arms of two Medieval Monks, offering a benediction to a wandering stranger.

Once the game of tiddlywinks had been packed safely away in its box, Hilary moved towards the back door and ushered the cat outside for its last minute wee. No sooner had she moved over to the stove to warm up the milk for their cocoa though, than the wretched thing was scratching at the door to be let in again. Once inside, it paused briefly to wind its wet body around her legs and then moved off to find the warmest place in the house to spend the night.

As they supped their cocoa, Hilary and Ronald voiced their concern about the strained relationship between their mum and dad, wondering where on earth it would all lead to. They tried analysing the situation, thinking what if anything they could do about it, but after a lengthy discussion, realised they were going round and round in circles and were no nearer to a solution to the problems that beset their parents than when they had begun the discussion. After a while and reluctantly, they admitted that they were not actually in a position to solve or even improve the situation, in any way. This was something that only their parents could sort out, and all they could do was to stand by and hope against hope not for a miracle exactly but for some kind of compromise between the two grownups.

It was still raining steadily when they took themselves off to bed, and as Sally snuggled down and drew the covers up to her chin, she listened with a feeling of ease and contentment to the sound of rain on windows and the low whistle of wind through window frames. While she waited for sleep to overtake her conscious thoughts, her imagination drifted lazily away, along a labyrinth of intricate and complex pathways, the ones that absented themselves during the hustle and bustle of the day.

For some reason, a blurred image of Hengist and Horsa, about whom she knew next to nothing, but whose very names had fired her imagination, drifted in. According to Jumbo James they were early Danish invaders, maybe the very first Anglo-Saxons, though whether that was fact or legend he had not been absolutely sure. They belonged in the dim and distant past when very little had been written down, many stories and myths perpetuated solely by having been passed down from mouth to mouth, generation to generation over eons of time. (down through the ages). Another figure, easily recognised from the front cover of one of the Headmasters books, floated across her mind's eye. It was the stooped, squat figure of Pilgrim, plodding through a desolate countryside, with a rucksack on his back, a mood of grim determination depicted in every simplistic stroke of the artists brush. This lone traveller moved purposely forward, his sights clearly set on a distant horizon, grimly facing unknown perils that would beset him along the way. Strangely, she could feel the benign and comforting spirit of Deffy and Bill around there somewhere, like two old Guardian Angels covertly watching over this special traveller on his journey into the unknown. She watched this image fade slowly away into the hazy distance with some regret, but before she had time to lament its demise, another began its journey across her senses. Through the dark mysterious landscape, a masked Highwayman appeared, and although he rode like all the demons of hell were after him, continued to float hazily, steadfastly across her inward eye like some strange compelling mirage. And riding at his heels, not in visual aspect but in some deeper, impressionistic realm, came Tom, Dick and Harry, allegedly fellow Highwaymen and victims of the practice of land clearance by the Gentry. This vicious practice drove tenant farmers and their families from the land, causing abject poverty and had driven many of the men into the dangerous game of highway robbery for which the penalties were very severe. Although absorbed now almost into the realms of folk law, these men had lived and suffered the consequences of the road they had been forced to take. They had indeed lived life on the very edge.

A dream like vision of another Highwayman, as he rode through ribbons of moonlight over a purple moor began to drift in and out of her thoughts, with accompanying images of cobbled pathways and an Inn situated on the very edge of nowhere, and the maiden living in isolation within its imposing walls. Her imagination recoiled from further exploration of this tragic poem. As far as she was concerned, this gallant Highwayman would be riding for ever and ever over the purple moors astride his trusty horse, to the maiden who weaved a red love knot into her long black hair.

Then as her imagination hovered between dream and reality, an angel floated by, paused for a mini second then evolved slowly into the blurred image of the Lady of Pevensey Church, an aura of grief still surrounding her like a lacy shroud.

Although the rain had stopped by the time Hilary and Sally made their way back home the next morning, it was still windy and very wet under foot. As Sally dodged the puddles along the lane, she contemplated the drowned worms, gross and bloated and quite disgusting floating in them, and shuddered. She was mindful of the important job of work they did. O yes! Dad had told her many times about the way they aerated the soil. How they took compost materials and such like into the ground, chewed and excreted the stuff, which made the ground more fertile, or something like that. She also knew that they were a source of food for a lot of bird species as well, but she was still not able to overcome her revulsion for these squirming creatures. That painting she had once clamped her eyes on had not exactly helped to endear them to her, quite the reverse. In fact as she now contemplated the dead ones in the puddles, the image of those human skulls, with hundreds of worms threading themselves in and out of eye sockets, gaping mouths and bony nostrils, popped into her mind. She could see it as clearly now as the day she had first set eyes on the disgusting image. It was etched into her imagination now and would stay there for always she reckoned. Yuk!

She grabbed Hilary's arm and pulled her unceremoniously towards the bottom gate, chatting inconsequentially about this and that, and by the time they had reached the top gate, worms and their disgusting habits had been purged from her immediate thoughts. She breathed a sigh of relief as she walked into the scullery she saw the milk churns, rinsed and now perched upside down on the draining board. Pat, who was now sitting around the kitchen table eating her breakfast along with Dorothy, Jacky and Granny Cotton, had already collected the milk from the farm. That at least was one chore she did not have to worry about. She then moved towards the Primus table and lifted the tea-pot up off the large enamel tray to assess its contents. Having decided it would stand a refill, she removed the ruched, bobble topped cover that Aunty Nin had knitted for it, and added enough water from the simmering kettle on the top of the Rayburn for a few extra cups of tea. She knew without asking, that Gran would never refuse a refill no matter how many cups of the stuff she had previously imbibed, and with a bit of luck, there would be enough left in the pot for mum to have one when she had finished what she was up to in the copper house.

Once the table had been cleared of its debris, and the crocks and cutlery washed and stashed away in the old dresser in the scullery, it was decided that a visit to Deffy and Bill was long overdue. They had already checked the cake tins and decided that there was enough of Aunty Nin's seedy cake and mum's fruit one to spare, enough anyway to make the old men's eyes light up. Once a trip to the edge of the big wood had been mentioned, there was no going back as far as Dorothy and Jacky were concerned and their enthusiasm was hard to contain. After donning their coats and Wellington boots, they made their way outside stopping briefly outside the greenhouse to see what dad was up to. He was bending over the bench surrounded by an assortment of Hessian sacks from which he was selecting suitable seedling potatoes for next year's crop. Sally knew from seeing him perform this chore in the past, that at the right time, he would lay them out in trays and store them in the frost free attic with plenty of natural light around for them to produce nice fat, healthy shoots. She also remembered that he called the process 'chitting', and always emphasised the word as he reckoned it gave him an excuse to swear without actually swearing. He was a funny old stick but never idle, that was for sure. Nor was mum if it came to that. She was more than likely preparing the meat and vegetables for dinner and making pastry for the fruit pie pudding at the moment, in between popping round to the copper house to do the washing of course. She never even sat down for long enough to drink a cup of tea in one go, and made some silly excuse about having a round bottom or some such thing. Even when she looked tired out, she never grumbled. Now that was something that she, Sally would never be able to do.

As they made their way through the back gate and across the field, they kept a wary eye on the ram, which had been brought into the field recently. Luckily, this one had not shown any interest in them so far, had not even turned its thick neck around as they had passed by, but old habits died hard. Rams as they well knew, were unpredictable and past experiences had taught them to be on their guard. Also, having the little ones around made the older girls doubly careful and it was with a sigh of relief that they piled over the stile at the bottom end of the field and into the muddy lane. As they made their way along the track, they jumped over the small drainage channels, which had been cut across the pathway at regular intervals along this low lying area, the little ones with rather more enthusiasm than was good for the state of their clothing. It was fortunate that she had brought a fair sized bit of rag along, Sally thought to herself. It was going to take more than a bit of spit and polish to clean up these two miscreants.

They could see smoke escaping from the funnel on top of Deffy and Bill's old shack as they approached the place, and watched as the wind wafted it this way and that in a merry old game. Bill, who must have seen or heard their approach, came through the doorway and as he ushered them inside, the acrid smell that hit their nostrils was a clear indication that not all the smoke was finding its way up and out through that old funnel. As Bill took the cake from them, he unwrapped and sniffed it appreciatively, then offered it up to his brother to do the same. Although Deffy was even less communicative now than when Sally had first set eyes on him, neither he nor Bill has changed significantly in the intervening years as far as she could see. They had always been and always would be, as old as Methuselah.

As Sally watched the faces of her little sisters, she was transported back to her own early childhood when she had first started coming here with the older girls. She remembered so clearly, that wordless fascination she had had with the occupants and contents of the place, and which she now saw reflected in the expressions of the little ones. Their eyes were everywhere, exploring every rickety shelf, every crook and cranny that had been filled to the gunnels with an assortment of fauna and flora, collected in and around the big wood by these two old eccentrics. The skeletons of little woodland creatures, some part some complete seemed to particularly fascinate them, and they gazed on these curious specimens in wide eyes amazement. Bill watched them for a while, the ghost of a smile hovering around the corners of his mouth, and then produced as if by magic, his collection of wild birds' eggs. Although she was ready for this and had seen the collection many times before, Sally was as fascinated this time around as she had been when she had first set eyes on it. For the two little ones, it was a wondrous experience and they gazed in silent awe on the rows of fragile orbs, each unique in its own way, which had been collected over the years by these two old men, morphed now into and an integral part of the wood in which they lived.

It was with a degree of reluctance that they left the two old men to the sparse comfort of their raggedy shack, where the rain was now beating a series of sharps and flats, onto its old tin roof, and out into the muddy lane. It was colder now, a definite hint of what was to come over the next few months, in the increasing coldness of the wind as it hit their cheeks. They shivered momentarily as they accustomed themselves to the sudden change in temperature, took a deep breath of fresh air, and then heads down, set their sights on home. They were hungry now and would be more than ready for their dinner when the time came, and of course, there was also Sunday School this afternoon to look forward to. Before that however, there would be a bit of cleaning up to do. It would not be just the two little ones who needed a bit of spit and polish - and more. By the time they got home, they all would.

Spruced up now and trying to avoid the worst of the mud in the field and the puddles along the lane, the girls set off on the journey to the Manse and Sunday School, an assortment of wools, leather and other materials stashed away in bags dangling from their arms. As they were about to cross the main road and into Crazy Lane, Sally spotted Denis Crow freewheeling down Whydown Hill towards them and there was no escape. As he drew alongside, Sally drew in a deep breath in readiness for one of his ambiguous rants, but he just paused for long enough to fix her with a stare that looked just like he'd chewed on a stinging nettle with cats wee on it, and then peddled off down the main road. She watched him disappear with a sigh of relief. He unnerved her in some peculiar way that she had never been able to fathom, but at least he had spared them one of his rants this time. And he was not it seemed going their way, and for that she had to be thankful. She sometimes wondered what made him tick.

After calling for Ronald, Patty, Basil and Raymond, the youngsters made their way towards the Chapel, arriving just as Miss Smith, Olive and Daniel were setting out the chairs and other paraphernalia, ready for this afternoon's class. Mrs Smith could not be with them today, which was a shame. She so seldom missed a session. Other youngsters began arriving in dribs and drabs, and the early buzz of conversation soon developed into noisy chatter and clatter, as bums competed for the available seating. The babble ceased when Miss Smith held up her hand and after shuffling to their feet, stood with eyes closed, chins resting on chests, listening in silence as she offered up a brief prayer. They opened their eyes but remained standing as Olive moved towards the piano and struck up the introductory chords to the opening hymn, a particular favourite of theirs, joining in on cue and with rather more gusto than harmony:

> *"Jesus loves me this I know, for the Bible tells me so.*
> *Little ones to him belong, they are weak but he is strong.*
> *Yes Jesus loves me, yes Jesus loves me.*
> *Yes Jesus loves me, the Bible tells me so."*

They sang this religious song right through to its end without once referring to their hymn sheets and, once these preliminaries were over, set about getting down to the real business of the day; the making of gifts and small items of clothing to send to the Missionaries in Africa, of whom, off and on was Mrs Smith.

The contents of bags and pockets from the youngsters were soon deposited on the long trestle table at the side of the room, alongside the various materials already assembled there by Miss Smith, Olive and Daniel. The most striking and by far the most in volume, was the selection of wool now decorating the table, the crinkly ends escaping from each tightly wound ball telling its own story. What was hard to imagine however, was the amount of times this wool had gone through and survived the process of unravelling, hanking, washing and rewinding in its life, virtually impossible to second guess how many disguises it had assumed in its long secret life.

Miss Smith was gathering a small group of girls around her to demonstrate how to turn the heel in a sock, a complicated business as Sally well knew. She was lucky that she, Pat and Hilary had been taught this tricky manoeuvre by the older girls, Betty in particular, who had got this procedure off to a fine art. Actually it was not that difficult when you knew how, she thought to herself, as was the case with most things in life when you really thought about it.

Pat, Hilary, Patty and Sally turned their attention to the pieces of leather, already cut to size and shape by Pop Cotton, and ready now to be made into purses. He had punched holes at regular intervals around the edges to facilitate the long strips of leather with which to bind the pieces together, had explained the importance of keeping these strips of leather straight as you worked and explained the importance of and how to ensure a neat finish. They were keen to try their hand at this simple task, but quickly discovered as they proceeded, that this was not the easy option it had appeared when watching dad.

Some of the boys were busy sorting through the box of large curtain rings, buttons and safety pins, also the hanks of coloured plastic string that lay alongside. Keith Card who seemed to be in control here, picked up one of the metal rings and began to demonstrate the blanket stitch, which would cover their nakedness, emphasising how important it was to keep the uniformity of the twist as he pressed each stitch into precise alignment with his thumb. He was well on the way to completing his first brooch before the other boys really had a chance to get started, explaining as he went along how to secure the decorative button in the centre of his masterpiece and how to fix the safety pin on the back. The button was just one way of decorating the piece, he was telling them. They could weave their own pattern within the circle using the lengths of coloured plastic if they wanted to, once they got the hang of the thing. But it was a tricky manoeuvre and needed a bit of practice. And of course there were other decorative objects they could design from the materials that were in front of them he explained.

Sally watched the demonstration on and off, with half an eye while pursuing her own chosen handcrafted contribution. She was getting the hang of the weaving process on these purses now and was quite enjoying the rhythm of it. After a while her attention was drawn towards the tangle of old lisle stockings that had been tipped onto the far end of the table, and up to this moment, ignored by all and sundry. She could not for the life of her imagine how this drab and untidy mess of black, brown, cream and various shades of grey, could be transformed into toys and rugs as Miss Smith suggested. It would take some kind of a bloody miracle for that to happen she thought to herself.

Then she paused, contemplating the dexterity with which Olive was transforming some of the multi-coloured strands of plastic into an intricate and altogether pleasing work of art. Its elongated shape suggested a belt perhaps or even the strap for a bag of some kind. Whatever, its ultimate shape and eventual use was secondary to her determination to try her hand at this particular woven wonder, and her fingers itched in anticipation.

Some of the youngsters talked as they worked, discussing amongst other things, the various activities that had taken place in the Chapel over the past weeks. The Harvest Festival had been particularly successful, with contributions of fruit and vegetables and even one of fish, which they recalled, had stank a bit towards the end of the thanksgiving service. As they grinned ruefully at the memory, Miss Smith suggested that perhaps at the next festival, they would think about celebrating all four seasons in verse. Anyway, it would give them plenty of time to think up a few appropriate lines.

Once they had mulled over the past, the talk moved towards future events, focussing in particular on that most important date on the calendar - Christmas day. The Chapel would have to be decorated for this special festival, and they all anticipated the trips that would have to be made into the countryside to gather holly and ivy and if they were especially lucky, a few sprigs of the rare mistletoe. Miss Smith had promised to bring in plenty of those strips of coloured paper over the next week or two as well, which they would loop together with a smidgen of glue and make up into long, decorative garlands, or paper chains as they called them.

Before they knew it, the small hand on the clock had made its way around the dial a couple of times and they suddenly realised, it was very nearly home time. As they began to shuffle their handiwork together, albeit with a measure of reluctance, Miss Smith cleared her throat and they all looked in her direction then sat back down again. Unusually, she was sitting with her elbows on the table, finger tips resting beneath and supporting her chin, and was clearly waiting to ask them something.

"Have any of you given any thought to that play I've been asking you to think about over these past few weeks? She began. "I'm leaving it entirely up to you now as to what you choose as a theme, but I would be grateful if you would come up with a few ideas before long, so we can make a start on the preliminaries, like 'words' and what props and things we'll need." Her brief statement was met with a wall of silence, and as she rose to her feet to offer up the closing prayer, Sally noticed a smile hovering around her mouth as she looked around at them all.

"Do you know what you remind me of, sitting there like that?" she asked, her smile widening into a grin. "A lot of stuffed dummies, that's what. I've never seen you sitting there so still or so quiet before, ever."

There was a slight uncomprehending silence for a few seconds and then a murmur went around the room, quickly developing into distinguishable words, with one in particular standing out from the rest. "Waxworks." Once the word had been uttered, there was no going back. Why had they not thought of this before, they asked themselves and immediately began to plan the plot and dumb characters, enthusiastically with no thought to the time of day. It was several minutes before Miss Smith was able to get a word in edgeways, and as a consequence the closing prayer was offered up a bit later than usual. She however, seemed not the least bit put out by the delay. On the contrary, having instigated this debate, she actively encouraged the lively discussion that was taking place around her. By the time the youngsters left the building, the scene had been set, the preliminaries sorted and they went on their way well pleased with this turn of events.

They shivered as they left the comparative warmth of the building, instinctively drawing their coats and scarves more closely around their bodies as they began the journey home. The wind was definitely colder now than it had been on their arrival at the Chapel, and there was more of it. It whistled through the bare branches of the trees along the way, bending them to its will as it moved them hither and thither in a merry old dance.

Heads down and grouped up close together to mitigate the worst effects of the elements, the youngsters made their way down Crazy Lane at a speed of knots, the girls reciting over and over a little ditty that seemed appropriate and which for some reason, amused them:

*"I saw you toss the kites on high and blow the birds about the sky.
And all around I saw you pass, like ladies skirts across the grass."*

When they reached the bottom of the lane, they paused for just long enough to congratulate themselves on the successful outcome of the days discussions, and to count their blessings for the timely arrival of the Smith family with their infectious enthusiasm, their encouragement to each and every one of them. This family with its doctrine of forgiveness, they all agreed, were like no other family they had ever met.

Sedlescombe Saints

*David Gammon, Arthur Puxty, Len Larkin, Derek Bishop, Ron Hudson,
Doug Kenward, Roy Chapman, mascot Diggy Fuller, Phil Knight*

Sedlescome Saints

*Sid Puxty, Arthur Puxty, Jack Chapman, Roy Chapman, Tony Taylor,
Len Larkin, Phil Knight, David Gammon, Alf Larkin, mascot Diggy
Fuller (Robert)*

Jacky and
Dorothy Cotton

Clockwise from top left:
Pat Cotton, Marlene McCann,
Margaret James, Margaret
Cruttenden

Pat Cotton

Clockwise from top left:
Janet Powell, Dorothy Cotton,
Brian Winchester, Jacky Cotton

Janet Powell

Left to right:

Hazel, Jacky, Eileen Troughton, Sally, Dorothy,

Margery Freeman, Pat

Uncle Tom and Auntie Nelly

Pat

Sally aged 14

Hilary and Sally

Mr and Mrs
Lawrence
and
Eileen

Amy
Powell
and her
family

Basil
Beeching

Village Outings

*Country
Ways*

Tony as a soldier
aged 22

Mrs Taylor with son
Tony Taylor and Joy Phillips

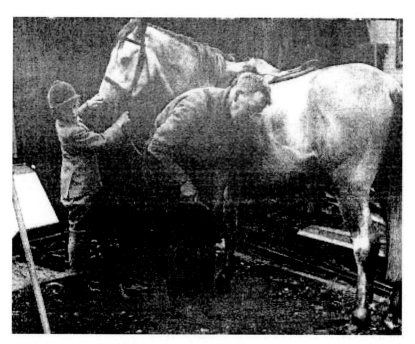

Mr Taylor the blacksmith

Mrs Garner, left, and Neil Farrow next to her

Mr and Mrs Farrow
Nelly, Neil and Jack circa 1921

The Wood family - left to right:

Hamish, Mrs Wood, Gavin, Mr Wood and Donald

Left to right: Donald, Hamish and Gavin Wood

*Dolly
and
Pop
Cotton
over the
years*

Chapter 7

The orange glow from the rising sun had gradually drained the darkness from the cold wintry sky, and for the time being at least, there were no snow threatening clouds in view. There was a cold east wind powering its way across the landscape though, the girls did not need dad to remind them of that. They would need their several layers of undergarments topped by their Gabardine coats to protect them from the worst of it, Sally thought to herself as she sat at the kitchen table eating her breakfast. They were well in the grip of cold old winter now that was for sure.

Christmas had come and gone, the decorations taken down and the ones that could be saved, safely stored away for another year. Sally was well pleased with the gifts she had received, the kaleidoscope with its 'patterns' of sheer magic in particular. She could not fathom how every twist or shake of the elongated box produced yet another glittering spectacle, yet somehow it did. She had also been given, as had her younger sisters, a tin mouse with a wind up key. They had had a whale of a time winding the things up and racing them across the kitchen floor, creating havoc and forever getting in the way, of Granny Cotton in particular. They had all been supplied with the usual and very useful crop of hats, gloves and scarves, which would be a Godsend on a day like this. The pink sugar mice they all received had soon been consumed, along with the blood oranges and chocolate drops. The tin whistles and the frog clickers that someone had thoughtlessly inserted into the little ones stockings however, had been harder to dispose of. The older girls had been trying to hide the blooming things away ever since, without much success. Dorothy and Jacky always managed somehow and eventually to unearth those noisy instruments. Tin mice were fun. Tin whistles and frog clickers however, were just down right maddening. Pat, Hilary and Sally had put together some homemade calendars for the grownups. They had painted and stencilled pieces of plain card, then suspended penny calendars onto the bottom with the aid of ribbon and a bit of glue. Sally had also knitted matching pixie hoods and mittens in red wool for Dorothy and Jacky, with white cross-stitched decoration around the rim and cuffs.

Having finished their chores Pat, Hilary and Sally were now back at the table, mugs cradled in hands, sipping their hot sweet coffee. The bottle of concentrate was still on the table beside them and Sally lifted it up and read the words on the label absentmindedly to herself. 'Camp Coffee and Chicory essence,' it said. Then she shook the bottle gently and watched idly as some of the dark liquid cloaked the top of the bottle before gradually slipping back down again. While they were still supping the beverage, dad came into the room with a thick brown paper package, which he deposited onto the table beside them.

"There's the seed potatoes I promised Mrs Pepler then. Better use that that old rucksack of mine to carry them along in. It's thick and strong and it'll protect them from the worst of this cold old wind," he said, as he moved towards the scullery door to remove the bag from its hook. "There, that'll do. The old lady'll know how to keep them frost free once she gets them," he added as he tucked the parcel away carefully into the bag and handed it to Sally. "Now wrap up warm, it's a lazy old wind out there and no mistake." As he moved away from the table, his mind clearly on the next chore he sniffed and Sally smiled to herself. She would recognise that characteristic sniff of his anytime, anywhere. He was a funny old stick, she thought as she rose from the table at the same time as Pat and Hilary, and began to don coat, hat, gloves and scarf. These warm outdoor clothes should protect them from the worst of the elements along with the lumps of bread pudding mum had carefully wrapped up for them in pieces of greaseproof paper, and which she now stowed carefully away into the rucksack on top of the precious potatoes.

As the girls made their way down the field, they could just make out the stooped figure of Pop Cotton beside one of the chicken coops as he tipped the feed from a bucket into one of the hoppers. He was buttoned up in that thick old jacket of his and beneath his baggy trousers, would be wearing a pair of those long, thick underpants, which made the youngsters giggle when they saw them drooped over the line above the Rayburn in the kitchen alongside Granny Cotton's old apple gatherers. Sally hoped he was wearing the pair of finger-less mittens she had knitted for him back in the autumn, but she could not make a detail like that out from this distance.

There was a thin, deceptively chilly breeze blowing through the bare branches of the trees along the way, with every twig etched starkly across the cold blue sky. The brown hedgerows were littered with leaves and dead foliage with here and there clumps of tough old cow parsley, stubbornly defying the elements by poking its fronds of bitter green herbage up through the cold, rigid earth.

As they were passing Gotways Farm, Sally glanced through the gap between farmhouse and barn, unable to see but imagining the little cottages that nestled in the lane just beyond. She wondered if mum's friend, little Mrs Edwards who lived there, would have braved the elements and pegged her washing out on a day like this, and reckoned she would, even risking the hot ache that would inevitably spread painfully though her fingers. Like mum there was nothing she liked better than to see her lines of washing flapping away in the breeze. Today however, any material with a trace of moisture in it would freeze into an elongated, amorphous shape and be hanging there on the line, stiff as a board.

Memories of the day, aeons ago now when she and her sisters had taken part in the capture of those demented horses that had escaped from this very farm, suddenly popped up into Sally's mind. The weather had been much the same as today, but with an even colder bone chilling wind, and she felt herself stiffen as she recalled the overwhelming fear she had felt at the time. Even now, she could see the bloodshot eyes of those horses as they had galloped towards her from the direction of New England Lane, could even feel the impact of the stiff frost laden grass as she had thrown herself over the hedge by the entrance to the track – and only just in time. Those horses had galloped over the very spot on which she had been standing just seconds before, driven by some primitive, primeval instinct – or maybe just sheer bloody mindedness, who could tell.

By the time they reached the top end of Kent Street, they were well into their stride and giggling as they tried to remember the words to one of Gracie Field's songs about an unfortunate youth called Fred Fannakerpan. Their efforts were pathetic to say the least, and only the last line on which they were word perfect was sung in unison, if a little out of tune as they attempted to imitate the unique quality of Gracie's voice:

"And that's the last we ever saw of Fred Fannakerpan,"

As they approached Carpenters Barn Farm Sally looked briefly towards the large house on the left where the dentist, Mr Holiday lived, hoisting her bag more comfortably up onto her shoulder as she did so. Unsurprisingly there was little sign of life in the large garden surrounding this grand house, apart from a noisy gathering of rooks, cawking and squawking in the coppice of tall trees to the side of the property. During the war, she remembered having walked this way with her older sisters, turning off along the lane which ran down beside it, and making their way home via Hart's Green. There had been a rumour at the time, that the King had just made a visit to Hastings, but it had all been hush, hush and they had discussed this bit of secret information in low whispers just in case someone might be spying on them. She could not remember now if it had ever been confirmed, but she supposed that it did not really matter now. What she did remember though were a couple of speeches, broadcast by the King (8th May 1945?) at the end of the war in which he had told the country:

'The second world war was fought to liberate people from Nazi and Japanese tyranny.' And:

'We kept faith with ourselves and with one another. We kept faith and unity with our great allies. That faith that unity, have carried us to victory through dangers that at times seemed overwhelming.'

Now those speeches had really made an impression on her at the time.

Reg Sellens who always played 'The Last Post,' lived along here somewhere she suddenly remembered and as she recalled the strains of this haunting dirge, the hairs at the back of her neck began to prickle. Remembrance Day was always a sad solemn occasion, accompanied by a similar aura of grief to the one that had surrounded the lady they had seen at Pevensey Church. Here however, the people were united in their sorrow, not set in a time warp of isolation as she had been. There was a feeling of empathy, community, amongst the congregation of the village, which somehow bound them together in grief for the loss of loved ones. She had noticed this same instinctive show of unity in times of acute stress and suffering in a painting of all things. According to dad, it was a representation of just one of the chilling incidents that had taken place during the time of the Great War. It showed a group of allied soldiers all suffering in various ways from the effects of poisonous gas. Those blinded by the deadly stuff, heads swathed in bandages, were leaning on and being guided by comrades whose injuries were less obvious. Others lay on the ground clutching at their chests their breathing clearly restricted and painful, some leaning into the supporting arms of fellow soldiers. Starkly realistic though the painting was, she had not recoiled from it. Man's inhumanity to man was here certainly, but also and most importantly was a united spirit of survival over adversity, a profound and enduring expression of comradeship.

In no time at all it seemed, they were walking past the low cut hedges that flanked the low road leading to Ebden's Hill, with the fields of Irelands Farm on their left, and the old Farmhouse itself sitting in comfortable isolation way across those fields. For the Cain family who owned and ran this farm, the work was hard, the hours long, but as with most farming families, the hard relentless grind was somehow taken in their stride. Peggy and John, the two youngsters in this family, helped with the day by day chores such as the milking of the cows before and after school, and were also involved with the wheat harvest and the cutting of the grass meadows, with the resulting hay stored and used as winter fodder for the livestock. Mr Cain had also operated a milk delivery round in the area at one time, which had lasted until the sheer pressure of work on his farm had forced him to abandon that particular enterprise.

They paused briefly at the entrance to Moat Lane, pondering over the origins, the subtle record of history stored within the acres of woodland across the road, which for some reason they had never actually been into. Rumour had it that the Romans had had a settlement there and if you knew where to look, the signs of their occupation were still there. As they made their way into Moat Lane, now sucking on the Victory V lozenges that Hilary had just passed around, they promised themselves a rummage around in this secret place when the weather had turned a bit warmer. They would make that project a priority they all agreed, and to seal the deal, Sally tied a knot in her hankie, held it up for inspection with mock solemnity and then popped it back up her sleeve again.

The remains of the clumps of giant hogweed, that had held proud dominion over every other herb and wild flower in the summer hedgerows along the way, were now reduced to an untidy mass of desiccated sticks. To the practised eye however, many of the larger dried out pieces of stem were ideal for making pea shooters, and proved irresistible to the girls who bent into the hedgerow to extricate a few from the thin but spiteful brambles that lurked in the undergrowth. After a quick trim with a penknife, they stowed away the missiles, then rubbed their hands together to re-circulate the blood to their chilled fingers before replacing their mittens.

They began to step it out again, bending their heads instinctively to protect themselves from the full effects of the north-easterly, which felt colder and more biting now that they were now heading into it. Here and there along the lane where the trees had been pollarded, their stubby branches stuck up like the gnarled arthritic knuckles of an old Ogre, and Sally grimaced. The observation reminded her of the tale that had scared the living daylights out of her when she had been a small child. Even now she shivered as she recalled the story of the giant with his penchant for human flesh, that of children in particular and was suddenly conscious of their proximity to the alleged burial place of this monster. By the time they reached Mrs Peplers little cottage however, the Ogre had popped back into a recess of her mind, along with other vague, half-forgotten memories, all awaiting a particular signal that would bring them instantly and starkly back into focus.

After a tentative knock on the front door, which unsurprisingly brought no response, they made their way around the side and to the back of the little house where they guessed the old lady would be. And there she was, busy as a bee as she moved around the various coops and sheds in her large back garden that housed her menagerie of livestock. She was wearing a long black coat tied up at the waist with a length of binder twine, and beneath the hem, the toes of her wellies were just visible. After acknowledging their presence with a brief nod, she continued her ministrations, ladling out food and words of encouragement in equal measure to her little friends. As they stood beside the fence watching her, one of her old goats ambled up alongside, raised his head and began to scrutinise them with the strange unblinking eyes of some medieval torturer, and Sally shuddered involuntarily before quickly averting her eyes. She moved away leaving Pat and Hilary to scratch the top of his head, and wandered towards the gaggle of geese and ducks and assorted chickens all chucking away as they vied with one another for a share of the sustenance that Mrs Peppler was scooping from one or other of the battered buckets around her feet. The old lady could do with another pair of mittens, that was for sure Sally thought to herself as she looked at the scruffy old pair she was wearing. Now that was something she could do. It would only take her an evening and she already had enough wool from that old navy jumper she had unravelled a while ago, to make her at least one pair of fingerless mittens like the ones she had made for dad. She was startled out of her reverie by Mrs Peppler who having finished her ministrations, for the time being at least now turned her attention to the girls.

"Is it me tatties you've got in that there bag?" she asked, her breath coming out in little puffs of steam and clearly visible in the thin, cold air, as she pointed towards the rucksack on Sally's back. Then without waiting for a reply, began walking towards her back door adding over her shoulder, "best bring 'em into me scullery before we all get froze to death. Cold as charity it be out here."

The girls followed, shuffling through the faded green door and into the fuggy interior. After lifting the potatoes carefully from the rucksack without damaging the bread pudding, and depositing them on the table top, Sally's eye was drawn towards the window, fascinated by the way its drab net curtain made the wintry sun look muddy as it struggled to filter through. After contemplating this strange phenomenon for a few moments, she looked at the little glass bowl that was sitting on the front of the dresser, where it had sat since the first time she had entered this little cottage. It was always full of sugar lumps, its set of wish bone shaped tongs on top and always seemed incongruous, the height of luxury in this otherwise frugal, vernacular abode. She never, ever refused a cup of tea from this lady. The chance to practice and perfect the knack of clasping the sugary lumps in the teeth of the tongs and plopping them one at a time into her cup of tea was an opportunity not to be turned down lightly. That the actual beverage was always a mite too sweet and tickled her throat when she swallowed it was a small price to pay for this experience.

They watched as Mrs Peppler removed the potatoes from the brown paper bag, and laid them out in a wooden box lined with newspaper, much as dad always did. No doubt she had also got a light, frost free place to store them in until the Spring, when she would find a place in her large fertile garden in which to plant them. She would also no doubt, cast a brief but critical an eye over the fat sprouting buds on the tubers from time to time, to check their progress and to make sure they remained strong and healthy until their internment. All the while she stood there, her old cat was winding itself in and out and around her ankles, purring loudly as it tried to claim her attention. Then suddenly without any warning, the thing jumped from ground to draining board and onto the windowsill, dislodging a box of soap flakes, which spilled out some of its contents as it dived towards the sink. The girls jumped out of their skin, glued to the spot for a moment. Then they moved swiftly, instinctively towards the back door and opened it, thus providing an escape route for the traumatised cat. As it scurried outside, the girls began to scoop up the spillage as best they could, ladling it into the first thing to hand, the brown paper bag from which the potatoes had just been evicted. They did not linger. After a few hurried words of commiseration, Sally grabbed her rucksack and they all beat a hasty retreat through the back door, high on the heels of the luckless cat.

The wind pounced on them as they turned back into the lane and they huddled together for just a couple of seconds to wind their scarves more closely around their faces and to psych themselves up for the long journey home, then set off at a tidy pace towards the Sprays Bridge area. Just a short distance down the lane they came upon the caravan that had once housed an old lady, but which was now derelict, and in spite of the cold they stopped to examine and lament the sad demise of this one time home. As Sally peered more closely at this spooky old caravan however, with its overgrowth of brambles and other invasive vegetation, she could have sworn she saw the raggedy bit of net curtain in the window move, and not with the wind she was sure about that. There was something else here, another presence, and she shivered as her imagination conjured up a long bony finger behind that almost imperceptible movement. Just a finger that was all. Her mind and imagination was unable or unwilling to further substantiate this strange entity.

She dragged her eyes away with a mixture of relief and reluctance and moved on down the lane with the other two girls, and in no time at all they were walking alongside the fields of Hoad's Farm. She liked this farm, on which the Pelling family lived and worked. She liked the atmosphere and the friendliness of this family who were never too busy to pass the time of day with the youngsters. They were a bit like Mr and Mrs Farrow really and the Partridge and Gosse families as well if it came to that, and not a bit like that grumpy old farmer, Watson or whatever his name was, who had moved to somewhere in Kent, ages ago now. Good riddance to him and to those maniacal dogs of his she had thought at the time and nothing she had heard about him since then had persuaded her to change her mind.

It did not take her long to locate her favourite silver birch tree. She had seen it from way back down the lane. As she moved closer however, she could see its pleasing shape in more detail, and noticed how its thin twiggy branches drooped and moved only sluggishly in spite of the cold east wind. This was a magic tree if ever there was one, she reckoned along with that other tree that guarded her little sister up in the old churchyard in Sedlescombe.

They were nearing Spray's Bridge now, and Sally's heart missed a beat as a huddle of cottages came into view, reminding her of the war time tragedy that had struck this tranquil place, shattering the lives of those affected by it. It was in Plum Tree Cottage, right here in this sleepy little Hamlet, that Basil Beeching's mum had died so tragically, the victim of wanton strafing by an evil German gunner, and even now, the sheer horror of it was still vividly imprinted on her mind. For the whole family, she knew it was still a stark and almost unimaginably painful memory, and for Basil in particular, something that would continue to haunt him, probably for the rest of his life. Life could be very cruel, and she had noticed that it was often the nicest people, like Basil, who seemed to suffer the most unnecessary suffering and unhappiness. She found this cruel injustice very difficult to fathom, and yet in spite of what he had been through, Basil remained one of the nicest youngsters she knew.

When they reached the bridge they paused beside its low brick wall for a short while, and looked down into the shallow stream with its rust stained pebbly bottom, a characteristic of many streams in and around Sussex and a reminder of the Elizabethan iron industry. They did not expect to see any sign of life along its banks or in the slow flowing water, nor did they spot any. Many species of wildlife would either be in hibernation or at the very least, hunkered down in some well-chosen snuggle in weather like this, awaiting the first signs of Spring and the welcome call of Mother Nature.

They took the steep incline from the bridge up into the Hart's Green area at a tidy pace, stopping now and again for Pat to get her breath back after a paroxysm of coughing, her legacy from the severe bout of whooping cough she had suffered a while ago now, and from which it was taking her an age to recover. Apart from the distress caused by these coughing fits, they relished the challenge of climbing the steep hill, an added benefit of which was the feel of the blood circulating through their veins, bringing life back into their toes and finger tips. By the time they reached the cottages at the top of the hill where Sylvia Gain and her family lived, they were warm as toast.

They stopped near the cross roads at Hart's Green, for just long enough to agree the route for the last part of the journey home, then decided to pop into the Lawrence's anyway, just to see Eileen and perhaps be offered a nice mug of hot cocoa to help them on their way, and they were to be lucky on both counts. Though the ground beneath their feet as they crossed the field was hard as Newgate's knocker, the cottage was cosy and warm and as they sat with their hands cupped around the delicious brew, and munching on the wedges of bread pudding mum had provided them with, they knew they had made the right decision. They chatted about this and that and to start with, discussed the older girls who were courting now. Freda and Hazel were walking out with John Stuart and Albert Soan respectively, both of whom were known and approved of by the younger girls, for their wit and sense of humour as much as anything. Betty's boyfriend Ron Green though, was not a local lad. He had been born and bred in Watford, but as a regular in the Royal Air Force, travelled quite extensively. However, from the first time the girls had set eyes on him, they had taken an instant and instinctive liking to this kindly, unassuming man who clearly adored their sister. That Betty reciprocated those feelings was patently obvious in the way her eyes lit up every time she looked in his direction.

As they talked, they were aware that sooner or later they would have to leave the warmth and comfort of this little cottage and face that cold east wind once more. Also, they were anxious to get back in time to see Climmie, mum's friend, who with her cropped black hair and exotic make up, was a very unusual looking lady indeed. They had discussed the possibility that she might even wear artificial silk knickers, now wouldn't that be something they said. She and mum had worked together at Caves Café years ago, and the bonds of friendship they had forged at that time had remained as strong and enduring as ever. They would chat and often giggle about their experiences in the old days without once repeating themselves and it was at these times that Sally realised that her mum had had another life, another existence before the one that she herself was now a part of.

As they hurried back down the field, Sally looked towards the pond and was sure that tucked away in the reeds over on the far side, she could see a couple of little dab chicks or moorhens. So still and quiet were they however, that they could just as easily have been paper cut outs from one of Dorothy or Jacky's books, and she grinned to herself. The expression of utter concentration and seriousness on the faces of her little sisters as they struggled with the task of setting up the various designs, was indeed a sight to behold.

The path leading from the lane up to the primrose secret, though criss-crossed with straggly bramble and other dormant vegetation, was clearly visible to their canny eyes. In just a few weeks' time, the ground beneath the sparse scattering of trees in this special place would be transformed from dull green into a magic carpet of creamy yellow. The youngsters would then be picking individual blooms to their hearts content with seemingly little or no impact on the harvest. They would be turning them into little leaf edged posies tied up with assorted bits of wool and dangled from little fingers, some of which would no doubt, making their way to the Buchanan Hospital where the girls would sell them for a few coppers and donate the money to the Hospital or to the Chapel's Missionary fund.

They looked for Mr Lawrence as they passed by the house and large gardens in Cottage Lane where the Stafford family lived, but there was no sign of him. They knew he would be around there somewhere, Eileen had told them so. If he had any sense they reckoned, he would be in one of the large greenhouses on a day like this preparing the enclosure for the sowing of seeds for this summer's crops. That he managed to keep this vast garden in such good order, summer or winter, was a source of wonder to them. But then dad had always held the view that Mr Lawrence was just about the best gardener he had ever come across, and this opinion was endorsed by Uncle Tom, mum's brother, a keen and expert gardener himself.

As they walked briskly towards the top of Crazy Lane, Sally glanced towards the verges and into the hedgerows along the way, and with the conversation dubbed down now to a sporadic word here and there, she was able to let her mind and imagination drift away. She knew that in just a few short weeks from now, winter would fall away from the landscape just like old Death's cloak and the seemingly lifeless area of hedge and ditch along here and in just about every other country lane would be lush and teeming with life. Buttercups, celandines, anemones, violets and primroses would seemingly morph into ragged robin, red and white campion, ox-eye daisy, dog rose and a host of other flora of diverse shape and colour. And the white dead nettles would be swarming with butterflies. She half closed her eyes and took a deep breath, and in her imagination, the characteristic and pungent smell of the flowering wild parsley tantalised her nostrils as it vied with lilac and a multitude of other blossom for its share of pollinating insects, and she sighed. Mother Nature was a truly remarkable, resourceful old lady, who could be depended upon to work her magic season after season, year after year. She never let them down.

As they came through the bottom gate, they could see dad walking across the field ahead of them. With his head down to counteract the weight of the sack across his shoulder and the cold east wind, he looked for all the world like old Pilgrim, Sally thought and grinned to herself. He paused and turned around as they hurried towards him, then stood back as they opened the top gate for him to pass through with his heavy load. She noticed with some satisfaction that he was indeed wearing a pair of the fingerless mittens she had knitted for him quite recently, and guessed that on his feet and hidden by those old wellies of his, were a couple of pairs of ancient socks, with multiple repairs to heels and toes. She always tried when she mended his socks, to weave the pattern evenly and without the lumps that would cause discomfort and even blisters.

"There, that won't hurt where it is for a while," he said as he swung his burden from shoulder to the ground in one thankful movement. "I'll take it round to the greenhouse once I've cadged myself a cup of tea. I know there's one on the brew, cause your mother called out to me a few minutes ago," he added as he rubbed his hands together to relieve the cramp. Then as he opened the door and stood back for them to precede him, he sniffed. "Smells like the wick on the old stove over there needs a bit of attention." And he pointed towards the valor stove at the far end of the scullery, the vapour rising from within the fat belly of this squat bow legged stove, distorting the air waves above its perforated top. "How was the old lady then?" He asked as they made their way to the kitchen. Before they replied however, they paused to breathe the warm air, laden with mouth-watering aroma's deeply and gratefully into their lungs, and by then he had moved on with a cup of tea in his hand.

"How long do you reckon it's going to take you to finish that cardigan Sal?" asked Hilary, using her knitting to gesticulate across the table towards her friend. "You're brave that's all I can say. That two-ply wool you're using 's not much thicker than dad's upholstery thread and that's a fact. It's what they make vests and so forth with isn't it, though you don't see many vests that colour I must say."

Sally held up the section of cardigan on which she was working then craned her neck around to inspect her handiwork. It had taken her an age to progress up to and passed the armhole reduction back section of this garment, but as far as she was concerned it had been well worth it. The fine light green wool and slender needles plus this combination of stocking stitch and moss stitch, had brought a pleasing delicacy to this embryonic cardigan. And best of all, she, Pat and Hilary were using brand new wool, in colours of their choice and purchased from the Scotch wool shop in Hastings, with the proceeds from their work in the hop picking fields. They had for once been able to bypass the tiresome chore of unpicking and rewinding the wool from old jumpers and cardigans, with that stubborn resistance to attempts to rid it of all its wrinkles.

The girls were sitting around the kitchen table, the thick socks encasing their feet giving them some protection from the inevitable drafts around the place. The lamp in the centre of the table flickered from time to time, distorting the shadows that lurked around the periphery of the large room, its glowing mantle however, providing them with enough light for their needs. The intermittent plop from somewhere within the belly of the old lamp was subsumed by the click and clatter of knitting needles, and by the general chit-chat and constant movement within the room. The little ones, having tired of trying to emulate the older girls, had abandoned wool and needles, and were moving around the place, skittering from one game to another, just like dust hole fairies. This activity ceased as if by magic however, when the conversation around the table was turned deliberately and for the sake of a bit of peace and quiet, towards early childhood memories of films they had seen. They knew this discussion would capture the imagination of the little ones. They began with the adventures of Bambi and his mate Thumper, a tale of an enduring friendship between a fawn and a rabbit. If Sally's memory served her right, she and Hilary had seen this enchanting film in the building at the bottom of the village, which had been a Chapel in an earlier existence if its ecclesiastical architecture, its heavy oak door and arched mullioned windows were anything to go by. The little ones were quiet as the proverbial mouse as they listened for the umpteenth time to the adventures of these two pals, grinning at the enacted antics of Thumper as he attempted to turn his mate, the shy timid Bambi, into a fine, confident Stag to be reckoned with. Their silent participation ended when it came to an imitation of the rabbit's squeaky voice and the little fellow's favourite trick of thumping the ground to signal danger or when his excitement just got the better of him.

And then it was Pinocchio's turn. This wooden puppet brought lovingly and skilfully to life by the old wood carver, Geppetto, was a favourite amongst all the family. Even Granny Cotton would stop and listen when this tale of a carpenter, a puppet, a cricket and a cat was being told, the twinkle in her eye lightening up that rather stern countenance of hers. As the tale unfolded the little ones sat quietly, passing their fingers over their noses from time to time to check that no drastic change had taken place in its size and shape through some inconsequential fib they might have told. They were ready however, as the older girls knew from past experience, to intervene immediately if the smallest detail was left out. The story of Pinocchio and his mates, Jiminy Cricket and Figaro the cat moved steadily forward, from the puppets creation through one adventure or misadventure after another, through thick and thin, and the little ones remained wide eyed and silent throughout. They listened to the villainous actions of the wicked showman Stromboli, then Pinocchio's heroic rescue of his creator and father figure, Geppetto from the jaws of Monstro the whale, both fascinated and scared witless in equal measure. When Pinocchio with a little help and encouragement from his mates, achieved his ambition to become a real Son to his beloved Geppetto, they visibly relaxed, their sigh palpable.

As Sally looked towards Granny Cotton, she saw her absentmindedly smoothing over her eye brow with her little finger as she listened to the retelling of this imaginative tale, then her thin lips began to move as she silently mouthed the words of the first verse of the Jiminy Cricket song, along with the girls:

'When you wish upon a star, makes no difference who you are.
Anything your heart desires, will come to you.'

"Fancy a game of tiddly winks then," said Hilary once the tale of Snow White and the seven Dwarfs had been expounded upon and a few heartfelt comments on the genius of Walt Disney and his team of animators had been made. Then she grinned as Dorothy dived towards the sideboard, and popped up with the tattered box of magic in her hands. This was clearly a signal for Granny Cotton to make her exit, and as she did so, casting a silent but deadly glance around the table at the circle of animated faces, the long abandoned knitting was moved carefully from table to sideboard to make way for the dice and counters. This manic game was accompanied by renditions of favourite ditties, some repeated over and over again, which as mum remarked as she moved about the room, were enough to try the patience of the most patient Saint. They saw a grin spread across her face however, when it came to Jacky's turn to try her skill on a tricky tongue twister – at speed.

'I said he was mad, he said mad I said yes.

Cotton Reels and so Forth

He said who I said you. He said me? I said yes he said Oh.'

When after countless spittle laden attempts Jacky finally got the thing right, mum patted the beaming youngster on the back and congratulated her. Her face fell at mum's next words however, uttered after a quick glance towards the clock on the mantle- piece then back towards the two highly excited red faced youngsters.

"Now then you two, you'll have to calm down a bit before bed time else you'll be awake half the night," she said. "Just put that game away and perhaps one of the girls will tell you a story if you ask them nicely, something that'll calm you down a bit. How about Cinderella or something?"

Just in time, thought Sally as she heard the outer door close followed by the click of the scullery door heralding the arrival of their dad, his characteristic sniff as usual preceding him. He would expect a bit of peace and quiet once he had turned the wireless on to listen to the latest news bulletin.

The bare sycamore trees at the back of the house had long since faded into darkness by the time Hilary and Sally left the house and began to walk briskly arm in arm down the field. Sally was wearing one of the thick pleated skirts that Aunty Gladys from Eastbourne had sent to her and was grateful for the protection it afforded against the cold north easterly wind. It had arrived, along with a similar one for Pat in a neatly wrapped brown paper parcel and each one had been carefully folded and layered with tissue paper to prevent creasing and to keep the pleats in place. All the clothes, outgrown by their cousin Anne or just surplus to requirement and passed on to them by Aunty Gladys, arrived in the same immaculate order. Being an only child had its advantages certainly, and having a selection of beautiful clothes was one of them, but she would not change places with Anne for all the tea in China. Mind you although her cousin was fussed over by her mum, she did not behave in any way like a spoilt child, on the contrary. She roughed and tumbled with the rest of them when she came to stay, and willingly shared a bed with whoever and wherever a space was available. Sally grinned to herself as she reflected on the differences between life at Sylvian, which was always buzzing with activity and the conditions that prevailed in the neat house in the old town at Eastbourne, where everything was ship shape and where the single bed she occupied when she stayed there, even had its own electric table lamp sitting on a small chest of drawers alongside, wearing a pretty shade.

As the girls shivered their way through the back door, they knew at once that Ronald had beaten them to it. His overcoat was draped over one of the chairs in the warm kitchen and they could hear him moving around in his bedroom. He had turned the wireless was on, which was unusual for him and they stood still for a few moments listening to the strains of 'South of the border, down Mexico Way' as it came over the airwaves, moved somehow by the words and melody of this plaintive, romantic song.

"You're late, I've been back ages. Look, I've already got the milk in the saucepan ready for a hot drink, and the Ovaltine's on the side over there," said Ronald, as he came through the doorway. "Don't want this on now, do you?" He added, switching off the wireless almost before they had shaken their heads, then moved towards the table and sat himself down on the over-coated chair.

Immediately, the image of a poster advertising this popular beverage in tablet form, popped up into Sally's mind. 'OVALTINE. CONCENTRATED FOOD TABLETS. For all outdoor occasions,' was the caption, with a healthy looking couple smiling out towards the passers by. She really must try them sometime she told herself, to see if they were as tasty and gummed your mouth up in the same way as Horlicks tablets did. Perhaps Hilary could get some from Mr Brann, the Grocer for whom she worked. It would be worth a try, she thought as she sat down at the table and watched her friend move over towards the cooker.

As they sat sipping their beverage, the girls listened to Ronald talking about the fun he and his mates had had in and around the village during the day. They had stayed in and around Mercy Dengate's farm and fields for ages he said, playing Cowboys and Indians with the bows and arrows they made from sticks and bits of wood rummaged from the hedgerows. Then after cadging a hot drink and a sandwich from one of the houses in East View Terrace, they had made their way off and into the various pockets of woodland surrounding Hurst Lane. They had identified several likely places for the camps they'd be setting up once the weather warmed up a bit, he told them, possibly the best of these situated on part of Sir John and Lady Newton's estate. This couple however, in spite of their lofty title, were kindly disposed towards the village youngsters, so that would not be a problem.

On the way home, they had waylaid Bangy, which had culminated in a short but chilly sojourn around the Pump. Ronald had gleaned a bit more information about Gorselands and its one time Windmill from this little old man who seemed to know just about everything there was to know about the village. As he continued to talk, Sally became conscious of the similarities between Ronald and cousin David Johnson. They were both avid readers, with a quest for knowledge and sticklers for detail.

She remembered a conversation that had taken place during one of her cousin's rare visit to Sylvian quite recently, with his mum, Aunty Cis. Not only was David well-read she'd realised, but he had also clearly gleaned a lot of knowledge from discussions with his dad, Uncle Frank, an astute, highly intelligent man, who shared the same Socialist beliefs and convictions as dad and his Brothers.

The discussion that particular evening had begun with general chit-chat amongst the youngsters as they had sat around the kitchen table, mostly connected to the day's activities. Once the grownups had sat down with them to enjoy a cup of tea though, it had moved away from childish recollections and anecdotes onto a broader themed discussion.

She remembered one name in particular that had cropped up that evening, and as she sat sipping her warm drink and listening with half an ear to the conversation between her two friends, she reckoned it was one she would not forget in a hurry. Thomas Paine, a social reformer and in dad's words, a brave and remarkable man was the name, imprinted now and forever on her mind and imagination. His influence, through pamphlets and books he had written, had spread far and wide, even to America it seemed where he had fled when his views had been considered too radical in England. David, for whom this topic was fresh in mind through recent discussions with his dad he'd said, mentioned one particular pamphlet entitled, 'The Rights of Man,' probably this man's most famous or according to some it seemed, infamous publication. It emphasised the stark inequalities and injustices in society, with powerful governments and the rich on one hand and the wretched poor on the other. A society in which he had observed, scarcely any but the poor are executed, where age was going to the workhouse, youth to the gallows and where the poor were even compelled to support the fraud that suppressed them. Still, as dad had said at the time, though there was still a way to go, getting this far towards a fairer society was down to a few astute, brave and articulate people like this man, who had jogged the process along. As she thought about it now, she reminded herself for the umpteenth time, how lucky she was to be living now and not in those far away days when it seemed the conditions you were born into you had no way of escaping from. It was just down to Fate or the will of God or some such thing. Since then she had begun to see her beloved plodding ploughman winding his weary way across the darkening landscape in a different light. Although Grey's Elegy was and always would be her favourites ballad, she now saw past the depiction of a rural idyll to the hard and relentless grind of working men and women in those days, viewing the landscape and all that had lived and died within it, with glasses not quite so rose coloured now.

Chapter 8
Summer 1949

Winter was now a distant memory and spring had morphed slowly and seamlessly into summer. Thankfully the weather had pulled its socks up in time for Carnival in Hastings today Sally thought as she hurried across the field to fetch the milk from the farm. She had left a scene of excitement in and around the house as preparation for this event took place, the first of its kind since before the war. She was on her own today. Pat had volunteered to do the pumping and had already made a start on this tiresome chore when Sally had left the house. Dorothy had been at her elbow, anxious as always to have a go. She'll soon get tired of that when she has to do it seriously and on a regular basis, Sally thought to herself and grinned. Actually, although she always moaned about this task, she did not dislike it as much as she made out. It was just that she always had other things to do when it came to her turn to do it that was the trouble.

As she walked her mind drifted from Carnivals and chores onto other incidentals, and by the time she had reached and was clambering over the stile at the top of the field, it had settled on thoughts and memories of the week she had spent with the Saul family in Eastbourne, during the Easter holidays.

She remembered the journey over to Eastbourne as though it were only yesterday, recapturing the mood of excitement coupled with trepidation she had experienced as the train had rumbled its way across the Pevensey marshes. She had watched the sea birds as they wheeled circled and dived across the morose, grey clouded sky, then gazed beyond this aerobatic display towards the rolling, mist shrouded Downs.

Aunty Gladys and Anne had been at the station to meet her and after a brief discussion, decided that in spite of the possibility of rain, they would take a chance, and walk down to the sea front. After stowing her case away in left luggage, for which service Aunty passed over a few coppers, they had walked out of the station and straight into the hustle and bustle of this busy town. Sally grinned as she recalled an incident that for some reason had caused amusement between them as they began to walk down the main street towards the beach. Just in front of them and walking along as though she were the cat's whiskers, was this hoity-toity lady with the price tag dangling from the hat she was wearing. As she disappeared through the doorway of a shop, they speculated on how long it would take for this oversight to be quietly brought to her notice by some public spirited individual, or perhaps discovered by the lady herself as she admired her image in one of the many dress shop mirrors. Their attention however, was soon diverted away from the unintentional foibles of this lady, towards a large poster in a shop window, which Anne had spotted. The words: 'A la Mode, when Great Grandma was a child,' was printed in large letters at the top of the poster, while below were a selection of images of ladies from the olden days, decked out in the most extraordinary costumes. This was right up Anne's street. Her favourite subject at School was Art and Design and she was particularly interested in fabrics and their application in the world of fashion. The minimalist fashion of the 'Twenties' had been her all-time favourite until the New Look came along which, with its extravagant femininity, a natural reaction to the austerity of the war years, she adored. As she had scrutinised the poster, with its fashions of a bye gone era however, she had remarked at length on the pleasing shape and intricacy of designs. As far as Sally was concerned these long, flowing, narrow-waisted frocks, were the most highly impractical items of clothing she had ever seen, and she would not have been seen dead in any one of them. How you could be expected to climb a tree or play a game of hop-scotch or skipping in any one of these fussy frocks, let alone breath, was beyond her comprehension. But then her talented cousin saw many things from an artistic rather than a practical point of view. Now the man who had been standing on the pavement beside them chewing on his moustache as he waited to cross the road was a lot more interesting to study than fashion, Sally reckoned. That he had more on his mind than just the act of crossing over from one pavement to the other was apparent in the set of his shoulders and the nervous jerky movement of his upper body. She had continued to ponder on the obvious burden of worry or misfortune that beset this troubled little man as she and Anne had made their way across the echoing surface of the Pier, playing a penny machine here and there while Aunty Gladys sat sipping tea in a nearby café. However, by the time they had left the Pier and made their way back to the station to retrieve the bag from 'left luggage,' thoughts of worried little men, fashions and hat labelled ladies had been replaced by that familiar feeling of excitement tinged with home-sickness she always felt when parted from her family and friends. As the bus had trundles its way towards the Old Town though, the latter feeling began to ease as she and Anne discussed possible outings and activities for the week ahead, and by the time they reached 46 Mill Road, the house in which she would be staying for the week, she had been in high spirits.

The highlight of the visit as far as Sally was concerned was a trek over the South Downs with Anne and Uncle Frank Saul, their efforts in tackling the slopes more than compensated by the spectacular scenery to be viewed from its rounded summits. They had stopped to comment on the massed sea of cowslips, already in bud and about to decorate the chalky slopes on which they thrived with their delicate beauty. Uncle had told the two girls about a legend associated with this nodding, yellow headed flower. According to this strange and ancient tale, St Peter had dropped the keys to Heaven after discovering that there was another set in existence, and the first cowslip had sprung from that spot, spreading its progeny far and wide. If you examined the arrangement of the clumps of flowers on their long stalks, he told them, you would see that they did actually resemble a set of keys. She had stored this ancient and fascinating legend in her memory along with others, like Hengist and Horsa and Sir Gerwain and The Green Knight, and the many others she had read about over the years.

They had dropped down from the higher slopes from time to time to investigate one or other of the little villages that were tucked away in pockets of isolation within their folds. They had wandered around the Churches then the Churchyards with their ancient leaning gravestones for ages, trying to decipher the lichen splodged inscriptions on the memorials to those long departed country folk, and the words of 'Greys Elegy' had inevitably made their way into her mind and imagination. However, on that day she had mouthed the words silently to herself as she examined the sparse, often barely distinguishable words on these ancient stones, pondering the lives and ultimate death of these 'Rude forefathers of the Hamlet.' (shrouded in mystery). One memorial in particular in one of these Churchyards, dedicated to one, 'Fanny Christmas' had caught her eye and imagination. As she and Anne had examined and commented on the clearly inscribed wording, Uncle Frank had brought their attention to another dedication, clearly to the same lady but in this one, the T had been omitted from the surname. It was at the edge of this particular Churchyard that they had seated themselves and devoured the sandwiches that Aunty Gladys had packed for them. Sally grimaced as she remembered having bitten into one of Anne's sandwiches by mistake on one occasion, when tomatoes had been in season. She still remembered the acrid taste of the sandwiches, ruined as far as she was concerned by the lashings of salt with which her cousin insisted on covering the things.

As they had continued on their ramble, Uncle who seemed to know the hills like the back of his hand, pointed out various land marks and places of interest. One he described but which they would have to see on another occasion he told them, was the plantation of trees, designed in the shape of a 'V' to commemorate Queen Victoria's sixty years on the throne. It took up best part of a tidy bit of hillside he told them.

Towards the end of the ramble, she and Anne had begun to wilt and Uncle, sensing this, had serenaded them with his version of 'Suzanna's a Funifel Man,' complete with all its exaggerated snorts, whistles, blows and 'ide-illy-dows.' This all-time favourite piece of nonsense breathed new life into them and they had giggled their way through 'Sing lassies go-rings re-low,' along with him, the few words that made any kind of sense to them.

Another outing had been to Wannock Gardens, this time with Aunty Gladys who though witty and very generous, was not as much fun to be with as Uncle Frank. It had been a fine day, with a penetratingly cold easterly powering its way across the Downs, but in spite of this, she had doggedly followed the girls around - for a while. However, discretion soon overcame valour and she had shivered her way to the little tea-room where she had sat comfortably inside, sipping her beverage while they had explored this extraordinary garden. After her departure, they had made their way to the more informal part of the garden, drawn towards the rather enigmatic sign, which stated, 'Water Otter Feature.' Having investigated this curious thing on a string on a previous visit, they decided to stand to one side and watch the reaction from other youngsters, new to this game, as they approached the well. This varied, but for bold and timid alike, after a moment's hesitation curiosity overcame trepidation and with a quick jerk on the string, the battered old black kettle shot through the surface, with many youngsters visibly jumping out of their skins.

After a while, as the spiteful wind began to penetrate their clothing, they had turned reluctantly away from this fascinating game, and after a quick adjustment of hats and scarves, had hurried away to explore the rest of this multi featured garden. It was not long however, before the cold and hunger had driven them towards the little tea room, and she grinned now, her mouth-watering as she thought about the giant scone, with its liberal coating of butter and strawberry jam that Aunty Gladys had bought for them. It was delicious.

She had thoroughly enjoyed her holiday. The only time she had felt homesick was at bed time, when even the thought of a comfy bed all to herself with an electric lamp on the chest of drawers beside her, had not been enough to quell the sick feeling in the pit of her stomach. But then you could not have everything, she told herself. She remembered as though it were only yesterday, that feeling of excitement as the train had trundled her back across the marshes towards home. The weather had changed yet again, a heavy mist now cloaking the Downs and rendering the landscape grey.

By this time, her thoughts and silent reminiscences had taken her up to the back door of the old farmhouse, which was wide open and emitting aromas of a recently prepared breakfast, and she shook herself back to the here and now. After passing the time of day with Mrs Collins, she collected the milk from this kindly lady and hurried back home, her thoughts now very much on preparations for the day ahead.

Hilary only had to work for an hour or two this morning, Sally was telling herself as she hurried down the field. Mr Brann was a good boss and had told her that as long as she made up the orders and minded the shop while he delivered them to his customers, he would take over from her, and then she would be free to leave. As the journey from Staplecross to Sedlescombe was mostly downhill, she would be able to freewheel her bicycle most of the way. She would be home, changed and up to Sylvian in a few shakes of a dog's tail, she promised.

The morning flew by, with the inevitable last minute scramble to get the chores done and everything together in time. After double checking her, or rather her borrowed, ruck-sack for the umpteenth time, Sally hurried down the field with the other girls with mum's, 'just make sure you hang on to the little ones at all times,' ringing in her ears.

They did not have long to wait for the number 12 bus, and watched in silence as it lumbered around Pay Gate Corner before pulling slowly in beside them. They clambered on board, and as the conductor stood aside, made their way up the stairs, where luckily they found enough empty seats remaining for them all on the top deck. The number 84, which was due along shortly, would likely be just as heavily laden as this one, they told themselves.

By the time they had shuffled bags and bodies together, they were passing through Kent Street, and as Sally looked out of the window, she could see old Fred hobbling along the pathway. She smiled to herself, remembering the last time she had encountered this old fellow, which would only have been about a couple of weeks ago, and she had asked him then why he was limping. 'It be t' screws, in me awld leg' he had told her, adding, 'awld doctor e teld me it be down to awld age, en when I ups en asks 'im, ow comes then as both me legs be same age, t'other done give me no trouble, e couldn'a answer. Leastways not proper loik. E jest went from ass 'ole to breakfast toime to tell us thar were nowt e could do. Silly awld bugger. Jest cause e got a bit o book learnin, e thinks e knows every damn thing. Us awld folk es e calls us could teach im and is loiks a thing or two, I tells im,' and he had chuckled and wagged his finger under their noses before hobbling painfully away. Perhaps a week or two of this fine sunny weather would sort him out. She hoped so.

She glanced briefly towards Wayside as the bus passed by, and although there was no movement in or around the garden, she knew that her cousins

Peter and Ian would not be far away. They and their mates would be down the far side of the gardens where the old piggery's used to be, where the whole area had been meticulously transformed by them into a state of the art cycle speedway track, and practising like mad for upcoming competitions. They called themselves The Baldslow Boomerangs, and had become part of the recently formed and well organised cycle speedway club, to which Sedlescombe Saints, their own team belonged. The competitions between the teams so far, were being fiercely fought, often with only a whisker between competitors. There had been a couple of minor accidents but so far nothing more serious than grazed arms and legs, which was quite surprising when you remembered the seemingly reckless speed with which the boys negotiated those bends in the track. Arthur Puxty and Tony Taylor were past masters at these tricky manoeuvres, with knees and elbows an integral part of a balance mechanism, which allowed them – mostly - to corner at maximum speed. She grinned as an image of these two boys popped into her mind and imagination, dogged determination to win in every fibre of their being, speeding around the track as though old Beelzebub himself were up their tail. She and Hilary would be cycling over to Westfield soon to watch these two plus the rest of the Sedlescombe team, as they competed with the Wolves in one of their scheduled matches. That promised to be an interesting game – at the very least. As the bus trundled towards the stop at Silverhill, she was trying to work out if a team called the Hastings Harlots actually existed, as one of the boys had suggested. Then decided, that if the mischievous look on his face as he had added in the same breath, 'peddling their wares,' was anything to go by, then probably not. She was gullible she knew that, but she had learned to take what some of the boys came out with, with a pinch of salt. It saved a lot of embarrassment.

It took an age to get off the bus at Wellington Square, along with what seemed to be about twenty thousand others, mostly on the Carnival trail the same as they were. The older girls took Dorothy and Jacky's hands firmly in their own, remembering mum's last words to them as they had left home, and also the frightening experience they had had on the beach with Jacky that time. They made their way to the memorial and then on to the sea front, immediately becoming part of a scene of noisy animation, as people sought out the most advantageous position from which to view this exciting and long anticipated spectacle. Hilary bought a six penny programme from a lady dressed as Little Miss Muffet, who was grinning from ear to ear as she bobbed and zigzagged her way through the crowd. They then moved along the promenade until they too found a space from which they could get a decent view of this long anticipated show, and not before time. The first costumed revellers, from the comic to the grotesque were already in view, their raucous rants and rattles preceding them. The feeling of excitement was palpable. There were clowns, their garish make up guaranteed to both fascinate and also scare the living daylights out of those of a nervous disposition, many wielding curled up whistles which they blew into the faces of those in the front row. There were other participants, dressed up to the nines in all manner of costumes, many mimicking characters from Nursery Rhymes. One figure in particular, dressed up like a bag of liquorice allsorts caught the eye and imagination of the little ones as it wibble-wobbled past the cheering crowd. It seemed that this particular participant was receiving a goodly share of pennies begged, borrowed, cadged or even saved for this special occasion, into his tin on a string.

The Brass Band with its exaggerated drum rolls and flourish of trumpets and trombones, added to the cacophony of sound and sensation around them, and was closely followed by the first mechanised participants in the procession, with even more costumed figures running alongside. The sheer number and variety of the floats, some pulled by tractors, others displayed on open-backed lorries, was truly breath-taking, with slogans on each and every one of them. Amongst the latter, were a few vehicles printed up with familiar company names, Farrant and Reid and Adams and Jarrett two of the most recognisable of these.

Join the Hastings and St Leonards Ratepayers Association, announced one enormous placard, followed by displays by 'Hoover' and 'Seeboard' Hastings. Aboard another float, representing 'The Gay Nineties Club,' there was much gesticulating and hilarity contrasting somehow amusingly with, 'The Boys Brigade' who just marched solemnly past the cheering crowd. The Carnival Queen, done up to the nines in the regalia of a real Queen, caused quite a stir as she floated slowly past surrounded by her entourage. She played the part to perfection, right down to that strange, imperious back to front wave, practised and perfected by Royalty.

There was a windmill perched precariously upon the back of one lorry, while another displayed a cardboard cut-out of a very large open hand holding some contraption that was hard to define, with the proclamation, 'Willing Hands to Serve You,' beneath it. There was another representing the SSAFA Appeal, 'Every penny will help,' it said. It was the nursing scene however, that caught Pat's attention, and she took in every detail of the smart uniforms and the feeling of caring compassion and efficiency that had been captured so completely within this mini dedication. (Tribute).

And still the flotilla of variety and imagination continued to file slowly past. A gentleman impressively decked out in a highly colourful and decorative costume, caught the eye and admiration of the crowd as he walked solemnly past, a long handled ceremonial axe angled across one shoulder. "Look, a Beef Eater," someone called out from the back of the crowd, creating a bit of a stir, and although the portly fellow continued to look straight ahead as he marched, there was definitely a twinkle in his eye.

There were so many floats and individual costumed revellers milling in and out of the crowd, it was difficult to fully appreciate one scene or character before the next processed slowly past. 'Our Way Grand,' announced one placard, the rest of the message missed as Sally's eye was distracted, involuntarily drawn towards yet another animated, colourful character, and the float had moved on and away from where she was standing. 'Damn,' she muttered to herself, trying to work out if it had been the Hastleons float on which these few words had been written and if so, what meaning the second part of the message would have given to those first few cryptic words. Perhaps now she would never know. However, the parade was still in full swing and her attention was soon drawn towards a figure covered from head to thigh in crepe paper, which was already showing signs of wear and tear. Luckily she still had a few coppers left from the ones mum had given her, and she popped these into the tin he was holding out, grinning as she watched him try to control the bits of capricious crepe around him with his other hand.

The WVS float brought a spontaneous cheer from the crowd as it passed by, and rightly so Sally thought to herself. Members of this organisation had worked tirelessly to support victims of the war, particularly those caught up in the bombing raids over cities. They had been right there in the thick of things, alongside firemen, medical staff and police, to offer comfort and reassurance as well as practical help. They had offered copious quantities of tea and sympathy, yes, and so much more.

'The Winkle club,' announced another float with yet another group of colourful characters on board. One chap standing up and above the rest was holding a horn shaped mega phone up to his mouth, reminding folk about the open air dancing along at Winkle Island in the Old Town this evening, amongst other things. This character was obviously well known in the town and drew several wise cracks from members of the crowd, especially from fellow Old Towner's or Hastinger's, as they were referred to.

Eventually the procession began to fizzle out, with the inevitable milling and noisy interaction between spectators, some following the tail enders while others, like the girls, drifted away to seek a respite from the relentless noise and manic gyrations of both participants and audience in this parade. The home-made streamers that Dorothy and Jacky had been waving around with such enthusiasm just a short while ago, were beginning to look decidedly tatty now, their hazel twig handles clearly visible through the layers of crepe paper with which they had been covered, the fronds frayed and hanging limply down. Even when they reached Dimarco's and were sitting around a table in this busy café, they were still clutching the things as though to relinquish them would break some spell and destroy the magic of the occasion. However, once glasses of lemonade were placed in front of them, the urge to quench their thirst became overwhelming, and the magic wands were reluctantly put to one side as they raised the cool clear liquid up to their parched lips.

Once they had slaked their thirst and rested for a while, the girls left the café and made their way towards the Memorial, drawn by the buzz of excitement around that auspicious relic. The atmosphere of high-spirited revelry was infectious, and with the little ones held firmly to the sides of the older girls at all times, they soon found themselves part of the vocal exuberances, the ebb and flow of tightly packed bodies.

They watched the antics of one gyrating youth in particular, who was so thin that when he turned sideways he looked like he'd buggered off, as the saying went and yet another who was struggling unsuccessfully to perform a handstand up against the Memorial. Then Sally's attention was drawn to the edge of the crowd where a woman, her face red and shining with sweat, was in the process of delivering a snifter of snuff up into her nostrils. A vision of Philly Brooman doing the self-same thing popped up into Sally's imagination and she grinned. She had heard or read somewhere that Queen Charlotte who had been married to one of the King George's, had also used snuff, and she shook her head in disbelief. That any right minded person indulged in such a filthy habit, beggared belief. There were nowt so queer as folk as old Fred would say, and she had to agree with him. But then, smoking cigarettes was not normal or even safe, she reckoned thinking fleetingly of old Sniff and Spit. If the adverts were anything to go by however, certain brands were actually good for you. She was thinking about the poster with the caption, 'CRAVEN A. For your throats sake,' that she had seen quite recently. That sophisticated young lady with long, blond wavy hair gazing out towards the world looked healthy enough she reckoned.

Suddenly she moved, pulling Dorothy with her as a lad with enough body odour to kill an elephant sidled up alongside and grinned at her. She had seen him somewhere before, at one of the cycle speedway events if she remembered rightly, but she turned away before giving any sign of recognition, fingers crossed. This was neither the time nor the place to renew such a flimsy acquaintance, and would she want to anyway, she asked herself, at the same time feeling just a wee bit guilty.

The older girls were not sorry when Dorothy and Jacky began to flag, limp hand holds and drooping wands the first sign of their fatigue. The excitement of the past few hours had taken its toll and they were ready now to return to the peace and quiet of the countryside. They calculated after a quick check with the Memorial clock, that they had a good fifteen minutes to spare before a number 84 bus was due to leave the square, which would give them ample time to visit the lavatories behind Woolworth's and make themselves comfortable for the homeward journey. As they disentangled themselves from the hurly-burly of this high spirited revelry, a comment made by Uncle Frank on that memorable Downs walk day in early Spring, popped up into her mind. 'Just think about the Coal Miners underground in all that dust and grime on a day like this,' he had said, plus other comments about struggles and rights that she had not really understood at the time. Now for some reason and in a totally different environment, the impact of those words suddenly hit her like a stone. Imagine working down there in the bowls of the earth, cut off from daylight and fresh air, day after day facing unimaginable dangers, she thought with a shudder.

Who in their right mind would chose to do such a thing? Certainly from now on a piece of coal would be more than just something you chucked onto a fire.

Once they had visited the lavatories, they very nearly took the short cut through Woolworth's and onto the square that way. However and just in time, Hilary reminded them of the old superstition about it being unlucky to enter via one door and exit through another, so just to be on the safe side, they decided to walk the long way round. The bus was already standing in the square with the driver and conductor on board, and as they climbed onto the platform, an overwhelming smell of mothballs assailed their nostrils, propelling their feet up the stairs and on to the top deck. 'Whew,' they all said in chorus, sucking a mouthful of unpolluted air back into their lungs as soon as it was safe to do so. There were surprisingly few passengers on board, a lot people obviously staying on in town to participate in the evening's festivities, and they were quick to take advantage of the extra elbow-room. When the bus chugged away from the square, they were sitting very comfortably, and by the time it had reached the Pier, the two little ones were fast asleep.

The conversation between them to start with was all about the Carnival with its magical mix of colours, sounds, movements and the acrid fumes from overheating engines. Sally's one regret was the absence of any bagpipe playing Scotsmen in the procession. From the first time she had heard the haunting wail of this strange musical instrument, she had been enthralled by it. This feeling was enhanced by the picture she had seen of a 'Highlander' in all his regalia in one of dad's books in the front room, the majesty of the man in complete harmony with the misty mountains and magical landscape over which he was gazing. One verse of an accompanying poem sprang into her mind alongside the image, and she began to recite the words silently to herself:

> 'My heart's in the Highlands, my heart is not here.
> My heart's in the highlands chasing the deer.
> Chasing the wild deer and following the roe.
> My heart's in the highlands wherever I go.

Suddenly her full attention was captured by the conversation, which was taking place between Pat and Hilary. They had made the natural progression from Carnivals to Concerts and were now talking about a School Concert that was still talked about even though it had been enacted in the early years of that last war. It was Pat's rendition of 'The Skye Boat Song,' one of the songs on the programme, tying in so astonishingly with her current thoughts as it did, that had caught her attention. Freda had been talking about the Concert quite recently, about the plays, the ballet, the scenes and songs, which she told them, had involved rehearsals galore and a lot of messing about. She had mentioned her role as Maria in 'Twelfth Night,' alongside Derek Forrest, Frances Moore, Frank Chapman, Jean Angel and Molly Woodgate, which had involved learning a lot of lines and remembering where you were supposed to be standing on stage at any one time.

Joy Phillips, she told them, had been a buttercup alongside Peggy Woodgate, and had also taken the part of the Golliwog in the 'Madamoiselle Fanchette from France' play. Tony Taylor had played the part of a Chinaman. Silvia Pack, Patty Winchester and Dorothy Simmons had been poppies, Bettine Kenward, Ivy Simmons and Ada Smissen had been bluebells, and Janine Vallor had been the fairy in the Ballet.

She said that 'Aunt Merrily's Picnic Party,' starring Daphne Mann, Dorothy Simmons, Kathleen Wilmshurst, Allen Deeprose and Brian Thomas, had gone down well with the audience but had caused a bit of a stir backstage beforehand, as one of the props had gone missing. Luckily it had been found, only just in time, beneath a pile of coats.

You had to hand it to Freda, her memory was fantastic and she had a way of bringing things to life, when she was in the mood, Sally thought. Then she grinned as she remembered a couple of songs from the show, 'Tit Willow,' and 'Three Little Maids from School' that they had tried to sing along with her recently. They had been completely out of tune, had only remembered a word here and there, and she had got a bit cross with them for giggling their way through it. Ah well, it would not do for all of us to be the same, she thought to herself.

"Look, there's Uncle Jack," said Pat suddenly, pointing through the window towards a figure walking down past Wayside towards the Monumental Stone Masons and The Willows where he lived. "He's seen us, look," she added waving madly towards the now stationary figure one arm raised in the general direction of the fast retreating bus. As they sank back onto their seats, they began to discuss the reason for their Uncle's fragile state of mind, how one experience in particular had brought about the change in his character. In 1942, A Bristol Blenheim aeroplane, on its way from Goddington airport, had crashed and burst into flames very close to the school his children and niece attended. He had been one of the first on the scene and had helped to drag the badly burnt bodies of the crew from the wrecked plane, and a combination of that horrific experience plus the close proximity of the crash to the school, with its unimaginable consequences, had been an experience from which he had never recovered. Until that time, he had been a carbon copy of his brother, Uncle Fred, quick witted and with a 'wicked' sense of humour. Since then, and making matters even worse, he had fallen from the back of a lorry, hitting his head on the ground and suffering severe concussion, and it had been touch and go at the time as to whether he would actually pull through. He still worked though, and was always on hand to give his brother a hand, which was especially useful when Fred sustained a poisoned finger, eventually cured with a dose of Penicillin. Sally thought about the bit of advice he had given her the last time she had seen him. 'Don't forget, the size of a rod or pole is the length from the back of the plough to the nose of the ox.' That was it, and she now felt obliged to carry that bit of information around with her, probably for ever. When she and her sisters visited 'The Willows,' where he lived with his family in one of the cottages, they often wandered over the waste ground on the far side of the gardens. If you looked carefully, you could still see signs of the brickworks that had occupied the ground for goodness knows how long, and a few gnarled fruit trees, the remnants of an old orchard, still bore enough fruit to feed the birds and lots of other wild creatures – and to supply Aunty Ivy with enough fruit to turn into apple pies, if she were not mistaken.

Sally carefully avoided the deep dark well in the back garden, its location imprinted in her mind but tucked way away in a tiny recess within her imagination where all those other hateful things of life resided. It reminded her of the one at the bottom of the Winchester's garden, which always made her shudder. However, the old Copper, which she reckoned could be even bigger than the one at Sylvian, was to wonder at, and it sometimes puzzled her as to where they got enough wood from to feed the monster. But the best feature of all at The Willows and a wonder to behold was the biggest and shapeliest lilac tree Sally had ever seen. Its glowing colour and sweet smelling flowers attracted the most amazing host of butterflies, which feasted from dawn to dusk on its nectar in the spring and early summer. She could see it now as it had been just a few short weeks ago when she and Pat had visited. They had stood beside the front gate for ages watching these beautiful insects as they dipped their thread like tongue in and out of the flowers. As she thought these thoughts, she was suddenly transported way back to that cold winters day, and her encounter with those tiresome horses. As she and her sisters had made their way home through the wood and across the frozen field, Hazel had sung the song, 'We'll gather lilac in the spring again' to them. For some reason, the memory made her all goose pimply.

Then naturally and seamlessly her thoughts moved on to Uncle Fred Sansom, and in particular his unique sense of humour, his definition of the Oozlem bird with its beak in the sand as it whistled out of his assole, always made her laugh. She had listened as he and dad had discussed the importance of the Indian Army during that last war, the largest volunteer army ever, they reckoned. They said something about it having helped to hold Rommel back while Montgomery regrouped, or some such thing. It was during this discussion that Uncle Fred had mentioned a mate of his who had been badly injured in one or other campaign they were involved in. 'For Christ's sake don't die here, the ground's too bloody hard.' He'd urged him. His mate had pulled through. He, Uncle Fred, had had a few jobs since leaving the Army, a spell in the Fire Service being one of them. He also kept a few pigs, and for quite a while, had picked up the swill in an attachment fixed to the back of his old iron frame bicycle. He fed something called Tottenham pudding to them as well, whatever that was.

All of a sudden it seemed, they were in Kent Street, and as the bus stopped to allow a couple of people to alight, Pat and Hilary began to rouse the little ones, which was proving difficult to say the least. They managed to get through to them eventually by reminding them that Aunty Ethel, Uncle Cecil and little Stephen from Stanmore would be at Sylvian by the time they arrived home. It was the mention of the name Stephen that actually brought them round. He was the little brother they had never had, and they thought the world of him. As soon as the bus drew to a standstill for them all to disembark at Black Brooks, they were off, and before the older girls had reached the bottom gate, were through the top one and running towards the scullery door.

They were all very fond of this family, with Aunty Ethel a particular favourite. Uncle Cecil and dad had worked together in London at one time, and the conversation between the two men was similar to the discussions that took place between dad and his brother's Alf and Fred, when they got together. This evening, Sally pricked up her ears when she heard them mention Uncle George, and his road to Socialism, and on the same journey sadly, his loss of faith in organised religion. One experience in particular had upset him. He had taken up the cause of a group of people whose rent had been hiked up unfairly by their landlords. He had put their case forward with what he considered to be a fair deal for all parties but had been ground down by what he referred to as a well organised brotherhood of affluence, or just the system, said dad. He had been devastated when he had lost this particular case, never ridding himself of the guilt he felt at having let his friends down. The premature death of this seemingly caring, astute and very articulate man, had had a devastating effect on the whole family. But as dad reflected, although he did not live to see it, George could perhaps have paid just a small part in bringing about a bit of a change in the system.

After a while, the two men got up from the table and wandered off to do the rounds, still trying to put the world to rights. As they passed by the scullery window, Sally saw Uncle Cecil beating a clenched fist into the palm of his other hand to make a point.

Once the little ones were fast asleep mum, Aunty Ethel and the older girls took themselves outside and sat on the underground tank, chatting as they slowly supped a welcome cup of tea. After a while, the conversation, prompted by Sally, took a gigantic leap from family affairs to films and film stars. She could not wait, she announced during a brief lull in the conversation, to see the film, 'The Red Shoes,' the performance of its Star Moira Shearer in particular. From the time she had heard about the film and had seen the poster announcing the forthcoming 'event,' all those long abandoned fantasies of becoming a Ballet dancer herself had resurfaced, and in moments of solitude, she allowed herself once again to indulge those dreams. Of the other stars in the film, like Robert Helpmann and Leonide Massini, she knew very little, they were just names to her. Her interest and passion lay in what she knew would be a truly magical performance by the young and talented star of this extraordinary film.

She dragged her thoughts reluctantly away from reflections on this particular film, and listened with growing interest as the grownups began to talk about the stars of an earlier era. Mum who was a few years older than Aunty, began her trip down memory lane with the name Rudolph Valentino, and if the sparkle in her eye as she talked about this man was anything to go by, then he would most certainly have been the heart throb of his day, and still idolised it seemed by lots of women of a certain age. She talked about his films then his early death as though she had been on intimate terms with the man, as on one level perhaps she had. She paused for a few seconds, then continued with reminiscences of other film stars, all quite famous and popular when she had been a girl, she told them. The names Gloria Swanson, Mary Pickford, Carmen Miranda and many others followed, and then she mentioned someone called Phyllis Dare, who had been the singer of sentimental and patriotic songs, she told them.

The trip down memory lane continued with Aunty Ethel bringing in the names of other film stars, some recognised by the girls from posters they had scrutinised or films they had seen in one or other of the cinema's they had visited. Sally was sure that Ingrid Bergman, one of the actresses she mentioned, 'an actress with a talent to match her beauty,' aunty said, had starred in a film she and Hilary had seen at the Deluxe Cinema. Or was it the Regal? Whatever, it would certainly not have been the Roxy, or the flea pit as this scruffy cinema in Silverhill was usually called, and for very good reason she thought and grinned. The pong in there was something awful, just like someone was smoking bus driver's gloves, as Basil observed. Mind you, not all youngsters were put off by its shortcomings. Some were prepared to part with a tanner for a seat up in the God's, or rather the chicken run, the common name for this wire netted enclosure. It had been constructed thus to protect those on the lower decks from bombardments from above, she'd been told. The Gaiety Cinema in Queen's Road on the other hand, was quite smart and very popular; on a par with the Ritz Cinema in Cambridge road, she reckoned. Both were particularly busy on Saturdays, when youngsters would queue round the block if necessary to get the cheapest seats for some must see film. She was sure she had seen a film starring Myrna Loy in the former, and certainly one starring Lana Turner in the latter. Then there was the Orion of course and the Curzon, where the penny drinks were the best in the world, she thought as the names of other popular stars popped up in quick succession. Many like Dana Andrews Hoagy Carmichael, Teresa Wright, Virginia Mayo for instance, she recognised mostly from old posters; others however, she had never heard of. Two very popular stars, amongst young and old alike, were Fred Astaire and Ginger Rogers, and rightly so she thought. Their dance routines were magical, absolutely out of this world as the saying went. And then of course there was Gene Kelly, a particular favourite of hers. The list of Stars went on and on.

The discussion continued, moving seamlessly away from films and famous film stars, with Pat now enthusing about the open air bathing pool along at the Marina. During the summer months, no matter whether the weather was hot cold or merely indifferent, the pool and surrounding area would be heaving with bodies. She was talking now about the bravery or sheer foolhardiness of the youngsters, many only knee high to a grasshopper, who after scrambling one after the other up the stairs and onto the top deck of the diving frame, would plunge without apparent fear, into the deep water below. She and Sally were now brave enough to belly flop into the water from the first springboard, and were already psyching themselves up to join Hilary, who had recently conquered the next one up with something akin to a passable dive. The diving boards here however, were bigger and higher and altogether more daunting than the ones at the White Rock Baths, and would take a bit of getting used to, they all reckoned.

When Pat mentioned the sticks of liquorice root they mostly bought and chewed on while they were sitting around the pool, Sally winced. She hated the stuff. It was just like chewing on a dead sock she reckoned, and wondered sometimes how she managed to chew her way through it without actually heaving. On the other hand, the fish and chips, all wrapped up hot and steaming in a bit of old newspaper they often treated themselves to when they left the pool, was bloody delicious. The memory of the aroma from that freshly opened steaming bundle, hit her nostrils now with enough impact to make her mouth water.

She pricked up her ears when she heard Aunty mention flying ants, and pulled her skirt instinctively up at one side as though the little winged creatures had actually surfaced around her. For some reason they favoured the area around the underground tank on which they were sitting, emerging in their thousands at some critical stage in their life cycle, usually when a thunderstorm was brewing. As they emerged, they performed some ritualistic dance or display, turning this way and that, before tentatively trying out the novelty and strength of their wings. Another little creature that fascinated her in its own way was the glossy blue black dung beetle, though its diet left a lot to be desired as far as she was concerned. She had watched them working their way over cowpats, and had wondered what on earth they were up to. Mum told her that they and a lot of other small creatures like them were natural scavengers, and played an important part in tidying up the waste that larger animals left behind. Sally had never looked at it that way. Evidently, the dung was used as an incubator and larder for the larvae as well. Mum said that the male ferried the dung to his mate who formed the stuff into a little ball and then laid a single egg inside. It seemed that both male and female were involved in the protection of their offspring, though how on earth someone had come up with that theory was beyond her. It made her realise though that all creatures, large and small had some purpose in life. Even the worms that frightened the living daylights out of her were the food for moles and hedgehogs and other animals, and they also aerated the soil, so it was said. The more she learned about the resourcefulness, the ingenuity of Mother Nature the more awesome the old lady became.

Mum and Aunty Ethel were discussing world affairs now, and some of the names they mentioned she remembered from articles that had cropped up in the Newspaper from time to time. Though they had registered in her mind at the time and she still remembered them, she found the names strange and quite difficult to pronounce, her tongue somehow inflexible and uncooperative as she tried to enunciate them. She tried the names out now gingerly and in a whisper; Chiang Kai-Shek, Chou En-Lai, Ho Ying-Chin, Mao Tse-Tung, and found that if she took her time, they were not so difficult to pronounce after all. For some reason, this confusion of names brought back a name and memory from the distant past that had attached itself to her mind and imagination, and would be there forever she reckoned. 'Yamamoto,' she mouthed to herself, remembering the impact the news of the death of this Japanese General had had on her. Even now she could remember in vivid detail where she had been when she had heard the news of his death near Bouganville Island, how devastated she had been and who had told her. What she could not fathom, however, was how this stranger had managed to reach an almost mythological status in her mind over the years, when she was all too aware of the atrocities committed by a regime in which he had clearly played a very important and influential part. How could she possibly continue to have this conflict of emotions when accounts of those acts of unbelievable cruelty, sanctioned by some Imperial Guard or other, still returned time and again to haunt her. It was a question she was unable to fathom let alone answer. She felt deep down however, that the man had not been as evil as the regime in which he served. She knew somehow that he had been part of something that had got terrifyingly, brutally and overwhelmingly out of control.

She breathed a sigh of relief when the conversation moved away from the discussion on Far Eastern affairs to something more light-hearted, dispelling at once her morbid thoughts. She often wondered how the conversation got from one subject and on to something seemingly quite unconnected, but she was not complaining, especially when, as now the subject was one in which she had an interest. Aunty was talking about one of the Lyons Corner Houses, in which she and her sister Aunty Lily had dined recently during a rare visit to the West End of London. By the way she was describing the place, Sally reckoned it could be the very same dignified restaurant in which she and Aunty Nin had feasted, the place in which she had first encountered something called etiquette. Sally could not imagine either Aunty Ethel or Aunty Lily committing the sin of cutting rather than breaking the roll that would have accompanied their soup as she had done, and would have known exactly what to do with the crisply starched serviettes standing to attention beside every place setting. However, that was as maybe. What had caught Sally's attention was the word 'Nippy's,' that according to aunty was the name by which the smart pinafored and bonneted waitresses were known. That name made them seem more human somehow, more friendly and approachable, which meant that if she were ever to dine in that illustrious café again, she would not feel so self-conscious and inhibited by that thing called etiquette,' or so she hoped.

She was sorry when at this stage, mum and aunty stood up and began to collect the cups and saucers together, saying something about having to check up on the little ones. Perhaps it was just motherly instinct that had brought about the almost abrupt end to the conversation or perhaps the discussion on restaurants and waitresses had triggered some reflex action. Who knew what went on the mind of adults. Still, after a busy day, it was good to just sit here and watch as the rays of the setting sun reached out, painting a silvery pink halo around the edges of the trees and covering the western sky in a rosy glow. She was not sorry she was not tripping the light fantastic on Winkle Island this evening. She was content just to sit here with her family, and watch the day give way slowly and reluctantly to the night.

Chapter 9
Autumn 1949

The sun came up in an orange glow, wearing a dark cloud like a giant eyebrow. "It'll be raining cats and dogs before the mornings out," Sally muttered to herself and to any other interested body as she moved away from the kitchen window and sat herself down at the table to eat her breakfast. Best get up to the farm and get the milk before it starts, she thought to herself, though with any luck it would be an hour or two yet before it started sulking. They had had a lot of rain recently, with the underground tank at a healthy level and the tanks around the house full to overflowing. She thought back to that hot dry spell back in the summer, when with the shortage of water, the tomato plants had been rationed to within a whisker of their lives, and the family had been 'forced' to wash in a thimble full of water. The frugality forced by the hot dry conditions had certainly improved the flavour of dad's tomatoes if that were possible, though she preferred not to dwell on the effect it had had on their own personal hygiene.

There was already washing on the line she noticed as she hurried towards the back gate on her way to the farm to fetch the milk. Mum was taking a chance she thought to herself, then grinned when she noticed a pair of Granny Cotton's old apple gatherers on the line, alongside a pair of dainty rayon, or artificial silk knickers belonging to Freda. The old lady's warnings about the dangers of inappropriate clothing had been completely ignored, she noted wryly though with very good reason, she reckoned. The navy blue knickers she and her sisters wore were warm and comfortable enough, and these pocketed bloomers, along with her frequent brush with those vicious old stinging nettles, was as far as she was prepared to go to ward off the screws. As she walked across the field and looked about her, she noticed the ragged remains of the bird's foot trefoil

159

amongst the clumps of grass, and although faded to a shadow of their former selves, were as dear to her as ever. An image of Queen Mab with her retinue of fairies and other tiny creatures always popped up in front of her when she saw them.

Aunty Nin had arrived at Sylvian on Friday afternoon and would be staying with them for about ten days mum reckoned, and although a bit on the bossy side, she did help mum with a lot of the boring day by day chores. She was also very kind in a gruff sort of way, Sally reminded herself as she strode towards the farmhouse; with the patience of Job when it came to assisting the girls with their sewing and crochet. Then there was that memorable trip to London of course, with all those fresh, stimulating experiences, where she had been treated by her aunty to the knickerbocker glory and that juicy fresh peach, and had been taken to some posh cinema by her, to see that hilarious Laurel and Hardy film. She grinned to herself as she recalled the antics of the two men as they had struggled up the stairs with that piano, the thing becoming increasingly less of an inanimate object and more like some stubborn mule.

More recently of course, and just as interesting in its own way, had been that day trip to Hove with Aunty Nin, where she had noticed and been quite fascinated by an interesting building close by the railway station. 'The Dubarry Perfumery Company,' it was called, its name picked out in attractive green and white mosaic lettering, with the names of other products, like cream for manicure preparations and fine toilet soaps, alongside. Knowing that Jumbo James had lived in or around this area at one time, she had asked him about this building with its attractive façade. He had told her the little he knew about the building and its purpose, and had then proceeded to scare the living day lights out of her with tales of a ghostly female apparition that was supposed to haunt a particular area of the building. A draft of cool air always preceded the arrival of the shrouded lady he said, with those in the room frozen to the spot as she hovered briefly in and around them before floating past and vanishing into thin air. The experience of all witnesses to this extraordinary happening, described it in exactly the same way, he said. Was this just a figment of the imagination, a trick of heightened sensibilities at dead of night, the bewitching hour, she asked herself. Or was it perhaps that through some experience just before death, the spirit of this lady found itself unable to move on until released by some human action, or by divine intervention, an expression she'd heard somewhere. But then she was letting her imagination run away with her yet again, when of course the purpose and highlight of their trip to Hove had been to visit friends of her aunty's, Mr and Mrs Rosengarten. Sally, their daughter, had been away at the time, and Aunty Nin, her one time Nanny, had been really upset to have missed her. There had obviously been a very strong bond between the two of them.

They had gone straight to the shop owned by the couple, whereas she'd opened the door, a strange musky smell had hit her nostrils, which was reminiscent of dad's cured rabbit skins, albeit in a sweeter, more refined sort of way. Once inside however, this sense was subsumed by another sensation. Her eye had alighted on and been captured by the sleek beauty of the fur coats and jackets on display, and she had experienced an overwhelming, irresistible urge to stroke them.

There were fur hats and gloves and the most amazing stoles there as well, among the latter, several adorned with a tiny animal head at one end and a tail at the other. Her curiosity had been well and truly aroused, and it was as she moved closer to get a better look at the top end, that she realised that the little wide eyed creature looking back at her was a fox. All at once she had felt a bit sad for the little old chap. Her mesmerised gaze had continued to move from one item to another in this plethora of fur and stunning workmanship, and even now she could visualise in detail and recapture the magic of this extraordinary collection.

After a while, she and Aunty Nin had departed with Mrs Rosengarten, leaving the shop and its customers in the capable hands of her husband, and had walked the short distance to the couple's home. The house was not an extension of the shop as she imagined it might have been, but as she looked around her, had seen and been struck by some of the beautifully carved, ornate furniture in and around the place. Dad would love this, she had thought to herself at the time. He would really appreciate the skill and dedication of the craftsmen who had created these unique and beautiful works of art. What had really caught her eye though, had been the tapestry fire screen depicting a scene from Romeo and Juliet that had been standing on the hearth in the front room. When she had mentioned it, Mrs Rosengarten just told her that it had taken 'a lot of patience, perseverance and gritting of teeth.' As Sally had examined the woven tapestry more closely, she could see the reason why. This fine piece of needlework was made up of thousands of individual stitches in multiple shades of wool, each one carefully and painstakingly woven into the backing material. Indeed a work of considerable merit, she reminded herself. She also reminded herself how kind and caring and very interesting these people were. She was able to appreciate and understand why her aunt was so fond of this family.

There were a number of large birds dipping and diving over fields of stubble in the distance, she noticed as she climbed over the stile at the top of the field with the cans of milk balanced carefully in her hands, and she paused for a few seconds to watch their antics. They were feasting on the scattered grain, the inevitable residue from the harvest in late summer, she reckoned. They also seemed to be riding the currents of air and getting in a bit of exercise before that rain, foretold by the red sky earlier this morning, started good and proper. That reminded her, she would have to look out Hazel's old gabardine mackintosh, which she hoped still fitted her, and she'd ask dad if she could borrow his old sow' ester or whatever he called that thing he wore on his head when the weather turned wet and windy. None of them bothered about umbrellas. Unless you were the one holding the thing and were right underneath, the rain always seemed to drip off the edges and run uncomfortable down the back of your neck no matter how careful you tried to be.

Dorothy and Jacky were playing with mum's pig ornament, Sally noticed as she walked through to the kitchen after depositing the milk carefully onto the draining board in the Scullery, and she clucked disapprovingly. As she rushed to remove this knock-kneed, pigeon toed work of art from their careless hands, mum stopped her, reminding her about the hours of pleasure she and Pat had derived from the same such activity, when they were small. Sally had to admit albeit reluctantly, that she did indeed have a selective memory when it came to her own childish behaviour in relation to that of her younger siblings, but that precious pig had to be protected somehow. Perhaps a bit of bribery would work, it was worth trying anyhow.

"How about if me and Hilary take you for a walk up in the woods," she suggested hastily. "She'll be here in a minute or two and it'll be ages before it starts raining. The old Ram's not in the field yet, though Mr Collins reckons it will be in a day or two. I just hope it's docile like last year's one was, and not a blasted maniac like the one we were stuck with the year before. Scared the living daylights out of us, that did, didn't it? All except dad of course. Nothing scares him. Now it'll just up to the wood and back again, we haven't got time to see Deffy and Bill this time," she added just in case they started wheedling.

Having successfully caught the youngster's attention, she rescued her precious pig and put it carefully back on the shelf where it belonged. Then with an audible sigh of relief, she began to get together coats and wellies for the little ones and for herself the Gabardine raincoat, which she found hanging behind the scullery door. Dad's old sow' ester would have to wait, she thought to herself as she saw Hilary hurrying up the field.

It was quiet when they entered the woods, with just the rustle of leaves and the occasional plop of a dropping acorn. And the monotonous five bar call of the wood pigeon's, 'take two cows booby.' For a short while the little ones responded to the atmosphere, content just to shuffle in the leaves as they walked alongside the older girls. After a while however, they began to venture further afield, picking up acorns and any desiccated leaf that caught their attention, and their increasing excitement and enthusiasm soon rubbed off on the older girls. They all joined in a game of hide and seek, and as the only cover hereabouts of any significance was amongst the clumps of ivy, the little ones were allowed mostly to don 'the magic cloak of invisibility.' They pushed this advantage to the extreme at times, and shrieked with delight when the older girls came within a few paces of them and peered around looking for them with exaggerated puzzled frowns on their faces. The youngsters were in their element, and it took a deal of persuasion, bribery almost to bring this game of pretence to an end. It was Hilary's promise of a visit to Deffy and Bill's little hut, possibly next weekend that finally brought about their reluctant acquiescence. Also, the rain forecast by the rosy glow in the sky this morning, was now dripping down through the bare branches of the trees, and becoming increasingly hard to ignore.

The high spirits and non-stop chit-chat continued when they left the woods, along with the persistent rain and rising wind. Once in the field however, the little ones ran on ahead to show mum the acorns, and leaves and the few shrivelled sloes' they had collected from the wood, clearly in harmony amongst themselves and with the rest of the world. Once again mum's precious pig had worked its magic, Sally thought to herself and grinned, remembering other occasions when this strange phenomena had occurred. How dearly she wished she knew the identity of the mysterious potter who had fashioned this curious clay creature with its undeniable charm.

The conversation amongst the Black Brooks youngsters as they made their way up Crazy Lane towards Chapel Hill, was almost exclusively about rehearsals for their concert, which were now in full swing. 'The Sedlescombe Wax Works' they called it, the title of this rather strange and unusual play, causing a few raised eye-brows amongst those with little imagination. By the time they had shaken off and discarded their wet clothing, and entered the little room adjacent to the Chapel where their Bible classes were conducted, there was a full complement of budding actors assembled within its now rather restrictive confines; and it was a job to get a word in edgeways.

A semblance of order was restored when Mrs Smith, Miss Smith and Olive entered the room, the bundles of old sheets they were carrying, almost though not quite, concealing their identity. These 'props' were the only ones they worked with at the moment, apart from the massive, rusty old iron key with which the exhibits (dummies) were mobilised, thus allowing them to perform their jerky actions. All the parts had been allocated and it was now down to each individual to perfect the action specific to their particular character, and most important as Olive told them was that they got the timing right.

As Sally waited for the action to begin, she studied the motley bunch in this room, each chosen to represent one or other worthy worker or Artisan as dad would have called them, and grinned. Sitting with their heads together just like the biblical David and Jonathan were Ronald Elkins and Ray Winchester, who were Farmer and Shepherd respectively. And John Hullock was a Blacksmith. Pat was a Milkmaid, her costume already stitched and waiting for the big event. Ann Pope and Patty Winchester were Nurses, the big red cross on the costume of the latter leaving no one in any doubt about the worthiness of her cause.

Basil Winchester was a Policeman and what he lacked in stature he made up for with his actions. A born actor and comedian was Basil and he was bound to raise a chuckle or two from the audience no matter what he did. Daniel Smith was a Vicar and the only one apart from the buyer and seller who was allowed a voice in this play. He had already perfected the mock pious monotone, for some reason associated with this worthy calling and she hoped she did not get a fit of the giggles when he got up and said his bit. He was a good sport and she would hate to put him off his stroke. There was nothing for it but to rekindle the memory of those diabolical wax works she had seen in the chamber of horrors at that Madame Tussauds place in London that time; that should do the trick. Those gristly exhibits were enough to wipe the smile off her face and stop that compulsive chuckle in her throat forever. She moved swiftly and decisively away from such thoughts, thinking instead and with a sense of relief about her own contribution to this show. She had been allowed to represent the Women's Land Army, with the caption, 'food comes first,' on her costume. She was made up with this part mostly she had to admit because of her cousin Connie who, towards the end of the war, had done her bit towards remedying the ongoing food shortage. She was very fond of her cousin.

Hilary Elkins and Frank Richmond were the seller and buyer respectively. The banter and haggling between the two as each exhibit was revealed, was both realistic and comical. At the moment they were doing their best along with Olive and Miss Smith, to get some semblance of order within the ranks.

As she continued to participate in the chaotic rehearsals for the show, she thought back to the Harvest Festival here in the chapel, where so much local fruit and vegetables and even fish had been donated. The service accompanying the festival had been arranged and conducted by the local youngsters, with a lot of help from the Smith family. Each child, clutching a handful or armful of a particular victual, or in one case a piece of coal, had paraded alongside the congregation, reciting a word or two in praise of their particular gift of food, the one holding up a fistful of fish causing a few stifled giggles from the audience. She, Hilary, Patty and Ann had been chosen to represent the four seasons, which had entailed each having to write and recite a short poem or piece of prose of seasonal celebration. She remembered the time she had spent trying to convey in just a few words, the essence of her allotted season, and just reciting the words slowly to herself brought back the magic of the occasion. 'I come to remind you of summer. Of long warm days. Of picnics in the hay field and by the sea. Of dragonflies and butterflies and bees - and the song of the birds.' Patty's poignant autumnal poem told of chestnuts and falling leaves and the departure of the swallow, while the emphasis in Ann's poem was on snow and vigilant Shepherds and bulbs hiding their faces down under the cold earth. Hilary had spoken about primroses and violets and wild birds nesting in hedgerows, conveying the hope and optimism of this special season with the words, 'nature bursting with energy.'

The simple white dresses they had worn for the occasion had been made for them by Miss Smith, as had their wide silk sashes, in colours reflecting the season they were representing. The sashes had adorned their upper bodies, angled around their backs then draped from left shoulder to right hip where the ends had been tied together in a neat bow. That splash of colour had been their only adornment.

At the end of the festival, Mr Smith had offered up a prayer of thanksgiving, conveying in a few words what with some agents of God seemed to be a yawningly slow process. It had been clear from the start that the philosophy of this family was that actions spoke louder than words. They practised what they preached, choosing to follow the teachings of God through Jesus and his disciples in deeds, rather than to deliver endless sermons. True Christians they were according to mum and dad.

Once the rehearsals had come to an end, there was just time for a couple of hymns and a short closing prayer before home time. Before the youngsters donned their damp coats, however, they 'offered up' a helping hand with the tidying up and a rough folding of the sheets they had been using, those with the longest journey's then running off home in the wind and rain. It was the few who lived on Chapel Hill and those from Black Brooks, who helped with the carrying of the cumbersome bundles from Chapel to Manse, avoiding the puddles on the path more by instinct than an ability to see their feet. As they approached the door of the Manse, Sally heard the unmistakable voice of Paul Robson coming from somewhere within the building. Mr Smith, in a rare moment of leisure was playing his favourite gramophone records she realised, immediately and immeasurably grateful to this practical yet sensitive man of God for allowing her another chance to listen to the deep soulful voice of this unique singer of Negro Spirituals. She performed the task of passing the bundles from hand to hand automatically as she listened to the strains of 'Ol' Man River' and 'Just a Wearyin' For You,' then 'A long ways from home,' feeling that strange yet familiar sensation this singer and his songs always provoked in her, and she knew that Mr Smith felt the same. The pathos in this rich deep voice moved him, pulled at his heartstrings in the same unaccountable way as it did with her, of that she was certain.

As they left the building, the effect of the rising wind and ongoing rain, brought the brief moment of introspective thought to an end, and in no time at all she became an integral part of the huddled group of youngsters, all bent on reaching the dry comfort of home in the shortest possible time.

They moved into single file at the junction between Chapel Hill and Crazy Lane as a motor car approached from the direction of Cottage lane, then paused to allow it to pass. At the wheel was Orson Button, or to give him his full title, Halson Conway Button, which according to Dad Cotton sounded more like a benediction that a name. He stopped however, and wound down his window, offering them a few words of commiseration, albeit in his usual bantering fashion. He was the youngest of the Button boys and the expression, chalk and cheese came immediately to mind when comparing him with his two older brothers, Sid and Claude. He had been blessed or cursed with a head of thick red hair, a ready wit and a temper that flared then subsided in the blinking of an eyelid; and he could talk the hind leg off a donkey. His nickname for obvious reasons was Ginger Nut; behind his back of course. The youngsters had never quite plucked up the courage to test his reaction to this blatant reference to that startling hair of his face to face. They knew from experience that a wicked sense of humour combined with a quick temper was a volatile mixture with a reaction that could go as easily one way as the other, especially when there was a personal element involved as was clearly the case here. It had never entered their heads that he might know of the nickname and be amused by it.

Pat and Sally sniffed the air in unison as they entered the house through the scullery door, recognising at once the acrid aroma of baking chicken feathers; and the smell was stronger in the kitchen, even though a couple of top windows near the Rayburn had been propped open. It seemed ages ago now that Sally had heard mum mention the need for a couple of eiderdowns to replace the ones that were thread bare, and she herself had noticed that the one on the bed she shared with Pat, was leaking feathers all over the place even though it had been patched several times. This was dad's job and that it did not exactly fire him with enthusiasm, was made perfectly clear by his declaration that he would rather clean out a dozen chicken houses caked with droppings than mess about with those blasted things. As he said, it was one thing stitching the outer casing of the things and getting the feathers inside, quite another trying to keep an even distribution of those feathers as you stitched the sections into place. At least mum was doing her bit by getting the feathers ready for him, she thought as she moved around the kitchen, and in no time at all she was not even noticing the sickly scent.

By tea-time, the feathers along with their offending smell, had been removed from the Rayburn and been replaced by something a lot more to the liking of the youngsters. It was herring roes on bread for tea, and the pan was now on the primus stove, with the soft succulent delicacies sizzling away within its ample girth. The girls were already sitting at the table, their bread covered platters in front of them, awaiting and anticipating a dollop of the tasty fare. When Dorothy slid from her seat and wandered off, no one took the least bit of notice of her, least of all the older girls. They were a lot more interested in food than in the antics of one of the little ones, and as mum dished up, began to tuck into the food in front of them with appetites to match the size of the portions. The first inkling Sally had of anything untoward was a scuffling and muffled squeaks from the seat beside her, and as she looked sideways, an astonishing and comical sight met her eyes, plus a dawning realisation of Dorothy's motive for leaving the table. Pat was wearing her tea. Her sneaky sister had crept up behind her and at the crucial moment, had popped a large brown carrier bag over her head. The perpetrator was now standing behind the chair, convulsed with laughter while Pat, momentarily frozen into an unbelieving silence, sat with soft squidgy roe dripping from her hair-line, right down to her chin and beyond. The result of the little trick had obviously surpassed even Dorothy's expectations, and her mirth proved contagious. Even Pat after she had been cleaned up and served with another portion of her favourite dish, was able to see the funny side of the situation, albeit with a measure of reluctance and a stern warning to her naughty sister, the latter endorsed by mum. It was a waste of good food, as well as a vexatious trick to play on her sister she was told sternly. Even as mum was speaking, Sally feared it would not be the last time her little sister would catch one of them out with a well-planned trick. She really would have to keep an eye on this budding practical joker.

By the time the washing up had been done and the dishes stacked away on the old dresser in the scullery, Dorothy and Jacky were in bed, and after sorting out their clothes in readiness for school and work the next morning the older girls settled down in anticipation of a bit of peace and quiet. The lamp in the centre of the kitchen table popped and flickered as air currents, or draughts as the girls preferred to call them, played around it distorting its flame, but they were used to this. The functional old thing cast enough light for them to sew, knit or read as they sat around the table and that was all they were bothered about. Freda and Hazel were knitting, the clicking of their needles and the sporadic chit-chat between them not distracting Pat and Sally one iota from the books they were reading. Pat was well into the 'Wind in the Willows,' the best book ever, she reckoned, but then she made the same comment about a lot of the books she read. Sally grinned as she listened to her sister's comments on the ongoing adventures of the characters she was reading about, reminding her of her own enjoyment of this fascinating story. There were the delightful Mole and Ratty and Badger, who seemed to spend an inordinate amount of time rescuing their friend Toad, always on some wild goose chase, from tripping over his own ego. Then as in most adventure stories, there were the dubious characters; here in the guise of Stoats and Weasels and Ferrets, and other creatures from the wild wood, who stalked the unwary traveller and for whom Toad was a natural prey. She had enjoyed every moment of this story. She was now in the throes of reading the Charles Dickens classic Great Expectations, which she had borrowed from the school library, a book she knew a bit about but which she had never actually read from cover to cover. She was finding the story challenging, but also fascinating in a strange kind of way. It had a disturbing ring of reality about it somehow. She had been scared to death by the sudden appearance of the convict Magwitch, popping up in such a God forsaken place like that, but after the initial shock, had felt quite sorry for the wretched fellow. Miss Haversham on the other hand, with her tenuous grip on reality, continued to scare the living daylights out of her. There was something about those weird psychological games she played with those closest to her that was particularly unsettling. On her obsessive search for revenge, this strange damaged woman, had taken a pathway from which there was no turning back. However, as with all Dickens' stories there were many twists and turns here, the difference between good and bad not always clearly defined she realised. It was certainly giving her brain a bit of exercise she thought, as she continued to follow the fortunes of the characters, Pip and Estelle in particular, with some trepidation.

As she looked up to get a bit of light relief from the somewhat dark content of this book, she was just in time to see dad picking a piece of tobacco absentmindedly off his tongue as he sat at the table with his newspaper propped up in front of him. He was not actually smoking right now. He usually savoured one of those thin, more spit than baccy roll ups of his when he was in the throes of one or other of his outdoor chores. They must have been particularly useful when he was in the process of cleaning out those stinky old chicken coops she reckoned, wrinkling her nose at the memory of those ammonia ridden hutches. This was a chore that she got lumbered with from time to time, and it was not just the pong that offended her sensibilities, but also those horrid, hot weather mites that seemed to thrive in the stench. All life forms it seemed had evolved to fulfil different needs and conditions, and as dad said, if it were not for scavengers, the world would stink to high Heaven.

The blustery day was certainly turning into a blustery night, Sally thought as she and Pat shivered their way around the side of the house towards the lavatory to pay their last respects for the night. If they did need to relieve themselves between now and the morning, it would have to be with the 'aid' of the small bucket at the side of the bed, but thankfully this rarely happened. As she waited for her turn, she shone the torch around half fearful at what might be lurking in the deep dark shadows beyond the narrow beam of light. In her heightened state of awareness, a vision of mischievous Goblins and Gremlins and Leprechauns, danced to within a whisker of the beam, then with silent laughter and incredible agility, dodged back into the inky shadows. She forced her mind away from such fantasies, and with a deep energising breath, sought to replace those images with ones of a lighter hue. Luckily the first thing that popped up into her mind was a poster advertising Dorma towels that had caught her attention recently. She grinned as she pictured that trio of plump happy youngsters as they tripped off to the bathroom, soap in one hand, the thick fluffy towels they were carrying in the other, trailing across their little fat feet. The caption, Family Favourites could just as easily have been a reference to the happy youngsters as to the towels they were carrying, she thought to herself. This thought sustained her until she and her sister were safely back in the scullery, rinsing their hands with the aid of a bit of carbolic soap and a trickle of water from the old tap. They spent too many hours pumping the stuff from underground to top tank to waste water even when there was an abundance of it as now, Sally thought to herself as she shook then sniffed her hands appreciatively.

Chapter 10
Winter 1949

Sally woke with a start. She must have overslept she thought as she hopped out of bed and up to the window in a bit of a panic. Then she sighed with a mixture of relief and wonderment as she looked out onto a cold, frosty landscape bathed in silver moonlight. She gazed at the waning moon, the fine haze of fluffy whiteness around its orb adding an air of mystery to the already magical scene, and sighed yet again. There was a mysterious world up there and no mistake, she thought as she shivered her way back beneath the bedclothes again. Morning was not that far away now, she reckoned. She would stay awake until she heard dad moving around in the kitchen, then pop out and share a cup of tea with him before getting dressed.

As she lay there, her thoughts turned to the dress rehearsal for the Waxwork Show that had taken place in the village hall recently, and uppermost in her mind, that overwhelming compulsion she had had to sneeze. It had started with just a slight tickle in her nose, but had soon developed into an eye watering, life and death struggle almost to stifle the impulse. A bit of pressure on her top lip would normally have done the trick but that simple expedient would have been out of the question for obvious reasons. Everyone knew that the fundamental objective when enacting the role of a waxwork dummy was to sit there, stock still, without moving a muscle. Perhaps it was this thing called mind over matter that had saved her bacon this time. She would just have to hope the same thing worked for her when it came to the actual performance, she thought as she shrugged her thick cardigan around her shoulders and made her way to the kitchen for a cup of sweet milky tea.

With Christmas nearly upon them, there was a lot to do and think about and mum in particular never seemed to get a moment to herself. As well as the day by day chores like housework and cooking and the constant battle to dry the mountains of washing that came her way, there were all those extra jobs, which were an integral part of this special and exciting celebration. With this in mind, Pat and Sally had decided that once their basic chores were done, they would take the little ones to the Big Wood with them to gather holly, which would give her a bit of space for an hour or two. It was very cold outside, and although the wind was not that strong, it was one of those lazy ones that went right through rather than around a body. They would need to wear their warmest clothing today, plus at least two pairs of socks in their wellies. And whatever happened, they must not forget to take dad's secateurs with them.

The rough grass along the lane was stiff with hoar frost, which crackled beneath their feet as they made their way along the track and very soon they were passing alongside Beanford farm, its ancient cat slide roof wearing its share of the white stuff. They spotted several old birds' nests amongst the twiggy vegetation in the hedges along the way, which, when built and in occupation, would have been well hidden amongst a thick camouflage of lush green leaves, and pretty nigh impossible to see. The familiar smell of wood smoke hit their nostrils as they continued towards the wood, and in a short space of time, Deffy and Bill's little shack itself came into view, a comforting spiral of smoke wafting from the chimney, or rather that thin tin funnel adaptation of theirs that seemed to work. They hesitated outside then decided not to disturb the two old men for the time being. However, realising their presence would most certainly have been observed, Pat tapped then put her head around the doorway, and in no time at all, an arrangement had been made for them to call in on their way home.

They noticed an old rusty plough rotting away in the course grass, not far from the edge of the wood, and wondered how long it would take for the two old men to find a use for this corroding metal, and why indeed it had not already been recycled by them. Then they moved away, shuffling around in the brown desiccated leaves, which lay like a thick layer of rusty confetti around their feet. There was no hurry. They were well warmed up now and eager to explore the wood for a while, before seeking out the red berried holly trees. With many of the trees around them now leafless and bare, it was easy to pick out holes in the trunks, or in the crotch of a tree where a thick branch had fallen away. Many of these holes they knew would have been hammered out with dexterity and hard headed determination by woodpeckers as nesting sites in which to rear their young. Now however, other little creatures would most likely be tucked up safe and sound within these snug abodes, a tiny hibernating dormouse for instance or some other small creature seeking sanctuary from the raw coldness of winter.

The leaves of the rhododendrons or dendyrodens as Jacky called them, though limp and darkened by frost, were easy to spot. There were banks of these overgrown shrubs along one side of the track on which they were now standing, planted they had been told to decorate what would have been a much wider roadway when a large country house had been in occupation around here somewhere. However, although the youngsters had searched the area from time to time, they had failed to discover any clues to its one time location. They had come to the conclusion, reluctantly, that this substantial residence had simply been swallowed up and digested by vegetation, along with the humble abodes of the ancient villagers who had lived and died somewhere within this wood. The latter, according to local legend, had been victims of the bubonic plague that had ravaged its way through country after country back in the dark ages.

There was no sign of the bluebells, which in springtime would fill the big wood with colour and perfume. It was hard to imagine that at this very moment, each potential flower and elongated leaf would be resting within its tiny white bulb, ready to respond to that specific trigger, which would set each plant off on its perpetual cycle of growth, decline, decay and suspension. Dorothy always referred to them as blubbels and it was while she had been searching fruitlessly for them one raw winter's day that she had tripped and fallen into the slush and muddy water of a tractor rut. The older girls had rushed to her aid and had sponged her down as best they could, then hurried her along to Deffy and Bill's old hut, where the two old men, having summed up the situation in a glance, soon had things under control. Her outer garments had been removed and she had been hurriedly wrapped in an old piece of towelling and sat down beside the stove to keep warm while her muddied clothes had been cleaned and put to dry around her. Sally had not forgotten nor ever would, the taste of the hot sweet tea dished up to them that day in those strange frog-green tin mugs of theirs, or Bill's words as he had handed it to them. 'Warm the cockles of yer 'eart that will,' he'd said his eyes sparkling. At least that particular accident would not occur today, not with the ground so dry, and hard as Newgate's Knocker.

Luckily, the holly trees this year were laden with enough berries to satisfy the hunger of the largest flocks of birds, so the few branches the girls were selecting for their traditional Christmas decorations was not about to make one ha'p'orth of difference to them they told themselves. Pat and Sally set to with secateurs and, with a measure of caution, began selecting then clipping away enough of the prickly decoration to decorate both kitchen and front room. It took a bit more time for them to search for and carefully select a couple of small pieces dripping with berries with which to decorate the Christmas puddings, and these they passed over to the little ones for safe keeping. Then it was time to make their way home, with a brief stop at the little hut on the way.

It was Dorothy who spotted the scutty, or Jenny Wren in the leaf litter at the edge of the wood, and she stopped suddenly and stood on silent tip toe, pointing towards the little creature as it furtled about in the undergrowth. It seemed unaware of or perhaps unconcerned by their presence, its hunger driven forage overriding its fear of potential predators it seemed. It was still on its search for a hibernating grub or hardy insect two, to assuage its hunger pangs, when they moved reluctantly away. It was the first thing they mentioned when Bill opened the door to them.

Silence had broken out amongst them by the time they reached the bottom edge of the field, and continued as they climbed over the stile and on to the stiff grass, shuffling the holly from hand to hand as they did so. As they moved across the field, strangely devoid now of foraging chickens, Sally glanced upwards, searching the cold blue heavens for the sight and haunting cry of the skeins of wild geese that in cold winter weather, rode invisible/indiscernible pathways high above the ground. However, apart from a solitary crow and a ew unidentifiable small brown birds, there was little else to disturb the cold wide expanse of wintry landscape.

Pat opened the back gate, then hurried on ahead to open the copper-house door, where they set the holly carefully down beside the crock, which was now full of eggs and covered with that Waterglass or Isinglass preservative stuff. They removed their gloves as they walked towards the scullery door, and rubbed the tips of their fingers together to restore the circulation in the one and only part of their body that was not warm as toast. As they rounded the corner, they sniffed appreciatively, all at once conscious of their hunger as the aroma of roasting sausages hit their nostrils. "Yum, yum," Sally said out loud, as she anticipated of the feast of sausage, mash, beans and greens to come. And she could see the same expression reflected in the eyes of her sisters.

"Before you take your clothes off, perhaps one of you would pop down to the bottom shed and call your dad for dinner," said mum as they entered the kitchen. "He's down there making up replacements for a couple those of nesting boxes in the chicken sheds, and not before time he reckons. Even so, it must be freezing down there and all he's had all morning is one cup of tea and he didn't take his time over that either."

Sally did not hesitate, which was unusual for her. It would not take her more than a couple of minutes to get down there and back again, she told herself, and the sooner she did the deed, the sooner she would be able to assuage her hunger. She could hear the tip tap of a hammer as she approached the shed, and as she opened the door and moved noisily inside, dad turned around with a couple of nails in his mouth, and acknowledged her presence by raising his hammer. That curious box, which supposedly had been a tea caddy in its youth, was open on the bench beside him, and it was from this interesting container that he had been selecting suitable nails for this 'basic' job. It was cold as charity in here but he seemed oblivious to this. He was however, wearing a pair of those fingerless mittens she had knitted for him, she noted with some satisfaction. As she looked more closely though, she noticed they were getting a bit frayed around the edges, and made a mental note to knit him up some replacements before too long.

As she waited for him to come to a natural break, she looked around at all the paraphernalia in here, and wondered where on earth it had all come from, that battered enamel sign over there for instance. She could make out the words, ESSO. Royal Daylight Paraffin on its surface even though bits of wood had been stacked alongside. It was similar in a way to the one in Mrs Floyds shop up the road, advertising Pratts paraffin, which was even more the worse for wear. There were many pieces of ancient battered furniture, donated by various acquaintances grateful to find a home of sorts for items that were of no further use to them. One section of the long bench on which he was working, had become a permanent area for the mending of shoes, with that old iron shoe horse of his sitting solidly amongst bits of leather, boxes of nails, blakies and studs, and a box with REDFERN'S Rubber Heels stamped on it. Her eye lingered on the tin of glue or solution as they called it, the acrid fumes of which were strangely addictive. Just how much so was brought home to dad just a short time ago, when he had looked up from what he was doing, to find Jacky swaying over the open tin. Since then, it had been relegated to the back of the bench, and the girls were not allowed anywhere near the stuff. The mending of shoes was not one of dad's favourite chores and that was putting it mildly. However, although he moaned and groaned about this relentless and ongoing job, he always managed somehow to keep their shoes in a reasonable state of repair, as often as not she thought grimly, with an excessive use of blakies and studs, which he tip tapped into neat shiny crescents around heels and toes.

The toboggan she could see hanging from those thick horizontal supports at the far side of the shed had been made and given to them by Uncle Frank of course, and what fun they had had with the thing. If this cold weather continued and they got an appreciable fall of snow, it would be taken down pronto and pressed into service that was for sure. She remembered the expressions of fear, excitement and sheer delight on the faces of Ethel and Derek Thomas, as they had careered down the field at speed and out of control in the thing and straight into the hedge at the bottom. These two youngsters and their dad, had moved into one of the Black Brooks cottages with their Aunty, Mrs Petty after their mum died, and to start with had been very quiet and withdrawn. Perhaps being encouraged to join in the exploits, the general rough and tumble of the youngsters in and around the area had helped them to cope. She hoped so. Anyway, a major break-through she reckoned was when Pat had introduced them to that favourite tongue twister of theirs: 'We rattled our bottles in Rollaky's Yard. We rattled bottles an' all.' They had fallen about with helpless laughter, and it had continued to be their favourite ditty.

Dad was on his feet now she suddenly noticed, and grinned as she spied a dewdrop hanging from the end of his nose. Would he realise and catch it in his old hankie before it dropped off, she asked herself then decided, probably not.

His nose must be numb by now she reckoned, and without feeling he'd have no idea it was there. And she certainly was not about to tell him.

As they moved thankfully into the comparative warmth of the scullery, Sally noticed the iron propped up and cooling off at the end of the draining board, and as she walked through the doors and into the kitchen, she could see that old blanket still covering the small table in front of the window. Mum had been ironing, which was not one of her favourite chores. It looked as though, having seen them walking up across the field, she had abandoned that chore and had hastily moved the pile of sundry items to the far end of the table while she prepared to dish up the dinner. Sally noticed that on top of the pile, was one of Betty's embroidered tablecloths, and she could see at a glance that mum had taken particular care over this item. No doubt it would soon find its way into the front room and onto the large circular table in there, where the skill and patience that went into this intricately embroidered work of art, would be seen in its full glory. Her older sisters were very clever, she told herself.

A combination of fresh air, exercise and full stomach's had proved too much for the little ones who were now taking an unaccustomed forty winks. Pat and Sally, also weary from the exertions of the morning, settled down to do a bit of knitting and reading. Sally was reading 'A Christmas Carol' by Charles Dickens, described by Jumbo James as 'a ghost story and a moral tale. An indictment of 19th Century values' or some such thing he'd said. He did sound a bit like dad at times. Whatever, Charles Dickens always brought his characters to life, and particularly here she thought to herself. The stingy Ebenezer Scrooge for instance, with his conscience manifesting itself in visions of ghosts past, present and yet to come, with that particularly frightening visitation by the ghost of Jacob Marley. Just the thought of coming face to face with that shrunk shank and those ghostly apparitions, was enough to scare the living daylights out of her. His clerk, the underpaid and unappreciated Bob Cratchit on the other hand, filled her with awe and downright admiration. As she followed this small and kindly and mild of manner man through the pages of the book, she could not help but marvel at his stoic acceptance of his lot in life; the downbeat, philosophical way he dealt with the trials and tribulations that came his way.

And then there was Tiny Tim. Her heart went out to this little fellow who bore the pain and constraints of his crippled body with a forbearance that brought a lump to her throat. He was part and parcel of this indictment of 19th Century values, experienced by Charles Dickens and described by Jumbo James of course. This was just another example of the conditioning of poor folk to meekly accept the hardships of their lives; a by the Grace of God or consequence of lowly birth sort of thing she thought as she put the book down slowly and reached for her knitting.

Once they had had their tea and the washing up had been done, the girls sat at the far end of the kitchen and with the aid of a candle and a bit of bare wall, played the hand shadow pattern game. Pat in particular had got this game to a fine art, and Dorothy and Jacky were enthralled with the various animal shapes, the rabbits, cockerels the talking dogs, and even more so with the sabre tooth tiger, that she portrayed. When it came to their turn the results were even more interesting, with some of their shadow shapes obscure to say the least. Others however, were quite hilarious with one open mouthed gargoyle and another shape looking for all the world like the mad hatter in Alice in Wonderland, making them all giggle uncontrollably.

After a while, they turned to another favourite pastime especially with the little ones, which was to make melody with the aid of a comb and a piece of tissue paper. Sally kept out of this one. For some reason, the movement of her mouth along the comb made her lips tickle and caused her eyes to water, which was a shame really. She reckoned she could have created some decent tunes given half a chance. It was while they were in the throes of this game, that Hilary came through the doorway, and Dorothy and Jacky were on their feet in a flash and across the room to hug her. Very little persuasion was needed to get her into this game, and as Sally got up to get her overnight bag ready, sat down immediately in the chair she had vacated.

Hilary and Sally chatted away as they walked down the field, flashing the torch around from time to time out of habit rather than necessity. They knew this journey like the back of their hands. Sally was in a good mood and rightly so she told herself. Christmas was just around the corner, and she was going to attend Midnight Mass at the Church for the very first time, which was exciting to say the least. It was not that her faith was that profound, she still found it difficult to visualise some God like figure with dominion over all the earth, as it said in the Bible. Jesus however, she had no difficulty with. From as far back as she could remember he had been her hero. She had never suffered one moment of doubt about the existence of this extraordinary being, and after all it was his birthday they would be celebrating. As far as she was concerned he'd never died; he was around still in various disguises. Also of course there was the novelty and excitement of being out that late at night.

"There must be a million stars up there at the very least," she commented as she flashed the torch in the direction her thoughts had taken her.

"I wonder if anyone's counted them," Hilary replied, and for some reason they giggled, finding that concept inordinately amusing. Then their thoughts along with the flashing torch moved away from the Heavens and on to earth bound matters, with a discussion on what board and card games they'd likely be playing when Willie and Roy turned up this evening. Ludo, and a game of beat your neighbours out of doors, definitely they reckoned, and perhaps snakes and ladders. Heaven help them though they agreed if Roy should remember to bring his chess set along with him. That puzzling game always caught them out no matter how carefully they tried to cover their backs. One thought led to another and by the time they reached Windyridge, they were talking about Ken Monk, Willie's brother who, some time ago had contracted something called Infantile

Paralysis (Polio), which had left its mark on him To start with it had been mere conjecture/suggestion that he had caught this nasty disease whilst bathing in the Brooks. Very soon however, the speculation turned to a widely accepted view amongst people in and around the village that this was indeed the source of infection. Since then, the youngsters had been forbidden to put even one foot into the water, let alone splash around in it for hour after hour as they had done in the past; indeed from as far back as anyone could remember. No one questioned this order, though now and again, when the weather was hot and sticky, there was that almost overwhelming temptation to throw caution to the wind and just jump into that tantalisingly cool water. As far as they knew however, no one had ever succumbed.

Chapter 11

The wind stirred from the North and Sally shivered. It howled across the field from the big Wood as she made her way to the farm to fetch the milk, bending the coarse grass to its will. Winter had set in with a vengeance she realised as she looked towards the cold blue sky with its bits of raggedy clouds and birds that were being blown hither and thither as they tried to ride the gusty currents created by this bitingly cold wind. Right now she felt a kind of empathy with these brave little creatures, even though she knew there was no comparison between their struggle for survival and her own. She at least had a comfortable bed to sleep in and always knew where the next meal was coming from. They on the other hand, lived in a state of uncertainty. For those and most other wild creatures, life it seemed was a constant struggle against the odds. She moved her toes around in her boots and snuggled her fingers up in her mittens to minimise the effects of the cold, then set off towards the farmhouse at a tidy old pace. As she walked up the track, she searched the field to her left as she always did, for sight or sound of Mr Collins' geese, but the noisy creatures were nowhere to be seen. Some she realised were destined never to squawk again, their flesh served up and enjoyed as part of the Christmas feast, their plucking's put to one side to be made up into goose feather beds at a later date. The survivors if they knew what was good for them, would be hunkered up somewhere safe and sound and away from this cold old wind.

Thoughts of sacrificial geese turned her mind fleeting back to the festive season and for a few moments, away from the discomfort of the icy wind. She relived the experience of the Mid-night Mass, which had been all and more than she had hoped for, though as much for the magic of the hour as the ceremony itself, she admitted to herself. Luckily, the lack of sleep had not diminished in any way the enjoyment of Christmas day itself, and images from the day began popping up behind her eye lids and tumbling over themselves like characters in some old Charley Chaplin film. Then her thoughts moved on to Hilary's party on Boxing Day and she recalled in amusing detail, the silly games they had played, which though repeated year on year, still brought the same measure of excitement and anticipation with them. 'Blind man's buff' had been brought to a reluctant halt when it threatened to get out of hand, and 'pass the parcel' had been almost as wild. 'I sent a letter to my love and on the way I dropped it,' on the other hand, had been conducted in an almost leisurely fashion. Her imagination settled for a few moments on one in particular, the trembling shove ha'penny board game, and she grinned wryly as she pictured the expression of fear and excitement on the faces of the little ones as they sacrificed themselves up to this wobbly experience. Even to this day, she remembered the fluttering in her stomach as the folded scarf was tied around her eyes, and she was guided onto the talismanic board and seemingly spirited away like Aladdin on his magic carpet. She had long outgrown this particular game but her experience along with pretty well all other participants, had been captured on Mr Elkins' Brownie No. I camera. This precious object was always stored away carefully after use in the box with a picture on its side of a little man with a fat belly and lucky legs.

She stopped briefly in the farmhouse kitchen for a chat and a warm up, before making her way back home with the milk. As she made her way carefully over the stile at the top of the field, she looked across the bleak landscape, and for some reason images of the warrior Beowulf popped up into her mind's eye. This epic tale she was reading about, which told of the tussle for good over evil had fired her imagination ever since Jumbo James had introduced her to this, as he put it, 'Old English Heroic Poem, set in Scandinavia,' recently. She shivered as an image of the monster Grendel presented itself, seeing him as a mirror image of the old Ogre at Sprays Bridge who had terrorised the folk from round about, but with even more evil intent if that were possible, and always it seemed in relentless pursuit of her hero. Good must eventually conquer evil, she told herself. Beowulf must surely 'overwhelm' his nemesis and rid Hroogar the King of the Danes and his people of this demon. It seemed like the struggle for good over evil had been around from time immemorial, and would likely go on forever and ever.

As she hurried through the back gate, she looked towards the sycamore trees with their bare branches moving around like a troupe of naked clowns. Then as she took a backward glance over her shoulder and out over the angry windswept landscape, she noticed that darkly ominous clouds had begun to gobble up the cold blue sky. The dark days of winter had arrived with a vengeance, and no mistake. Not that she was complaining. There was something about these days of biting winds and grey, moody, snow laden skies that appealed to her. If it were not for those blasted chilblains, and the draughts that whistled through the air bricks around the house, plus one or two other minor discomforts, like freezing temperatures in the bedrooms, thankfully alleviated somewhat by those hot flannel covered bricks mum placed in their beds, it would be her second favourite season. Fortunately, picking sprouts was not one of her chores, and for that she was eternally grateful. All too often, she had seen her dad trying to rub the life back into his fingers as he came through the kitchen door after plonking down a bucket of frozen sprouts onto the scullery floor, and he was no wimp. She placed the containers of milk carefully onto the draining board in the scullery with a sigh of relief. What she needed now more than anything was a decent mug full of steaming cocoa.

**

Hilary, Pat and Sally hurried up Crazy Lane towards the Chapel, their breath vaporising briefly before being blown away from their lips on the cold east wind. They were trying to memorise the words and mimic the Cockney accent Uncle Fred assumed when reciting the 'Brown Boots' song to them - with varying degrees of success. "Braan boots I ask yer, braa-a-an boots. Fancy goin' to a funeral in braan boots," they sang in unison. Then the words got a bit raggedy until they got to the line, 'e gived is other boots away,' where the reason for his sacrilegious behaviour, implicit in those few significant words became clear. The message was not lost on them and these words were recited almost reverently. They paused briefly at the top of the lane to get their breath back, and stood beside the farm gate and looked out over the barren landscape, where in the far and middle distance, the trunks of oak trees were silhouetted blackly against the gun metal sky. Then they turned away and within a couple of minutes, were shivering their way into the comparative warmth of the little room adjacent to the Chapel. Miss Smith and Olive were already there, but for once, they were the first of the youngsters to arrive, and hesitated for a few moments before removing their coats, hats and scarves. It was not long however, before sudden draughts from the opening door, announced the arrival of others.

After a short prayer and a hymn, they got down to the important business of ironing out a couple of minor hiccups in readiness for their next performance of the 'Waxworks' play, scheduled to take place in Robertsbridge next Saturday.

The crisp white sheets for this show were already stacked in neat piles on the side table, waiting to be loaded into Miss Smith's little old motor car. Sally loved the journey to this small, low lying market town with its habit of flooding during any appreciable fall of rain. She did not mind being packed like the proverbial sardine into one or other of the cars that ferried then to and fro, just as long as she was able to move her neck far enough around to get a glimpse of the twin fir trees along the way. She was not superstitious of course, that was for the likes of grownups. She just had this   conviction that something nasty would occur if she failed to perform certain rituals.

In the first show, which had taken place in the village hall in Sedlescombe, the old air raid rattle, used by Hilary to announce each exhibit, had stiffened up, and by the end of the performance she was visibly sweating with the effort of trying to turn the thing. Just a bit of soap around the handle would put that to rights, Miss Smith reckoned. Another shortcoming to be addressed was the positioning of the chairs, where more room was needed around each one to allow easier access for Hilary the seller and Keith Card, the prospective buyer of this collection, and would give the youngsters more room in which to perform their jerky movements. For some reason, Hilary's exaggerated two-handed struggle with the massive old iron key used to animate her waxwork dummies had caused a lot of merriment amongst the audience. To Sally however, this bit of rusty old iron exuded a kind of malevolence. She imagined it having been used in some deep dark dungeon in the olden days, and just looking at it reminded her of the chamber of horrors at Madame Tausaud's. Still, as long as folk continued to see the funny side of the whole charade that was fine by her.

By the end of the afternoon, they were warm as toast and feeling reasonably optimistic about the next show. An added bonus was the mugs of fortifying hot cocoa Mrs Smith had provided to sustain them on their homeward journey. As Sally supped her cocoa, hands clasped comfortably around the vessel, she offered up a silent word of thanks to Mr Farrow's cows for providing the milk for this special treat, and another to whoever had grown and ground the beans.

A scene of leaden skies and brooding silence, met the eyes and ears of the youngsters as they left the comparative warmth of the little room. The bitingly cold north easterly that had bedevilled them on the outward journey had dropped away. The cold now had an edge to it, with that characteristic and unmistakable tingling in their nostrils that announced the imminent arrival of a tidy bit of snow. Even as they lingered in the lane outside for their usual bit of chit-chat before going their separate ways, they knew that within the next hour or two, the first few thick flakes of snow would be drifting lazily down, and that by morning they would be looking out over a vast white landscape. The first appreciable fall of snow always triggered off a mood of excited anticipation amongst the youngsters, with few if any not smitten by the sheer magic of it all. Any small inconveniences, like frozen toes and fingers would soon be overcome or forgotten about as they snow balled and tobogganed or perhaps best of all, stepped out onto their mirror like and awesome slide down Chapel Hill

The girls hurried up the field towards the glow from the kitchen window. The weather was closing in more and more around them, and the light from the trusty old oil lamp was a welcoming oasis in the fast gathering gloom. The cold certainly put an edge on the appetite, Sally thought to herself as she opened the top gate, and her mouth watered as she anticipated tucking into the piles of cheesy egg they were having for tea, accompanied as always, by thick slices of bread and butter. She for one was more than ready to do justice to the grub.

Chapter 12

After the snow and bitingly cold winds of deepest winter, it was a relief when a rise in temperature towards the end of February brought a spell of wet and windy weather. The constant mud across the field, reflected in the leaden skies bore witness to this change, as did the untidy heap of muddy wellies piled up against and around the scullery door. Today however, the sun had decided to show its face, and there was a palpable sigh of relief from the cold, wet earth and from the cat who having found a sunny spot near the greenhouse, was sitting there extracting every last drop of warmth from the thin wintry sunshine. The girls were on a mission. They planned to take advantage of the half decent weather plus Hilary's rare Saturday off work, and cycle through to Bodiam to explore the ruins of its ancient Castle. They had been planning this trip for ages, having become familiar with the route and the outlines of this impressive structure on their trips to and from the hop fields over the years. Sally was now on her way to give the bicycles a once over, looking in particular for flat or soft tyres, a sure sign if there ever was one of a dreaded fast or worse still, a slow puncture. She glanced idly towards the sycamore trees as she made her way around the house then stopped suddenly in her tracks as something caught her eye. The spider's webs criss-crossing the windows of the shed over there, shimmered like silver threads as they caught the rays of the weak morning sunshine, and she sighed. Another magical moment to be stored away, along with the haunting cry of wild geese as they flew across a snow threatening sky, to counteract those old nightmares that plagued her from time to time, she thought to herself as she hurriedly gathered her thoughts and brought her attention back to what she was here for.

The fish paste sandwiches were already made up and packed away in dad's old rucksack by the time Hilary arrived, along with thick chunks of fruit cake. And surprise, surprise, dad had given them some of his best John Standish apples to refresh themselves with on the journey. All the girls needed to do now, was to fill a couple of bottles with the cold, sweet tea that mum had left in a jug on the side table and they would be ready to go.

As Pat, Hilary and Sally free-wheeled down the field, the mud escaping from the mud-guards on their bicycles splattered against their legs, but they hardly noticed. The thick socks they were wearing took most of it anyway. They were more concerned with avoiding the few brave hens that were now scratching through the soggy grass, searching for the odd worm or grub to supplement their diet of layers mash or whatever it was that dad was feeding them with right now. They cycled up through the village, noting idly but without comment, that the pump seats were unoccupied. Maybe later in the day a few brave souls would chance their bums to a soggy embrace with the rain soaked wood, but for now this favourite watering place stood in uncharacteristic solitary mode.

The first topic of conversation as they wheeled their bikes up Church Hill was the Waxwork play, or rather the surprising and favourable reception the youngsters had received from the various and varied audiences they had played to in and around the area. Luckily the inclement weather, the heavy falls of snow followed closely by a prolonged spell of wet and windy weather, had not brought about the cancellation of even one performance. True, the journey to and from Robertsbridge had been hairy to say the least, but exciting all the same for that, with the clanking of the chains on the wheels of Miss Smith's motor ringing in their ears as she had driven the little old thing slowly and carefully along the snow bound country lanes. They had won first prize for their performance in this little market town and had been congratulated for the originality of the subject, and for the entertaining and at times, amusing enactment of it. Hilary and Keith as seller and prospective buyer, and Daniel as the Parson, had been singled out for a special word praise. Daniel, the last waxwork to be unveiled and the only one to be given a voice, was particularly impressive and always brought forth a few stifled chuckles from the audience. Once he had clicked shakily into action, he raised his right arm in a short shaky open palmed salute, then offered up the benediction, 'God be with you' with mock solemnity albeit in a most suitable monotone. The girls tried, but as always failed to get the right intonation into this simple statement. It was quite frustrating. However, the conversation soon moved on and by the time they reached the top of the hill, they were well into a discussion on lucky symbols. How for instance did the luck of a four leaf clover compare with that of a rabbit's foot, they wondered There was no contest on this one as far as Pat was concerned. She would trust her luck to a piece of clover any old time she said. It smelled sweeter than a rabbit's foot and would keep for ages in an egg-cup of water, or even longer pressed between the pages of a large book.

As they peddled up the road towards Hurst Lane, Sally looked instinctively towards the house where old Beelzebub lived, but he was nowhere to be seen. He still gave them a wide berth, if he spotted them in time, even though it had been ages since they had chanted the bit of chuff, chuff doggerel at him. But then who could blame him really, she admitted rather shame-facedly to herself. They had given him a hard time for a while. Further on, she looked in the direction of a large house where old Mr Swanson lived. Luckily he too was nowhere to be seen. She could not stand the man.

At the Cripp's Corner junction they stopped and straddled their bikes for a few moments, as they contemplated calling into Mr Brann's shop to pass the time of day with the kindly old shopkeeper, who was also Hilary's employer, then decided against it. As Hilary pointed out, he would be busy at this time of day and would not really want them cluttering up his little shop. Once they had made the decision, they set their sights on the incline ahead, and peddled off towards Staplecross. The weather vanes on top of the Oast Houses along the way were barely moving, Sally noticed as she glanced to her left. Then as she looked further out over the rolling landscape, she spotted horses on the far away horizon, looking pale, almost transparent in the silver wintry sunshine. The magical moment was brought to a sudden and untimely end as she began to wobble, and she hurriedly brought her eyes and attention back on to the road ahead, thanking her lucky stars as she did so, that she had chosen to bring up the rear. She should have learned her lesson by now, she told herself, remembering the day she had stuck dad's old gardening fork through her wellie and into her foot. She had been day-dreaming then of course, same as now. One of the tines had gone clean down between her big toe and the next one and was oozing by the time she removed her sock. Mum had bathed the wound gently with one of her concoctions, and luckily it had healed in no time at all. She still had quite a scar there though to remind her of the incident, and would probably carry it to her grave she told herself solemnly.

The ruins of the old Castle they had caught tantalising glimpses of from the top road, came into full view as they free-wheeled down the last few hundred yards of the meandering hill into Bodiam. They hopped off their bikes when they came to the humpity bridge, parked them alongside and made their way towards the gateway and into the vast grounds surrounding the Castle itself.

As far as they could make out the place was deserted, apart from a few unidentifiable birds wheeling around, then dipping and diving to investigate a possible source of food no doubt. They paused for a few seconds on the way across the grass to investigate an observation bunker, a relic from one of the wars they reckoned. To them the squat building with its concrete mantle, looked modern yet paradoxically dated; incongruous and out of place in these surroundings. They eventually came to and walked across a bridge spanning the moat then paused briefly beneath the massive archway, which clearly had seen better days. Even in this state of crumbling decay however, they could see how heavily fortified the area around here would have been in its hey-day. They knew that any intruders, clever, brave or foolhardy enough to have breached the first lines of defence, would have had all kinds of unimaginable things rained down upon them from above. Sally shivered as her imagination once again got the better of her, and removing herself from the danger area at a tidy old pace, walked on and into a scene of partial walls, vanished ceilings and huge chunks of fallen masonry.

They stood for a while in silent study of what was left of this now derelict monument, from the regular apertures around its vast walls where doors and windows would have been, up to the ancient battlements far and away above their heads. Though ransacked and plundered, and weathered by centuries of wind and rain, this symbol of medieval strength and status, still retained an air of dignified grandeur. There was also a strange feeling of timelessness here somehow.

After a while, they began to move around, investigating various crooks, crannies and crevices, eventually coming across a large aperture leading onto a spiral of narrow, almost vertical stone steps. With hardly a moment's hesitation, they moved towards the stairway, and offered up the safety of their very life and limbs to the vagaries of fate - or some such thing. Many of the steps leading up and around the spiralling staircase, were worn away or broken, and it was with due care and attention to the placement of one foot after the other, that they made way up and away to goodness only knew where.

Sally's heart began to race as she followed Pat and Hilary up the stairway, not with exertion but with exhilaration. Climbing trees, even the most tricky, was a doddle compared to the challenges presented by this slowly disintegrating man made structure she thought. It was not just a question of finding a safe foot hold, but also deciding what the devil to hold on to. They stopped every so often, to re-evaluate the situation, well aware that it was not just the climbing but the descending that they had to take into account. Soon the way ahead became particularly ill-defined and they decided that it was just too dangerous to proceed, enough was enough. They shuffled around then huddled up together on a narrow ledge and looked up towards the battlements, still way above their heads. Bats, with their ancient folk-law connections, and with whom she had a love hate relationship, would certainly feel at home up there, Sally thought to herself, as she craned her neck to get a better view. And bad tempered old crows who seemed to have a hate, hate relationship with just about anything. Reluctantly, they turned away from contemplation of this fine example of crenulated defence, and with Sally now in the lead, began to make their way back down on to firm ground again, wisely giving up any pretence of trying to emulate mountain goats, and sliding back down on their bums for most of the way.

They lingered in and around this ancient pile of stones for a while, unable somehow to drag themselves away from its curious, singular embrace. As Sally looked around, she tried to reconcile the past with the here and now, finding it difficult to imagine that this derelict Castle had once been animated, a hive of activity. Back in the dim and distant past however, according to Jumbo James, aristocratic families had lived and died, dined and cavorted within its massive stone walls. Oh to have been a fly on the wall in those long ago, far away days of yore.

As they left the crumbling scene of Medieval life and prosperity, Sally could not resist glancing back over her shoulder from time to time to imprint this extraordinary place indelibly into her mind and imagination. Once right outside however, as she cast her eyes over the expanse of gentle countryside around them, she breathed an audible sigh of relief. There was no contest between any structure, however grand, and the living breathing countryside around her. Especially now that winter, having almost fulfilled its crucial cycle of rest and rejuvenation, was being nudged slowly and surely out of the way by spring. Soon hedges and ditches, woods and meadows would come alive with the sights and sounds, and optimism of an awakening landscape, with the magical notes of the dawn chorus to serenade them. What more could you wish for.

As they walked back across the wet grassy ground, Hilary looked at her watch, or rather the one she had borrowed from her dad, and was surprised as they all were, to discover that it was only just coming up to mid-day. It seemed ages ago that they had first offered up their bodies and minds to the vagaries of that ancient monument. Anyway, they were hungry and as the old bunker was close at hand, it seemed as good a place as any to sit and sup their grub.

Once settled and vaguely comfortable, Sally shuffled about in her rucksack and brought out the pack of sandwiches, pulled the contents carefully apart and handed them around. No one seemed to care how squashed and travel weary they were, or even to notice the small greasy globs of butter that were now decorating the brown paper bag in which they'd been stored. They just tucked in with healthy appetites, absorbing the accumulation of dust or rather the mud of antiquity on their hands, along with their delicious fish paste sandwiches.

As they munched away, they looked towards the river Rother wending it way through the valley beneath them, and tried to imagine how it would have looked in the olden days. According to Jumbo James, it had been wide and deep enough at one time to accommodate quite large boats, just like the river Brede through Sedlescombe had been. A Viking long boat would have had no trouble navigating its way along either waterway, he said. Mostly though it would have been used to carry general merchandise, like wheat and barley, bundles of sheep's wool and other day to day requirements, like tallow and vegetables and perhaps oils of various kinds and descriptions. Certainly, the occupants of the Castle here would have needed a regular supply of food, a lot of which would not have been available locally. Now both these waterways had dwindled to mere streams, where even in a small dinghy you would be hard pushed to negotiate their narrow confines, where, as Hilary remarked, 'you would need to keep your elbows well in.'

Next on the menu, were the John Standish apples, which before they devoured they decided to play three up with. With dad's beady eye several miles away, this was just too good an opportunity to miss. Hilary just had the edge when it came to accuracy and dexterity in this popular sport, with Pat and Sally not far behind, and before long they were taking it turns to demonstrate their skill in this game of throw and catch. There were a few anxious moments but by the end of the half hour or so of this energetic game, they congratulated themselves for having kept the apples in circulation at all times, and had thus protected them from any contact with the ground – just. Before they sank their teeth through the red and yellow skin and into the juicy flesh beneath, they gave them a bit of spit and polish then quietly munched away on the favourite item on their menu.

Once they had eaten their apples and taken a sip or two of the cold sweet tea, they decided that this was as good a time as any to try their luck, and test their mental map reading abilities on finding an alternative route home. After all, it was still early with plenty of daylight left to allow for a slight deviation here and there, they told themselves. Having made the decision, they hurried back to the humpity bridge, turned their bikes around and prepared themselves for the challenge ahead. 'An easy foot in an easy shoe, who cares a tuppeny dam where the road leads to.' Sally recited to herself as she pushed hard down on the pedals and rode off in the wake of her sisters, ignoring any slight misgivings she might have had.

Hilary it seemed, had a rough idea where they were going, and with Pat and Sally more than willing to follow her lead, they set off into the unknown. After a while, they found themselves on a stretch of undulating roadway with tall hedges and woods on either side, that seemed to go on forever, and they all breathed an audible sigh of relief when at long last this gloomy and rather foreboding stretch of road gave way to a view of open countryside.

They continued for what seemed mile after mile, passing a scattering of cottages and a village or two, then all at once, having spotted a decent vantage point, they came to a sudden halt. After propping their bikes up against the hedge, they moved towards a rusty old gate, which sported an even rustier old chain, and leaned over the thing to try to get their bearings.

They could see for miles and once Sally realised that Hilary had figured out approximately where they were, felt free to scan the countryside around them. Immediately her eye was drawn towards an area of tall pines and shrubby growth, through which a large imposing building could be defined. Even from this distance the house had a closed look about it, unlike Sylvian, which seemed to smile a welcome to one and all. She was sure it was hiding some dark secret and was haunted, and she wondered who on earth would choose to live in such an atmosphere of isolation and foreboding. Perhaps the place was guarded by a massive hound, with eyes as big as saucers, like the one Granny Sansom terrified the life out of them with when they were little. She felt the hairs stand up on the back of her neck at the memory and quickly removed her eyes and imagination away from such reflections, bringing her attention closer to where they were standing. It was only then that she noticed the rickety stile at the side of the gate, and beside it and partially obscured by hedge and coarse grass, a lump of granite with the word 'Footpath' carved into its ancient surface. Sally thought immediately of the couple, friends of mum and dad's from way back, who visited Sylvian on a fairly regular basis to walk and keep open what they called, 'ancient rights of way.' Some days they would use a bus or train to transport them to a particular area. At other times they would get up at the crack of dawn, pack their iron rations into small back-packs, and just walk until darkness drove them homeward. However, no matter how weary they were at the end of the day, they always found time and enough energy to pore over complicated maps and work out a route for the next day's foray. They were thin as lathes the pair of them, and yet they could eat even herself and her sisters under the table, which was saying something.

Thinking of visitors to Sylvian, reminded her that Aunty Nellie and family would be coming down for the Easter holidays, which was not that far away now, and this is where she and her sisters would be bringing Peggy and Eddie on one of those days, that was for sure. They relished a good long bike ride, and if their reaction to Pevensey Castle was anything to go by, visiting old castles was right up their street. She couldn't wait to see the expression on their faces when they looked around Bodiam Castle for the first time.

If she remembered rightly, Mrs Watson and her daughter Margaret were planning to visit soon after. They always arrived at around six thirty in the evening in their impressive motor car with Margaret very firmly in the driving seat. Mrs Watson was too old to drive anyway, and so tiny she would have been hard put to see above the steering wheel. For obvious reasons the journey from Croydon was always taken in easy stages, yet in spite of this, the time of their arrival could be estimated to within ten or fifteen minutes. This predictability meant that a fresh brew, set up on a tray with a freshly starched cloth on its surface, and accompanied by the obligatory thin china cups and saucers, would be ready and waiting for them. Alongside this would be fingers of shortbread or thin slices of fruit cake all neatly arranged on doily covered plates. When their visits coincided with the cucumber season, Mrs Watson always insisted on cucumber sandwiches for tea. This strange vegetable skinned then sliced as impossibly thinly as the bread and butter that accompanied it, was not a particular favourite with the girls. It tasted of nothing as far as they were concerned and yet perversely had a slightly bitter tang.

Now that little old motor car of The Watson's was something else. Though modest on the outside, it was surprisingly roomy inside and Margaret had ferried several youngsters comfortably to Rye and back in it on one occasion. Sally remembered the trip very well, why wouldn't she? A ride in a motor-car was a rare enough occurrence on its own, but an added bonus had been the sensation of sitting upright and proudly in the dicky seat at the back, alongside Pat, on that outward journey. The whole day in fact had been very memorable. They had walked along a succession of cobbled streets and narrow alleyways in Rye, absorbing the history of the place, while admiring the quaint and fascinating facades of its ancient buildings. They had sipped tea and nibbled cake in a posh restaurant, with Margaret enthusing about this small bustling town as she called it, with its feet set firmly and securely in the past. When she had begun to talk about the Wood family, those special friends of hers, Sally had pricked her ears up. They would be thrilled to bits with this place, she had said. Now as Sally leaned on the old gate, along with her sisters, it suddenly impacted on her that in a few months' time, she would be meeting the Wood Family for the very first time and knew, without a shadow of doubt, that this encounter would be something very nearly as special as meeting Hilary for the first time. That it had something to do with the three boys in the family, Donald, Hamish and Gavin had crossed her mind. She knew however, with a deep down certainty, that it went much deeper than this.

She suddenly came out of her reverie with Pat shuffling around in the rucksack and uttering the magic words, fruit-cake. "We'll have a cochel now to keep us going and eat the rest later," she mumbled as she lifted the crumpled bag and its contents free from its confines. "Just what the Doctor ordered," she said as she carefully opened it up and ladled its travel weary contents into Hilary and Sally's open hands. "Sorry it's in bits, but it'll taste just as good," she added as she scooped up a good handful for herself. Then they set too, remoulding the crumbs into biteable chunks with nimble fingers, and in no time at all were transferring them from hand to mouth with a rhythm and expertise, born out of years of practice. After they had licked the residual crumbs from their hands, they took a swig or two of cold tea, repacked the bag and were up and away forthwith, conscious all at once of the long trek ahead of them.

It was not long before the terrain began to change. From a long lonely road with little or no sign of habitation, a few isolated cottages began to dot the wayside verges, gradually increasing into the density of a small village. In the windows of one of the cottages alongside, were red chenille curtains with fringed pelmets, just like the ones in Mrs Harris's cottage on the village green, Sally noticed as she rode slowly passed. When she had a home of her own, she would decorate the windows in just the same way, she told herself. They spotted the little shop immediately and after dismounting and propping their bikes up against a wall, made their way towards the entrance. Jempson's as the store was called, was a veritable Aladdin's cave. It was a cross between Mrs Floyd's shop in Kent Street and Aunty Lylie's mart in Croydon, albeit a whole lot better organised and more upmarket. For a start, there were siphons of soda water here that would never have graced the counter of the other two, and it smelled a whole lot sweeter too. The adverts here were something else, Sally thought as she looked around, her eyes alighting on one in particular. 'Typhoo Tipp's Tea, 6d a packet (1/4lb). Relieves indigestion. Tannin – less. Leaf no stalk,' it announced, and with it, a picture of a Lady in a red dress with a large hat and an even larger parasol, that as old Fred would have said, 'could charm them birds orf them ther trees.' Her favourite advert was here as well, she noticed. There was the little girl and her grandmother, layered up in old fashioned garments and strange lacy hats, sitting at the table obviously enjoying a cup of tea. The old fashioned pattern on the table cloth was echoed in the china cups and saucers carefully balanced in the hands of the rosy cheeked duo, and up in the right hand corner was written just one word, MAZAWATTEE, which said it all for her. Then another couple of posters caught her eye. There were two young girls on one, both wearing crisp white pinafore's over long frocks, their curly tresses topped with floppy hats, and both were fussing over and feeding fluffy bunnies with some unidentifiable herbage. In the other, a young girl in similar attire, was kneeling down, her arms affectionately around the neck of a little black and white dog. Both posters were reminiscent of the Pears Soap advertisements she had seen from time to time.

She turned from contemplation of these works of art and advertisement suddenly aware that Pat and Hilary were about to choose between sherbet dabs and liquorice sticks to supplement the few bits of fruit cake they had left. "Sherbet dabs," she uttered without any hesitation and breathed a sigh of relief when Hilary grinned and placed three of the wee yellow parcels alongside the bottle of drink she was purchasing. Whew she thought, mentally drawing the back of her hand across her forehead. If she'd been a couple of seconds later, she could have spent the journey home sucking and chewing on those fibrous old liquorice sticks. It did not bear thinking about. And another satisfactory outcome here she suddenly realised was that Mr Phillips sold the same brand of drink as the one Hilary had just purchased. Therefore, she would be able to take the empty bottle back to him and get her money refunded. How was that for a bit of luck? She turned away, feeling quite satisfied with the whole proceedings, and spent the short time before their departure just wandering around this interesting store.

"There should be a right hand turning somewhere not far along this road," said Hilary as they retrieved their bicycles from against the wall and wheeled them back onto the lane. "We've still a long way to go, but once we find that lane, it'll all be plain sailing and so forth, no worries," she added. Her optimism was contagious, and they set off to tackle the long journey ahead quite happily and with renewed vigour.

They reached the crucial turning in no time at all and were soon peddling off down a lonely lane with breathtaking views over the open countryside. They were on a roll now and with their iron rations stored safely in their back-packs were, they told themselves, ready for anything. After a while, the open aspect gave way to an area of woodland, reminding Sally of a melancholy ditty that was almost as close to her heart as 'Grey's Elegy.' 'Lonely woods, with path's dim and silent. A haunt of peace, for weary hearted. There's healing in your shade and in your stillness balm, ' she began. Then as she began to silently mouth the words, 'here all who seek repose from the world's strife and clamour,' she saw in her mind's eye, that almost indiscernible mound on the far side of the Churchyard at Sedlescombe. All at once the trees that grew in and around the humble resting place of her little sister, the Aspen in particular, took on an even greater significance. Trees were special she had always known that. Right here and now though, she began to understand and appreciate the scope of their guardianship and protection, and she silently thanked them from the bottom of her heart for it.

After another mile or two of rhythmic peddling and sporadic chatter, the terrain changed once again, and they found themselves looking out over a landscape of small hedged fields, with a few scrubby oaks dotted here and there. It was time for a tiddle, a drink and a bit of light refreshment, in that order they decided and began to look around for a suitable spot to tarry a while. They soon spotted the ideal place, in the shape of a sturdy farm gate set into a thick hedge of hawthorn. Having parked their bikes, they were soon up and over the gate and squatting down behind the hedge for the first wee since leaving home, and it was more by luck than judgement that their bums escaped a painful assault from the bits of raggedy stinging nettle nearby. After adjusting their clothing, they hopped back over the gate to avail themselves of the next item on the agenda, and were soon passing the bottle of drink around from hand to hand, slurping noisily of its contents. It did not take long to finish off the remnants of fruit cake, and in no time at all they were into the sherbet dabs, dipping and sucking away contentedly on the thin bits of liquorice.

Pat was the first to notice the old birds nest in the hedge beside them, definitely a blackbirds she reckoned as she moved the thin twiggy branches aside to examine the desiccated remains. Then a moments lack of concentration as she withdrew her hand from the thorny trap, resulted in a deep scratch, which immediately began to ooze small globules of blood. "Don't worry, it'll be a pig's foot in the morning," Sally piped up hastily, this oft quoted saying popping from her mouth instinctively, more to cover up her own consternation at the sudden sight of blood than with any malice of forethought. Pat however, did not appreciate this aside one little bit, and frowned as she sucked away on her wound.

This was the right moment Hilary decided, to spring her little surprise on them, and reached down and pulled a package from her bag with the other two girls looking on in idle curiosity. "How on earth," Sally began as Hilary unwrapped the elongated package to reveal three sticks of liquorice. Then the penny dropped. Obviously they had been purchased at the last moment while her attention had been elsewhere, and been stowed away with that 'sleight of hand that deceived the eye,' she thought. It was not that she was particularly fond of this stringy substance but it had to be a darn sight better than chewing on a lump of paddywack any old day, she told herself. Anyway, it was all they had to sustain them for the rest of the journey, so she accepted her portion of iron rations from her friend's hand with a measure of gratitude.

Sally had lost count as to whether she was on her second, third or even fourth wind by the time her eyes registered that they were on familiar territory. At long last they had reached the outskirts of Westfield she realised with a jolt. From a road that had seemed to go on forever, they were now within three or so miles of home, and with that certainty came a sense of relief and excitement. As they peddled up the short slope towards the main road, they were tossing up between the Spray's Bridge and Cottage Lane route home, deciding quickly and unanimously on the latter, which was a lot less challenging. Also, as Sally pointed out, she was not in the mood to risk an encounter with a wicked old ogre, albeit a dead one.

They were soon cycling along the lane towards Westfield Place, where just a few cottages and an odd farmhouse dotted the landscape. They began to look for the clumps of Guelder or swamp roses as they called them, that grew in an area of boggy ground on the edge of this estate, and hawk eyes Hilary was the first to spot them. They stopped briefly and straddling their bikes, looked over the hedge to take a closer look at these trees, which for some reason had always fascinated them. Perhaps it was something to do with the rarity of the plant in this area, or maybe it was just its curious shape that had caught their eye, who knew. What they did know, however, was that the flowers and berries that decorated this tree in early summer and autumn were poisonous, so they always put a respectable distance between themselves and this overgrown shrub.

After steering their bikes back into the lane, they pushed down lightly on the peddles, coasting along past the Big House and on towards the Lodge at the top entrance to Oakland's Park with almost effortless ease. As they approached the junction between Chapel Hill and Crazy Lane, Hilary slowed down then came to a standstill with the other two pulling up close behind. "I've just had a thought," she said. "How about if we take a detour down into the village so's I can off load this empty bottle. The shop'll be closed by now but if I leave it round the back and tell Freda, I'm sure she'll get the deposit back for me. It's not that far out of our way any old how." And why not they all agreed. After all what was a bit of easy extra mileage like this after the marathon they had just undertaken, they said as they readjusted their handlebars ever so slightly and began freewheeling down Chapel Hill.

"Blow me down, there's old Sniff and Spit going along there," said Sally pointing towards the river-bridge. We've just missed him and thank the Lord for small mercies. He's such a miserable old sod he is and he's getting worse by the day."

"Well, he's fair, you can't take that away from him," replied Hilary, pausing for effect then grinning as she glanced briefly sideways and noted Sally's puzzled expression. "At least he hates everybody! The only thing he's got any interest in evidently is that canary of his. According to Roy it's a poor moth eaten little thing, a bit like that other bird he had, the one that came to a sticky end. Anyway, thank your lucky stars he's gone now, but just think how much worse it might have been if it'd been Denis riding along the road there. He'd have seen us for sure, and make no mistake, he'd have been off his bike and waiting for us before you could say Jack Robinson. Then it would have been 'I double donkey dare you this' and 'I double donkey dare you that,' until the cows come home. That was one of our favourite expressions until he cottoned on to it, wasn't it. Now we hardly use it, do we - I wonder why."

By this time they were approaching the bridge and slowing down, and within a few seconds were over and drawing up beside the Tithe Barn. While Hilary hurried around the side of Tanyard House to deposit her empty bottle in one of the crates stacked at the back of the property, Sally held onto the temporarily vacated bicycle by its handlebars, straddling her own comfortably as she did so. As she waited, her eyes wandered up across the village green, and she noted how unusually quiet the place was. There were just a couple of villagers in sight, and although their backs were towards her as they walked up passed the Pump House, she registered their identity in an instant. Mrs Bishop whose natural culinary skills made her realise all at once how hungry she was, was heading home alongside her husband. She had often wondered how Mr Bishop's nick-name 'Newt' had come about. As far as she was concerned he looked more like a benign pixie than a lizard any old day, but there you go. Spud Taylor? No she had no idea where that had come from either. Now Tony Powell's nick-name 'Spidder' she could well understand. He was thin and wiry, with the ability to go from stock still to the speed of lightening in an instant.

"That's better. That old bottle weighed a ton. The longer it was on my back the heavier it got," said Hilary, as she reappeared, ready to take charge of her bicycle once again. Sally nearly jumped out of her skin. She'd been miles away and the raised voice, that sudden interjection into her thoughts had scared the living daylights out of her. She took a deep breath as she relinquished the bike, then turned her own around in unison with the other two and prepared herself for the very last bit of the journey home. "Hang on, give me time to polish up me halo and so forth," said Hilary as Pat began to thank her for the way she had steered them through all those bewildering country lanes. "It was touch and go there at times I can tell you, a bit of a wing and a prayer kind situation you might say. " And she grinned as she now admitted how close she had come to getting the whole thing wrong.

There were now massive clouds building up, light in parts but all sporting dark grey underbellies. The rain that luckily had held itself in check all day was, it seemed preparing itself to deposit vast amounts of its wet self onto the damp earth and all that stood within it.

"Better get a move on or the rain and the Googly Moosh'll get us," said Pat, looking up and around as she pushed down hard on her peddles and set off towards cow-shit corner.

Chapter 13

'Spring is sprung The sun is ris. The bird is on the wing. Or is the wing upon the bird? I dus not know what which.' Sally mouthed silently to herself as she knelt on her pillow and peered through the bedroom window. At long last her very most favourite season had arrived, she thought to herself as she looked over towards the big wood, with its trees outlined and accentuated by the rays of the early morning sunshine. She took a deep breath then sighed contentedly as she prepared for the day ahead.

First there was the milk to be collected from the farm, but that state of affairs was soon to change. At long last, the status of that cow, which would provide them with all the milk they needed, had gone from a definite maybe to a certainty – or so she'd been told. 'Don't hold your breath,' mum had told her. As she dressed she thought about Hazel, now married and living with her husband Albert Soan in a little cottage at the top end of the village. She really missed her sister, and even though she was not far away, it was not the same as having her under the same roof. It brought back memories of Betty's departure from the family home all those years ago, which had been even more of a wrench. Betty had only been fourteen when she had left home, the same age that she herself was now, and London had seemed such a far away and dangerous place and had filled her with horror at the time. She could not imagine in a million years having the courage to do such a thing.

'Chop, chop, this won't get the poes emptied,' she said to herself, as she scrambled into her clothes. Then she hurried off to the kitchen to cadge a cup of tea.

After breakfast, Pat and Sally grabbed the milk cans and set off towards the farm to fetch the milk. As they passed through the back gate and Sally turned to fasten the thing, her eyes passed briefly over the washing lines. Before long they would be groaning under the weight of freshly laundered blankets, pegged out and over the taught wires, ready to receive their annual dose of fresh air and sunshine. The earth was coming out of its winter stupor that was for sure, she thought as she turned and squinted into and against the glare of the bright spring sunshine. Mother Nature would be taking a deep breath right now she reckoned, in preparation for the tasks ahead.

It was Saturday and the two girls, energised by the sunshine and the realisation that they had the whole weekend ahead of them, set off across the field at a tidy pace. Hilary was working of course so it would be late afternoon at the earliest before they saw her. In the meantime once the shopping was done, the rest of the day would be their own, 'fingers crossed and so forth,' as Hilary would say. An ear worm was driving Sally crazy. It had popped up into her mind suddenly and out of the blue as she had been eating her breakfast, repeating itself *ad infinitum* as was its wont, and had just stayed there. To drown out the wretchedly repetitive theme, she began at first to hum and then to sing a favourite song, hoping to drown out the offending refrain:

> '*Blow the wind southerly, southerly, southerly. Blow the wind south oe'r the bonny blue sea.*
> *Blow the wind southerly, southerly, southerly. Blow bonny breeze my lover to me.' She began.*

Her voice was wobbly with no trace of the haunting cadence with which Kathleen Ferrier would have delivered it, but she did not care. As long as it did the trick, she would be more than satisfied.

Mrs Collin's was alone by the time the girls puffed their way into the warm kitchen of the old farmhouse, the aroma of fried bacon and percolated coffee though still lingered in and around the place. The latter reminded Sally of Caves Café where her mum had worked all those years ago, and as far as she was concerned, was one of those things that smelled so much better than it tasted. She preferred the sweeter, less acrid taste of Camp coffee any old day. They had spotted Mr and Miss Collins around one of the cow sheds on the way in, and she was struck afresh at the contrast between the frailty of the kindly lady who stood before her, and the Amazonian strength and stature of the other two. That the latter came from good old farming stock as she'd been told, was pretty obvious, as obvious in fact as that the lineage of the former was of a somewhat less robust, more genteel nature. Chalk and cheese was the expression that came immediately to mind here.

Janet Powell and Brian Winchester were already ensconced around the kitchen table by the time they arrived home with the milk, and Sally breathed a sigh if relief. Their presence meant that she and Pat would be able to step it out on the way to village without the little ones tagging along and holding them up with their insistence on stopping every few yards along the way to look at this and that. The four youngsters were old enough now to play out and about without the supervision of one or other of the older girls; thank goodness and all the stars for that, she thought to herself. They were good mates, these lively youngsters, with enough wit and imagination between them to overcome any shortcoming, often surprising the older ones with the inventiveness of their games. The word bored, was just not part of their vocabulary. Perhaps this afternoon, she and Pat would give Jacky a bit of advice on how to transform that square piece of rag mum had given her into a neatly hemmed hankie, and maybe help Dorothy to stitch, stuff and decorate the pincushion she had started to make out of those few bits of felt, Miss Smith up at the Manse had given her. Then she grinned as she listened to their whispered words, recognising the ditty as one that she had taught them quite recently. 'There was a jolly Scotsman, who lived at Waterloo. The wind blew up his trouser leg, and showed his cock-a-do. His cock-a-do was dirty, he showed it to the Queen. The Queen was so disgusted she had it painted green.' She moved away from the table as they began to giggle, quickly disassociating herself from this slightly risqué rhyme.

The two girls walked briskly down the field, Pat carrying one of mum's large shopping bags, and Sally with dad's trusty old Rexine bag sitting comfortably on her shoulder. The shopping list they carried was not challenging in the least thankfully, the items on it light and easy for a change. They continued the brisk pace until they reached the top of Crazy Lane, where they paused beside the gate for just long enough to admire the view and to get their breath back. Then they began the descent down into the village with their legs now operating easily and of their own free will. As they passed the Chapel, Sally felt that familiar uplifting of spirit she always felt when passing by or entering this place of worship. It was certainly not one of those impressive monuments to a bye-gone era, like Pevensey Castle, Battle Abbey and the like, enshrined and stuck in some sort of solemn warp as they were. It had a warmth and friendliness about it, a living, breathing harmonious countenance, due in no small measure to its occupants she felt sure. She was looking forward to Bible Class there tomorrow.

As they walked across the bridge, the acrid smell of singed horse hoof hit their nostrils, reminding them that Mr Taylor was already hard at work in that little shed of his. The words of the Blacksmith song popped up immediately into Sally's mind, and she could not resist the urge to utter at least a few of them, with Pat for whom the words had a particular meaning, voicing them alongside:

"Here's a health to the jolly Blacksmith, the best of all the fellow's.
He works at his anvil while the boy blows the bellows.
Which makes his bright hammer to rise and to fall.

Cotton Reels and so Forth

There's the old Cole and the young Cole and the old Cole of all.
Twanky dillo, dillo, dillo, dillo, dillo.
And the roaring pair of bagpipes made from the green willow."

"Well I'll be blowed," exclaimed Sally as the ditty came to an end and she looked behind her. "Don't look now, but Denis is coming round cow shit corner, and looks like he's in a bit of a hurry. One thing, he can't be two faced or he'd be wearing his other one," she added turning back and giggling nervously. Quick, if we get a move on we can just get inside the shop before he gets here. I'm just not in the mood for his tattle today. Not that I ever am, if it comes to that," she added as having hurriedly opened the door, they almost fell through and into the little shop. "Whew, that was a close shave. We'll have to make sure he's not lurking when we come out, that's all," she uttered letting her breath out in a long sigh of relief. She could not resist the temptation to look back over her shoulder however, and then immediately wished she hadn't. As he cycled slowly passed, the look he gave her as he caught and held her eye, felt just like some singular, deadly embrace.

She turned away from her nemesis to hear Pat passing the time of day with Mrs Skilton, then as the little lady moved towards the door with her shopping bags, she leaned forward and opened it for her. As she turned away from the doorway, she saw Miss Dengate standing beside the counter. Her voice, overlaid with that characteristic and pleasing brogue of hers, was directed towards Reg who was serving her.

"What're tham thar things up there then Reg?" she asked, pointing towards a pile of packets on a top shelf behind the counter.

Tham thar things be packets of sugar, Miss Dengate," he replied immediately and without batting an eye-lid, and Sally blushed, knowing full well that the so called bags of sugar were actually packets of sanitary towels. By the puzzled expression on her face, that explanation seemed to mystify her somewhat, but she refrained from further questioning, turning her attention instead towards the girls who now stood beside her. Her eyes sparkled as she looked at them and as she grinned, Sally was struck once more by the strength of those extraordinary teeth of hers, and the size of the gap between the top front ones. She was such a friendly soul, genuinely interested in their activities and even more interested in what dad had been up to. The pair of them, she and dad, certainly had a lot in common, she thought. They were both down to earth practical country folk, and Sally did not use that description lightly. Although dad had not had his hands in the claggy Sussex soil for generation after generation as had the Dengate family, he was a countryman heart and soul, with hands the size of plates to prove it.

By the time Reg had finished serving her and had turned his attention towards the short shopping list the girls had passed over the counter, they were on to the subject of Mercy Dengate's old Billy goat, which was a bit of a handful

197

to say the least. He was sometimes to be seen grazing in the field near the Brickwall, and the youngsters, boys and girls alike, had learned from experience, to give the bad tempered old devil a wide birth. That the old lady was able to handle him so well was a source of admiration by old and young alike, and Pat was telling her so. "Oh 'e dunt give me no trouble," she replied. "He en me've got an understandin' see? He may be onery but he sartenly arnt stupid. Course 'e tried his luck when e were a young un, but some ken in thet hard owld head a his, soon inform im who be boss. Sarternoon e en me be going along to one of Gammons fields for im to have a maw on a bit're frash vegetation. E got a taste fer tham thar saplings that've seeded emselves alongside that hedge."

Sally could have listened to this old lady forever. Her words flowed so easily and naturally off her tongue, and alongside old Tom and George and Fred, she represented what remained of that old world of characters and commonsense. No wonder dad, who was a very good judge of character, spoke so highly of her.

After packing away and paying for her groceries, Miss Dengate pulled her chummy hat well down over her ears, then set off bag in hand, to retrieve her bicycle from around the side of the shop. The girls were not far behind, and after checking that Denis was not lurking nearby, ventured out into the open and looked up across the Green. They could see several boys clustered around the pump, with various bikes propped up here and there, and noticed immediately that Basil Beeching was one of them. He was head and shoulders taller than most of his contemporaries, a gentle giant if ever there was one. Denis was there, straddling his bicycle, and after registering his presence, Sally ignored him. She'd had enough of him for one day. They stood for a few more moments beside the boxes of assorted vegetables, sniffing in the delicate aroma of leeks as they tried to identify the other boys. Ronald Elkins was one of them and Ray Winchester and Michael Soan were another two, Then Sally spotted Diggy Fuller, and grinned. He reminded her of a mischievous Pixie. He had a knack of summing up a potentially humorous situation and acting upon it with split second timing. No wonder the Sedlescombe Saints cycle speedway team had chosen him to be their Mascot.

After a while, they turned away from contemplation of the informal gathering around the old pump, readjusted their shopping bags and set their sights on home. There were a few wind-dogs moving across the sky now they noticed and shivered. They had cooled right down they suddenly realised, and decided it would have to be the up Chapel Hill and down Crazy Lane route once again. A good pull up that old hill would soon get the blood flowing around their bodies and eventually warm up their hands and feet. They would cycle up to meet Hilary from work this afternoon they decided as they walked briskly towards cow shit corner. If they got their timing right, Mr Bran would be standing behind the counter when they arrived with a cup of tea in his hand, his little old van parked up outside. They could be pretty sure then that the worthy partnership between man and van had been fulfilled for the day, the boxes of groceries had been delivered to all those little cottages around the country lanes, and that unless anything unforeseen happened, Hilary would be free to leave the shop. Mr Bran was very good like that. By the time they reached the entrance to Farrow's farm, they had got their plans for the day and indeed most of the weekend sorted out to their satisfaction, and without any arguments for a change. "Touch wood and keep your fingers crossed at all times," Pat said and grinned.

They made the mandatory gate stop at the top of the hill, noting familiar landmarks that would soon be partially obscured by new growth as winter, now visibly withering on the vine, made way for spring. The girls were feeling upbeat and optimistic, and rightly so. The days were lengthening, the countryside opening up before their very eyes. Their favourite season was upon them, with Mother Nature hovering, magic wand in hand ready to begin the process of regeneration all over again. Old winter had had its moment of glory.

After several minutes, they moved away from the gate of contemplation, the content of their idle chit-chat changing in a split second from miracles to bodily needs as they did so. They were, they suddenly realised, desperate for a wee. With their shopping bags bobbing to and fro in time with their feet, they trotted off down Crazy Lane, anxious now to reduce the distance between them and the lavvy as quickly as possible.

"How about a nice mug of cocoa then," said Pat breathlessly as they hurried up the field a few minutes later. For Sally however, it was first things first and she sprinted the last few yards to gain access to the nearest lavvy, without bothering to reply.

It was Saturday evening, dark as Hades outside and Hilary and Sally were sitting around the kitchen table at Windy Ridge, deep in wool and conversation. Their knitting needles click clacked along with a satisfying rhythm as they chatted, with the pauses in either activity few and far between. They were talking about Old Thyme Dancing, a recent and very welcome addition to all those other activities that took place in the village Hall at Sedlescombe. At the moment, The Gay Gordon's, The County Cotillion, The Lancer's etc., were just names and a confusion of complicated steps to them. But in time, with a bit of luck and a lot of practice, they might just get the hang of it. 'Fingers crossed at all times, and so forth,' said Hilary. They could not imagine reaching nor did they even aspire to, the enviable level of expertise of Dulcie and Bill, who led and demonstrated the dances. Just mastering the steps would be enough for them. Ron and Ken Edwards and Cecil Taylor they reckoned were already up there with the best of beginners, with Mrs Bishop and Mrs Woollet not far behind. Luckily, these members were very helpful and enthusiastic, and with their support and encouragement, the girls thought they were in with a chance. Now the Polka, that was a different thing altogether as far as Sally was concerned, and she knew without any shadow of doubt that she would never,

ever get the rhythm of the darned thing. Talk about jumping around like a parched pea.

The girls were grateful to Ron and Ken, who lived in Kent Street and who always walked them home after these Friday evening sessions, and even more so, on dark moonless nights, when who knew what, lurked beyond the beam of their torches. They even walked as far as the bottom of the field with Sally, and waited for her to do her up and down torch signal at the scullery door, before they went on their way.

After exhausting the subject of complicated footwork, and more importantly, how to master the art of getting around the dance floor without making complete idiots of themselves, they moved on to something a little less demanding; for themselves anyway. The new programs and league tables for the Cycle Speedway events were due out shortly, and once they got their hands on one, they would be able to work out a schedule for Saturday evenings and Sunday mornings, always bearing in mind their necessity to be back in time for Bible class on Sunday afternoons. The teams participating in this new and exciting sport were divided into two camps, The Hastings League, and the Sedlescombe and District League. The former was comprised of teams from in and around the Hastings area, the latter (the name chosen because the Saints had been instrumental in setting the thing up), representing those from local village teams. The Baldslow Boomerangs, her Cousins' team, were in the Hastings League of course, and were bound to be in competition with the Sedlescombe Saints sooner or later, Sally realised. When this happened she reassured Hilary, although her loyalties were divided, she would certainly be supporting their home team. How could it be otherwise she said, when they had been around, if not immediately involved, when those first picks and shovels, had hit the stony ground around East View Terrace. They had witnessed the hard work and dedication that had gone into the construction of the track on this challenging ground, which seemed to have been the only sizable piece of land available to those cycling enthusiasts at the time. For Sally it was definitely a case of mixed emotions when it came to the actual races, with excitement fighting fear at all times. As she watched the speed with which the boys rode around the track, her heart was in her mouth. How they kept their balance let alone their nerve as they took those tight corners at such unbelievable speeds, defied the laws of gravity - or some such thing.

How the conversation moved from bikes to baccy, they had no idea, nor would they have bothered their heads about such inconsequential things. Sally had witnessed the process of turning a lump of brown organic matter into a pile of neat strands before she left home this evening, and was proclaiming yet again, her surprise at her Dad's ability to perform such a delicate operation with those chunky hands of his. She was describing in detail, how he had whittled

away at that thick wedge, stopping every so often to rub and loosely separate out the strands until they resembled the contents in one of those pouches of shag tobacco on display in Wilton's shop beside the Village Green. Hilary grinned as she listened, adding her own observations as soon as Sally took breath. The part of the process that puzzled her she said was how dad managed to fashion such neat and narrow cigarettes from his home grown tobacco and those delicate Rizla papers he used, be they the red, green or blue packaged ones. On the few occasions when they had persuaded him to let them have a go, the results had been disastrous. All they managed to roll were lumpy, spit laden, disintegrating bits of uselessness. And he always tut-tutted at the waste of his fag papers.

After a while, they dropped the knitting down onto the table, braced their shoulders and relaxed back into their seats for a few moments. It had been dark for hours, and although they had not bothered to check, assumed it must be very nearly cocoa time. Through the intermittent chatter, the clatter of spoons and crockery as Hilary performed the pre bedtime ritual, Sally was sure she could just make out the piercing, evocative cry of a scritch owl. It was a long way off, possibly as far away as the big wood where it was either preparing to quarter one of the fields nearby, or just warning rivals off its territory. To her it was as magical and mysterious a sound as the honking of wild migrating geese, or the unearthly wail of a night prowling fox. It evoked a strange emotion, akin to the one she experienced when studying those paintings on the front room wall at home. As she sat awaiting her night-time beverage she thought about them. She could see in her mind's eye, the wild beauty of those hardy highland cattle set in a landscape of hills and mountains that faded away into mist and rolling grey cloud, and sighed. Those tranquil scenes of solitude and isolation had always fascinated her, and she remembered how during the dark days of war, she had derived hope and comfort from the images captured and set within those simple frames. They were etched on her mind and imagination forever she reckoned, along with the mat that sat beside the veranda doors. Simply crafted from shredded lisle stockings, then woven into a mosaic of fawns, greys and black, that little rug had been her childhood magic carpet.

As Hilary brought the steaming mugs of cocoa to the table, Sally picked up the two bundles of knitting, hastily wound the woven bit around the needles, then removed the whole lot to the sideboard to keep it out of harm's way. Then they sat with elbows on table, mugs held firmly between cupped hands, and began to slowly sup the delicious brew.

After a short while of sipping, supping and intermittent chatter, Sally began to look beyond her mug, and grinned as her eye came to rest on a package with a Jolly Monk on its surface. 'Monk and Glass,' announced the container on which his image had been printed, and he stood there holding up a bowl of blancmange between cupped hands, and with the widest grin she had ever seen writ large across his face. Next to the Fat Friar, was a drab looking package, but looks were deceiving, as she well knew. 'Yum, yum, dried egg powder,' she said to herself, knowing that inside this dull rectangular box was a pale yellow powder, that when whisked up with a bit water, salt and pepper, made the creamiest omelette she had ever tasted; or with milk, even creamier scrambled eggs. She could even taste the difference when mum added a tablespoon or two of the stuff to her fruit cakes, and that was saying something. She almost wished the hens went off lay more often. There was a packet of jelly crystals alongside, but it paled into insignificance beside the other two, and her eyes and attention returned to her empty mug. As she absentmindedly swished it around, trying to create a meaningful pattern from the dregs of cocoa at the bottom, she thought of Granny Sansom, an expert at interpreting the strange formation of tea leaves. No wonder she stuck to that medium, she thought. Even she would be flummoxed by the residual sludge in this mug. Granny's speciality were floating tea leaves anyway, and it would have been pointless looking for one of those elusive strangers earlier on, even if she'd thought about it. Grains of cocoa did not float like tea leaves.

Once the mugs had been rinsed and set aside to drain and dry, they sat back down at the table again. They were tired but not yet ready for bed and having spied a pile of old Film Weekly's that Mrs Elkins or Jean had left around, sat chatting and thumbing idly through them. After a few minutes of gazing at pictures of uniformly hansom male stars, and the slightly risqué photos of female stars in silk lingerie, they put them aside and took up a couple of comics that Ronald had left around. This was more like it they reckoned as they opened them up and began to examine the originality of the animations, the witty asides. These imaginary characters exuded a vitality that was missing from those Starlets with their provocative poses, and the famous male actors with their Brylcreem'd hair and dazzling smiles. Ronald had much better taste than Mrs Elkins and Jean put together, they decided, and would tell him so in the morning. They just hoped he would not then insist on them perusing his Mechano magazines or whatever they were called. Those specialist publications that Ronald read and understood with such apparent ease were totally incomprehensible to them.

After a while, Hilary suggested a game of Cat's Cradle, and as she left the table to search out a suitable length of wool, Sally tidied and set the comics to one side, and moved a couple of chairs around to face one another. Once Hilary had tied the ends of the wool together and encircled the resulting loop around her hands, the game began. Within a short space of time, with the interaction of thumb and forefinger of both hands and the occasional use of their little fingers, they had exhausted all the traditional moves, including their favourite creation, the parachute. Then the fun began as the game quickly degenerated into a free for all, the moves increasingly bewildering, innovative to the point of stupidity. It ended as always in helpless fits of giggles and utter confusion with Hilary struggling to release Sally's fingers from the tight entanglement of knotted wool. Once the snarled mess was disposed of, they flexed their fingers to restore circulation, and after a short pause for breath, Sally followed Hilary willingly in one of her favourite finger games, reciting in unison with her friend, the ditty that accompanied the exercise:

> 'There's a church, and there's a steeple.
>   You open the doors, and you see all the people.
> There's the choir boys' going upstairs.
>   There's the Parson saying his prayers.'

After a few minutes of this simple drill, their fingers were pink and warm as toast, the life-blood restored to every finger tip. As they relaxed back into their chairs, hands resting loosely in their laps, the inevitable happened and they began to yawn. The long busy day was catching up with them and although they continued to chat for a while, they were more than ready for their beds. At the moment, Hilary was musing on the strange echo in Churches and other large and ancient stone buildings, the topic more than likely triggered by its association with the old finger game. As Sally listened, vaguely aware of the thought process that had brought about this meditative mood, she gradually began to sink into a state of drowsy introspection. After a while, the Lady of Pevensey floated into her mind and imagination, with that aura of grief still surrounding her like a shroud. As she drifted away, an image of Gandhi emerged and with it a few words from the speech made by Sir Stafford Cripps at the time of Gandhi's assassination: 'I know of no other man in our time, or indeed in recent history, who so convincingly demonstrated the power of the spirit over material things.' He had said. The poor old pacifist, who had fought long and hard to free India from British rule, must have seen and heard enough about the orgy of killing and destruction following that momentous event, to have made him wring his hands in horror and disbelief, she thought. Her mind continued to float along on a wave of introspection until Hilary tapped her gently on the shoulder. Then she roused herself, followed her friend through the minimum of bedtime preparation, before groping her way towards her little bed and slipping thankfully between the sheets. Her last thoughts before she dropped into a deep dreamless sleep were of mum and dad and her sisters, for whom she offered up a brief silent prayer. And of Sylvian.

Chapter 14

The cow had arrived. The momentous event had been witnessed by the whole family, who had gathered together beside the gate at the bottom of the field to await its arrival, moving to one side as the lorry lumbered along the lane and into the field. Uncle Fred Sansom was in the driving seat with his brother Uncle Tom, who had travelled all the way from Oxfordshire to give a hand, beside him. The girls had watched in silence as the men fitted a slatted wooden platform to the rear of truck, and as the creature had negotiated the temporary walkway, had passed their hands across their eyes to make sure they were not seeing things. She had soon dispelled any doubts and misgivings they might have had however. Totally unaware and unappreciative of her awe struck audience it seemed, she had moved across the field sampling the fresh green shoots, and had then showed her approval of her new home by producing the first of many fresh steaming cow-pats. It was at that moment they realised that she, Rosebud, was in all respects genuine and not just a figment of their imagination. The whole thing had been a bit of an anti-climax though to say the least.

This event had taken place a few weeks ago, and since then a rota of twice daily milking schedules had been established.

Sally however, having discovered that she was sensitive to Udsall, the disinfectant used on Rosebud's teats, was not part of the team. The allergy manifested itself in small watery blisters that itched like merry hell, rather like those horrid chilblains that plagued her in the damp, cold winter weather. She had accepted the situation with a mixture of guilt and relief, the latter definitely the stronger and overriding sensibility, for it had not taken her long to realise that milking cows was not half as easy as John and Porky Partridge, and the Land Girl at local Farms had made it seem. She had pulled and squeezed and struggled with the teats, managing to produce a skinny streak of milk, which had turned into a feeble dribble and had then dried up altogether. If there was a knack to it as she'd been told, then it had failed to rub off on her and her clumsy fingers. As far as she was concerned, getting milk from a cow's udders, was like trying to get blood from a stone, and Dad's efforts were just as feeble. Pat and Dorothy, who had been left to shoulder this odious responsibility, were not best pleased and who could blame them. If the boot had been on the other foot, she knew she would have shouted her displeasure, her accusations of favouritism, from the rooftops.

However, although watching Rosebud cropping grass in the field was still a novelty, Sally's attention moved quickly on to something of a different nature. Her thoughts were now centred on the ancient custom of Beating the Bounds, which was taking place around Sedlescombe today. In the olden days before the introduction of Tithe maps, this ceremony had taken place every seven years, with the sole purpose of impressing the boundaries of the parish unforgettably on the minds of rising generation of males. Since then however, with definition of parish boundaries no longer reliant on local knowledge, it was a symbolic gesture, carried out on a somewhat ad hoc basis. In fact the last time this ceremony had taken place, as far as she could make out, had been just before the start of that first terrible world war. As she moved around the kitchen preparing her iron rations for the day, she thought about the tales of suspicion and intrigue, voiced by ancient villagers like old George and Fred. They told of haphazard interpretation of boundaries in the olden days, with the moving of boundary stones and other dubious practices, carried out for the express purpose of benefiting their respective villages. She could not wait to learn more about the intrigue surrounding this age old custom.

It was a lovely day, warm and sunny with a gentle breeze, and as far as she was concerned, nigh on perfect for this long awaited ramble through the countryside. She had known it would be fine when she'd seen the red streaked sky last night. 'Red sky at night, Shepherds delight,' she had muttered to herself. She, Pat and Hilary were now on the way to the starting point, and not before time by the look of things. As they walked briskly passed Farrow's steps and looked over the valley, they could see that a sizable group of people had already assembled on and around the old river bridge ready and waiting for the challenge ahead. Mr Phillips, a leading member of the Parish Council was in overall charge of operations, and as they approached, they saw him struggling to uncoil a large rolled up map that was clearly proving too unwieldy for him. Jumbo James the Headmaster, quickly stepped in to assist him, and suddenly there were eyes, pointing fingers and advice all around the little man and his map. The first part of the boundary was soon decided upon and the map released to resume its tight coil, allowing Mr Phillips to adjust his little round glasses, and announce the start of the ancient custom of 'Beating the Bounds.'

A large contingent of villagers, of all ages and agility, had assembled by this time, and the company moved off in a buzz of excited chatter loud enough to alert the latest of latecomers to their whereabouts and ultimately track them down. Ron Elkins, Ray Winchester and Michael Soan, clearly buoyed up by the prospect of adventure raced ahead, and were soon up amongst the leaders. The girls were content to be and remain somewhere in the middle ground, where from time to time they were joined by other youngsters who chatted for a while and then moved restlessly off to seek other diversions. Suddenly, Willie Monk and Roy Chapman swept up beside them, red faced and out of breath. They had come straight from East View Terrace where they had been doing a spot of maintenance on the cycle speedway track, they told the girls once they had got their breath back. The conversation for a while was all about bikes and riders, and the tracks on which they operated, with a discussion on a newly released programme of forthcoming matches. According to the boys who obviously had had sufficient time to peruse this new pamphlet, some of the teams scheduled to compete against one another were evenly matched, with the race likely to be a close run thing. In other matches however, with one team so obviously superior to the other, the outcome was a foregone conclusion, or as Roy so aptly phrased it, 'a walk over, no contest.'

The chit chat within their own little group and all around them, flowed with an ease borne out of familiarity, with the occasional high spirited banter creating a few scuffles and loud guffaws here and there. When the leaders paused once in a while to consult map or memory, the horseplay ceased dramatically, and apprehensive glances were exchanged. The boys, aware that the ancient and dreaded ritual of bumping boys on boundaries they'd been warned about would happen sooner or later, knew and feared that any one of them could be singled out at any time to receive this humiliating and painful experience.

From the area of Oakland's Park and all through the lower reaches of the Brede valley, the pungent aroma of parsley and wild garlic predominated. Even as they veered inland, following a well-trodden footpath towards Jacob's farmhouse it lingered in the air, alongside the scent of pollen from tall grasses, which were frothing with globules of cuckoo spit. Before long, they encountered the first of several woods outlined on the map, and it was decided that this one was to be tramped through rather than skirted. It was cool and gloomy in here in spite of the warmth and brightness of the day, with shafts of sunlight penetrating the thick canopy of leaves only briefly, intermittently. Anything could be lurking in here Sally reckoned as she peered into its murky depths. If she squinted and allowed her imagination full reign, one of those strange fabled creature might be spied slinking through the undergrowth. A sly leprechaun, a goblin or gremlin, or even worse, the wicked old witch from Hansel and Gretel. She shivered, goose-bumps suddenly popping up onto her skin as her heightened imagination conjured up weird images of wraith like and scary phantoms. She was quite relieved when the wood thinned out to a clearing, and as she made her way through the thick encircling hedge and over the ditch on the other side, she chided herself for her stupidity. Any fantastical creature, no matter how frightening, would be daunted, nay terrified, by this troop of chattering humanity.

"Watch out, that could have been Tinker-bell you were swotting there," said Pat with mock severity as Sally swished an insect that was buzzing annoyingly around her face. "And listen, there's a cuckoo over there," she added, pointing over the field they were crossing, barely drawing breath between the two exclamations. The girls stopped momentarily in their tracks as the two bar cry of this elusive bird echoed across the meadow. No matter how often they heard the sound of this unique creature, it never lost its fascination for them.

By this time, Roy and Willie had moved on and the girls followed, walking crocodile fashion across this and other fields, eventually reaching a stile leading onto a lane. They were very close now to the Powder-mill Reservoir, the crossing of which was to be the highlight of the day, they reckoned. As they walked towards this large lake, there were exclamations of surprise and squeaks from the front runners, accompanied by a curious sort of dance. As the girls stopped and looked down, the cause of all this agitated movement became immediately frighteningly clear. There were thousands of baby frogs all around them. They were crawling through the undergrowth and all over one another and they were the daintiest, most fascinating little creatures they had ever seen. The girls looked at one another, then down at their feet as a disturbing thought occurred to them at one and the same time. Could there be one or more of these little creatures, lying squashed and lifeless beneath their sturdy shoes. Hilary was the first to break the frozen silence.

"Whew, that's a bit of luck," she said as she lifted first one foot and then the other, to check the ground beneath, and after taking a deep breath, Pat and Sally did the same. From then on, the progress was slow, the attention more on baby frogs than the little boats moored alongside the Reservoir waiting to ferry them all across the water.

It took a while, but at last the whole contingent was on the other side of the lake, safe and sound and surprisingly dry. As Sally scrabbled out of the boat, she looked back over the water, screwing up her eyes against the glare of the sun on its surface, and sighed with pleasure. The steady rhythm of paddles, the sound of the dip and plop of oars as they rose and fell over the water, resonated in her ears, and would do so forever she reckoned. In fact if expressions on faces, and those exclamations of sheer joy all around her was anything to go by, then 'a good time had been had by all.' It was clear that the pioneering spirit engendered by this experience would sustain them for the next hour or so, which was just as well. It was it seemed, all uphill for a quite a while now.

After a steady uphill climb, a boundary was reached, the crossing of which necessitated the bumping of some unfortunate youngster on its line of demarcation. Ron Elkins was selected, and though clearly annoyed and embarrassed by the whole thing, suffered the indignity with a stoicism to be proud of. There was an exchange of nervous glances amongst the youngsters during the short procedure, with the unspoken question of 'who will be next,' writ clearly on their faces. Then the group moved on and immediately, the incident was gone and forgotten about.

After traipsing steadily through more fields and farmland, lanes and woods, a loud hoorah went up when a stop for refreshment was announced. The girls sank to the ground with a sigh of relief, opened their bags, and began to shuffle around for their iron rations. Before they got that far however, quantities of food and drink appeared as if by magic, and after an initial moment of hesitation, was soon disappearing down the hungry, thirsty throats of all the weary walkers. It was quiet for a while, with just a low buzz of conversation from contented eaters, some sitting while others wandered around groups of co-boundary beaters, chatting and chewing as they went. Ron, Ray, Michael and their mates were among the latter. They plonked themselves down beside the girls for just long enough to enthuse about and enlarge upon the challenges of this adventure, and then wandered off again.

Once the boys had moved away, the girls examined their legs and arms for scratches and stings. The long socks and long sleeved blouses they were wearing had given them little protection from brambles and those tall, vicious stinging nettles, they realised, as they uncovered bare flesh and took stock of the damage. "I think we'd best look around for some dock leaves, don't you? Said Hilary, and winced as she rubbed her stings. "That'll do, better late than never," she added as having sought and selected a decent specimen, she spat on, and then delivered a dose of balm to the affected areas. They had just sat back, supporting themselves comfortably on propped hands, when the call came to 'press on folks.' There was an immediate stirring of bodies, a general dusting off of bums and they were on the move again. They joined the general exodus, just a bit reluctant to leave this area so soon. Popping-hole Lane, a favourite haunt of theirs was just a stone's throw away from here, with Cripps Corner and the shop in which Hilary worked, even closer. Hilary had cycled along the nearby lane countless times on her way to and from work, but as she said, as it was an uphill ride on the way there when she was fresh, and downhill on the way home when she was tired, she had no complaints.

The welcome break plus the victuals they had consumed manifested itself in a burst of renewed energy and enthusiasm, which was just as well. This leg of the journey was proving itself confusing to say the least. They had skirted woods, crossed fields and witnessed another bumping on another boundary, and yet they were coming up to Great Sanders House now, which was only just down the road from that refreshment area. Still they were not complaining. With Roy, Willie, Basil Beeching and Ron Hudson now walking alongside, there was never a dull moment.

The proximity to Hurst Lane also prompted a discussion on the origins of place names with recurring suffixes and prefixes. Hurst for instance, according to Basil, was the old name for a wooded area, while Coombe, as in Sedlescombe, meant a valley. He mentioned Eye, as in island, and Wold, an area of open countryside and several others, all with their origin or roots set in the dim and distant past. They were still on and into this interesting topic, when they reached and began to make their way through a coppice of scrubby trees and tangled vegetation. Then the conversation petered out as they realised that there was a challenge ahead that needed a bit of thought and concentration. It was clear from the start that the skirts and blouses the girls were wearing would be no match for the proliferation of vicious bramble and thick vegetation around them, so the boys took the lead. Their sturdy boots and long trousers gave them some protection from the criss-cross of prickly thorn and briar within this mini jungle. They just powered their way through and opened up a pathway of sorts for the girls, who emerged into the field beyond with a sigh of relief. It was interesting if not downright amusing to listen to tales of tumbles and forced retreats from dishevelled stragglers as they emerged from their ordeal. Most were grinning ruefully as they rubbed scratches and removed bits of twig and leaf from their hair and clothing, prompting a remark about pioneering spirit from some lippy lad nearby, who was laughing his head off.

Once the stragglers had got their breath back, there was a rough head count and the posse set off once again. Thankfully, the going was easy for a while. As they trotted down the grassy slope, someone pointed over and upwards to where a Windmill had once stood, sparking off a discussion on these old relics. This one had fallen into disuse and eventual decay ages ago, replaced it seemed by steam and then by electrically powered flour mills. The youngsters had heard about it of course, and had tried but failed to pin point its exact location. It was worth another try now they reckoned. From conversations with Bangy Smith and old Fred and George over the years, they had learned a lot about the importance of these wind powered machines and their counterparts, the Water Mills. Evidently they had been a feature of the landscape for centuries, and were used not just for the grinding of wheat and corn, but for many other purposes. They had played an important and significant part in the processing of gunpowder for instance, for which this area had been famous. Unfortunately, most of these old warriors, which had once been such an important and integral part of rural community, were now lost in the mists of time. Along with that mysterious village up in Battle Big Wood, Sally thought to herself.

The pace slackened somewhat as they began the steady climb up towards Whatlington, though the level of general chit-chat remained roughly the same. Suddenly, over and above the buzz of conversation, Sally could hear the strains of a song that had caught her attention and imagination from the first time she had heard it. 'Ghost Riders in the Sky,' it was called, and as she listened, she felt its strange and haunting power wash over her once again. She could not hear all the words or make out who the singer was, just that the soloist was young and male and was singing the song ever so slightly off key. She stayed in the realms of ghostly apparitions riding across endless skies for a while, coming back down to earth and reality as the group, after a gradual slowing down, came to a halt beside a Barn. The way forward it seemed was right through this old building, and as she lined up for the entry and exit, she noticed the sudden dearth of young males and smiled to herself. The lads had learned the hard way, where and when to keep a low profile, it seemed, and the tactics they were using were proving very effective. There would be no bumping of nippers on this particular boundary.

It took a while, but eventually all the walkers had moved through the barn and exited on the far side, where they found themselves on the edge of a wild flower meadow. It was decided, that this was as good a place as any to stop for a bit of liquid refreshment, and without further ado, bottles were raised and water, some likely spiked with other more powerful liquids, were gurgling down parched throats. Once Sally had had her fill, she looked across the field, and was struck as always by the colour and sheer variety of wild flowers in amongst the grasses in these meadows. She could see the soft pink petals of the ragged robin, the tall yellow rattle, poppies, clover, wild pansy and oxeye daisy, and even plantains, with their long stems topped by those curious snake-like seed heads. And wonder of wonder, out amongst the rye grass, oat grass, dogs tail and timothy, she spotted her beloved toddle grass, nodding away in the light breeze.

She turned and looked up as Hilary tapped on her shoulder, and was immediately captivated by what she saw. Over and above the small outcrop of trees towards which her friend was pointing, she saw and began to watch a couple of birds of prey, as they engaged in some sort of aerial display. Then others within the group, shading their eyes against the glare of the sun, began to gaze upward, drawn into and silenced by the performance they were watching. The birds, oblivious to the silent voyeurism around them, continued to perform this curious bonding ritual, soaring and circling, rising and dipping, connecting for a split second as they passed, then repeating the manoeuvres over again with the same artless grace. Even when the spectators turned away, the demonstration of love and commitment continued. The birds were still silhouetted against the clear blue sky, and still acting out this age old ritual.

After a huddled powwow the leaders were on the move again, and there was a hurried shuffling of bags and feet as the other boundary beaters prepared to follow them. After skirting a couple of small fields and passing some old farm buildings, Hancox House came into view. It was the first time Sally had approached the place from this angle and with the sun dipping down through the Heavens it looked like a scene from A Midsummer Night's Dream. She had no idea how old this delightful building was, or who had set the first stone in place. All she knew was that somewhere along the line she had heard the word Medieval mentioned, which suggested it was at least as old, or even older than Asselton House and the old Manor Cottages in the village. Like the old barn they had just left behind, this mellow house straddled the Sedlescombe/Whatlington boundary, and a prior arrangement had been made for access to and through the property.

From the time she walked up to and into the rambling old house, Sally was enthralled. Though clearly a house of distinction, this place was so much more than a sum of its furniture and fine wood panelling, its accumulation of books and pictures and curious chimneys. As she walked through, she could almost feel the spirits from its ancient past echoing silently down through the centuries. And the ghosts here were of a benign disposition without any shadow of doubt. Sir Alan Moore, the school Doctor lived here with his family now, though on this occasion he was nowhere to be seen. He was a tall angular man, kindly yet remote, and although she was always stupidly tongue-tied in his company, he seemed not to notice. She tried to linger, but impatient hands pushed her along, and suddenly and with a feeling of acute disappointment, she found herself on the pathway outside. As they moved away from the house, she turned and glanced back over her shoulder. As her eye took in its pleasing aspect, she tried to picture the artisan who had set the first foundation stone down into the claggy Sussex soil, and also some of the folk who had helped to shape this curious house, but the fancy failed her. Perhaps later when she had more head space, her imagination would bring these elusive images to life.

She now looked further a field and over the land surrounding the Hancox estate, which was farmed by the Winter family. The tenancy agreement, set up by one of Sir Alan's predecessors, had endured for many years and seemed set to continue. Aunty Peggy was closely related to the Winter family, and she and Uncle Fred Sansom were frequent visitors here. Her Uncle was particularly drawn to the place, finding it a bit of a refuge from the ups and downs of his own hectic lifestyle.

After a brief stop for refreshment, the company moved forward, some now looking weary and certainly the worse for wear. Just prior to their departure, Spilsteads Farm and Riccards Lane had been mentioned with the epithet 'last leg of the journey' offered up as some sort of incentive. Before they reached either location however, there was another brief halt while a sizable group of interested bodies stooped to examine yet another old stone marker with its camouflage of lichen and lush undergrowth. As they waited, Hilary suddenly dropped her bag to the ground and after shuffling through its contents, brought out a handful of Cadbury mini choc bars. "Whew, nearly forgot these," she said as she pulled them apart and handed them around the group within a group. Though soft and misshapen, the dark blue wrappers and bits of silver paper were quickly removed, and the contents were soon disappearing down happy throats. Ethel Thomas, who with her brother Derek had joined them back at the old Barn, reckoned they were life savers, and that slightly exaggerated citation was echoed by the others. Once they had sucked the residual chocolate from around their teeth, there was just time for a quick slurp of water and then it was back to 'follow the leader' again. As they moved forward, Sally took a moment to look back down over the rolling countryside from whence they'd come, feeling a sense of satisfaction and achievement. At least they were on high ground, it would be pretty well all downhill from now on. It was just a case of carrying on and putting one foot in front of the other, she thought as she gave herself and those around her, a symbolic and well deserved pat on the back.

At last the magic words, 'there's the Bowlings,' came from somewhere up front and spread rapidly down through the ranks. There was a perceptible sigh of relief, followed by an immediate tightening of the troop as those at the back pressed forward. There was a short period of vacillation when they reached the Brooks, with so many tired bodies struggling to climb over the stile. Soon however, the younger fitter folk, ever resourceful, found other ways of getting through and on to home ground. Once a measure of order had been restored, the contingent moved forward with a renewed spring in its step, past the Waterfall and then on and into the village.

Sally's eyes lit up when she looked up across the green, where even in the half light, she could see a sizable group of villagers milling around the old Pump House. As she moved closer, she could see Bangy, and beside him, old Fred and Tom and Jim. Even Bollocky Bill was there. No one but no one could mistake that hairy countenance she reckoned and grinned as she remembered the observation made by one of the boys. 'E's got enough 'air there to thatch a bloody stack,' he'd said, and that just about summed up the man and his shaggy fhizzog. A farmer he might be, but to all the youngsters he was and always would be, 'Bollocky Bill the Sailor.'

No one it seemed had expected to see such a large welcoming party, and expressed their surprise and gratitude as drink and a few victuals were handed around. For the youngsters it was crisps and lemonade. For the grownups though, the liquid provided, and which soon began to disappear down thirsty throats, clearly contained something a bit stronger than mere bubbles.

It was tempting to linger, to continue to participate in the jolly aftermath of this special occasion, but it was dark now and the effects of the days ramble was beginning to catch up with them, especially Ethel and Derek who were noticeably tired. Even Ron and Ray now standing alongside were flagging, and after putting up a token show of resistance, turned reluctantly away from the ongoing celebration along with the others. As the little band moved down across the green towards the river bridge, they were trying to remember the names of the woods they had skirted or walked through, and the farmyards and fields they had crossed. They were well along the main road before they were satisfied with the list, and giggled as they began to recite the words parrot fashion: Footlands and Jacobs, Hazel wood and Beech wood, Hancox and Dorrell, they began, with Ron and Ray adding an imaginary name here and there for good measure. Luckily, Paygate corner was reached before the singular spurt of energy petered out, and even as they prepared to go their separate ways, the boys were still churning out jokes one after the other. Where had this burst of energy come from the girls asked themselves as they moved away with the light-hearted banter still ringing in their ears. What they needed and hoped for now was the resolve to keep their own legs in motion lest they seize up altogether. They were also aware that for Pat, a bit of a rest and a good night's sleep were essential. She needed to be up bright and early in the morning to milk Rosebud. Also as Sally was about to mention before thinking better of it, the front room table had not received its regular dose of spit and polish lately, which was most unusual. This impressive round table was her sister's pride and joy and the regular polishing of it had been a willingly undertaken, self-imposed chore for as far back as she could remember.

As they walked up across the field, Sally was thinking about the scrag end neck of lamb stew, laden with vegetables, split peas, and pearl barley that would be simmering at the back of the Rayburn, ready and waiting for them. By the time she had reached the top gate, she could smell it and her mouth began to water. She just hoped mum would already have eaten that horrid asparagus, delivered to the house by Mr Rudge this morning. As far as she was concerned, it was just like eating a bag of snot.

Chapter 15

Sally was about to stir her tea when she noticed a single tea-leaf floating on its surface and hesitated. She studied it for a few seconds, wondering if indeed there was anything in the old superstition, that a stranger would cross her path that day. After due consideration, she stirred the leaf away, remembering that as she and Pat were off to Hastings this morning to replenish Dad's stock of machine thread, it would be many not just one lone stranger who would be crossing her path. She moved up to the kitchen window and was just in time to see dad sprinting across the field, rattling a bit of cow cake in a bucket to entice Rosebud into the milking shed. His little legs were going nineteen to the dozen, and it was easy to imagine him out manoeuvring his opponents when he had played for Crystal Palace football club all those years ago. She wondered if it had been at around that time that he had met Les and Dennis Compton who visited Sylvian from time to time and reckoned it must have been.

Pat was standing at the side of the shed and as Rosebud entered, she moved forward, bucket in hand to carry out the first milking session of the day. She was wearing a large white apron, one of dad's creations, and even from here Sally could make out the thick mustard coloured tape he had used for the halter and waist ties. She moved away from the window, feeing just a wee bit guilty that she had been able to side step this odious chore, and decided that straight after breakfast, she would get on with the pumping. Mum could help her with the priming, she decided. She could do that bit of vigorous pumping while Sally climbed up into the attic and poured water into the pipe attached to the tank up there. Once that business had been sorted out to her satisfaction, she turned her attention to Dorothy and Jacky, who were having a bit of an altercation about whose turn it was to use the fox faced egg cup. A compromise was reached by removing the cups to the side table, and while the little one's backs were turned, covering the cups over with a tea towel, then asking them to choose. Dorothy won, with the promise that it would definitely be Jacky's turn tomorrow.

Later, as she and Pat walked down the field, Sally sniffed the air, which was heavy with the promise of a thunderstorm. It would probably be an hour or two before the full force of it hit them, but it would be a good one, she could feel it in her bones. The weather had been unsettled, moody even for a couple of days now, so she knew it would culminate in a good old show of lightning and thunder. She remembered the evening last summer when she and Hilary had been caught out in one of the most ferocious thunder-storms they'd ever experienced. The thunder had had been rumbling around when they left home and had continued its low key threat as made their way towards the village, but it had not worried them unduly. It had seemed such a long way away, and their only chore had been to deliver handbags to two of dad's customers. Before they passed them over, they had gently fingered the soft leather, and had taken a few moments to examine and appreciate the workmanship in these utilitarian objects. They had then moved down through the village, stopping beside the old pump house to pass the time of day with the youngsters who were grouped around this well established meeting place. It was when one of the youngsters had looked and then pointed anxiously towards the heavens that they had decided to move on. As they were hurrying up Chapel Hill, the lightening began to flash followed by deafening thunder and by the time they reached the top, the first fat drops of rain had begun to fall. They had taken to their heels, sprinting down Crazy Lane and off by the old oak tree where, blinded by rain, and scared witless by lightening, they had ploughed through swathes of vicious stinging nettles. It was only when they reached home, breathless and dripping all over the scullery floor that they realised they had not sustained one single sting. A bloody miracle they called it. She reckoned they were not the only ones to have got a wet shirt that day.

As Sally was walking along the lane with Pat, she looked at the Lords and Ladies that grew up alongside the ditch year on year, and was struck yet again by their curious appearance. There were strange superstitions or old wives tales attached to these plants, with an alternative name cuckoo pint, supposedly being of particular significance. The leaves reminded her of the words, 'speckled and blotched,' in the poem 'Lord Randal my Son,' that she had come across recently. It was however, instinct and the strange odour given off by these fascinating wild plants, rather than superstition or the words of an unhappy love poem that had kept her and her hands well away from the things.

As she walked across the road, she thought she could hear the sound of thunder rumbling away in the distance, then decided it was more likely to be the sound of the bus trundling around cow shit corner. Sure enough, within a couple of minutes, the old number 12 rounded Pay Gate Corner and in response

215

to their outstretched arm, pulled in beside them. As they stepped up and into it, they heard the usual high spirited commotion coming from the top deck, and as there was at least one empty double seat on this lower one, decided to sit here for a change. Having hogged the window seat, Sally sat back to enjoy the sensation of effortless movement. Of course she liked walking and peddling, but this mode of travel suited her once in a while. It was an opportunity to give her undivided attention to the world around her, or what she could see of it. By the time the she had got herself comfortable, the bus had topped Whydown Hill, and was cruising down passed Gotways Farmhouse, with the countryside now opening up around them. The sun was still on show, though struggling now as dark rain bearing cloud began to move in, and the old wind meant business she thought as she looked out across the fields where the grasses were rippling like waves on an endless sea. There were still dog roses in the hedgerows she noticed, with the ox-eye daisy and foxgloves also enjoying their moment of glory; and even with this storm brewing, the white dead nettles alongside the hedge, were swarming with butterflies. Almost best of all she thought as she sent a mental message to the little creatures to seek a safe haven sooner rather than later, was that mum's peonies would change any day now from tight buds to a burst of vermilion petals. She loved this time of year.

The bus stopped opposite Carpenter's Barn, and Margaret Cruttenden and her mum stepped on board, both armed with spiky topped umbrella's. She and Pat hardly ever resorted to the things these days. For a start brollies had an annoying habit of turning inside out in any appreciable breeze, and also a tendency to get lost. The girls relied on their Gabardine rain-coats to keep them dry and apart from that weak spot around the neck, these mackintoshes did protect them from most eventualities. Anyway, with this storm looming, and the likelihood of some spectacular forked lightening in the offing, the last thing she wanted was a mini lightening conductor above her head as she walked around town. Nor did she want to poke someone's eye out with the thing if it came to that. She did like the umbrella song though, especially when dad, Uncle Alf and Uncle Fred sang it in that fine-tuned Cockney accent of theirs. But then she liked most of the songs they sang, Sonny Boy being another favourite, especially the 'when dare are grey skies, ah doan mind de grey skies. I'll still have you Sonny Boy,' bit. Those three, with their mastery of accents and natural talent for mimicry, plus an excellent memory, would have made a darned good Musical Hall act she reckoned.

The bus took a deep breath before tackling the challenge of Ebden's Hill, and by this time, the girls were well into a discussion on roller-skating. Why, Sally was asking, were Pat and Hilary able to keep their balance and even perform a trick or two on them, while she felt more like a chicken with St Vitus dance when she donned the blasted things. Pat likened it to learning to ride a bicycle, but as Sally reminded her, bikes had brakes. The only way she could stop the things from propelling her ever onward was simply to fall over or into a convenient hedge. That however, as she well knew, could be and often was, a painful experience. She was not looking forward to that session at the Roller Skating Rink in Hastings next week one little bit, even with assurances from Roy and Willie that they would have her whizzing around with the best of them by the end of the session. Yeh, and pigs might fly, she thought, knowing full well that she would more likely be spending most of the evening clinging to barriers, a wallflower. The most she could hope for was a bit of moral support and commiseration from a fellow cowardy custard. Mind you, Dave Burt would be there she suddenly remembered, and he seemed to have lots of patience. He lived in Brede, and the first time she'd seen him was when he had appeared at the cycle speedway track alongside Brian Martin. Since then, they had met up with him on a regular basis, and it had not taken her long to suss him out as a good 'un as dad would say. And he was sweet on Hilary, that was for sure. Anyway, it was time to change the subject she decided, and began to question Pat yet again on when she was likely to get the results of that exam she had taken a few months ago. If she had passed as Jumbo James expected then she would be off to the Grammar School in Bexhill in September. Sally couldn't wait. She had heard good things about this school, and who knew what interesting books her younger sister might be bringing home to study. She would ask her to keep an eye out for the one she'd been waiting to get her hands on for ages. 'The Water Babies,' it was called. She was sure this was the book with the Doasyouwouldbedoneby, and Mrs Doasyouwouldbedonebyasyoudid characters in it, which she thought sounded both amusing and meaningful at the same time. Just as she was getting into the subject, Pat suddenly grabbed her shoulder and pointed ahead.

"Blindo flippin top me, did you see that lightening, that was a bit too close for comfort," she shouted, and Sally very nearly jumped out of her seat. So engrossed had she been in books and strange characters that she had not noticed the bus turning from London Road and on to the sea front. "Wow," was the only word that escaped her lips as she looked out over a sea that was bubbling like a cauldron, with lightening dancing, darting, zigzagging like pulses of multi coloured quicksilver, over and above its angry surface.

"I don't like the look of this all," said Pat. "It's okay in the bus but what about when we have to get out of here. We'll get soaked and we could even get struck down dead by this lightening. It looks really, really dangerous out there." Sally could not have agreed more, she was also beginning to feel uneasy. Watching a good old thunderstorm from the safety of the kitchen or scullery at home was one thing, facing this angry beast with little or no protection was something else she reckoned. When the bus came to a halt in Wellington Square, they were sorely tempted to stay put, but necessity overcame trepidation. "In for a penny, in for a pound then," said Pat as she stepped off the bus and into the raging storm, with Sally close on her heels.

They ran along Queen's Road, with ear deafening thunder and forked lightening all around them, and burst into the Singer Sewing Machine shop, breathless and dripping wet. It was several seconds before they got their breath back, by which time Sylvia Upton had moved from the back of the shop to where they were standing, and had closed the door quietly behind them. The girls knew this young lady well and really liked her. She lived in a bungalow in Crazy Lane, and they often stopped and had a chat with her and her mum on their way to and from Bible Class. Dad reckoned 'they were a couple of good 'uns, the genuine article,' and he was a pretty good judge of character

Not surprisingly, they were the only customers in this usually bustling shop, and as Miss Upton busied herself with dad's order, felt free to wander around the plethora of sewing machines here. There was something deep down satisfying about the shape of and decoration on these utilitarian objects, Sally thought, and could not resist fingering them as she moved around the shop. Then her eyes moved towards and lingered for a moment on the boxes stacked up on shelves around the shop. There were enough spare parts here to fit any sewing machine that had ever been invented, she reckoned. Then she turned as Pat touched her arm and pointed towards a wedge of thick waxy substance, similar but in better condition than the piece dad had and which he frequently used to strengthen and smooth the thread he was using.

"That reminds me of what they used on thread before that stuff over there was discovered," she said. "Ear wax. Can you imagine? There was even a narrow spoon like scoop to get the stuff out of your ear 'oles dad said and he wasn't joking. As he said, at least you'd have had a steady supply of fresh warm wax to harvest any time you needed it. Yuk." She said with feeling and grinned then shuddered as she really thought about it.

Miss Upton, trying to suppress a grin, called them over to the counter. "Everything's here, including the needles for your Father's treddle machine," she told them. Something Sally had almost forgotten about. "At least that Rexine bag of yours should keep out most of the rain," she added as she placed the package inside. We'll soon find out, Sally thought to herself as she turned and contemplated the now relentless down pour. Still with that old thunder and lightning less fierce now, at least they were not so likely to be struck down dead. As soon as they left the shop they realised that it would have been pointless trying to avoid the puddles, so they just walked briskly back along Queen's Road, with the water splashing up and into their shoes. They were not far from Posner's now, and Sally just hoped that she would find what she was after in this shop, rather than having to traipse along to Plummer's or Mastin's. They shook themselves off as best they could before venturing inside, then immediately made their way to the underwear department.

"These'll do," she said, pointing towards a display of sturdy white interlock knickers with a bit of lace at the leg. "Me and Hilary want something to wear when we go Old Thyme Dancing. It's really for the 'Lancer's.' when our skirts go right up over our heads if we're not careful. Look they're only two and six, that's not bad, but I'll just get us one each for now. Hilary's given me some money for hers." Once the precious items were paid for and carefully stowed away on top of the other package, they lingered for a while. Although they were quite enjoying this moody weather, it was a chance to dry out a bit before they ventured outside again. As they mooched around, they noticed a display of sheer silk stocking, tastefully displayed on manikin legs. "What does this remind you of," asked Pat and Sally grinned knowing full well what she was on about. It was a shared image they had of Freda and the ritual she performed before she left the house to go somewhere special. The seams on her stockings had to be perfectly straight, and to achieve this she would turn her head this way to check them, then to make doubly sure, would also ask one of the girls to check them for her. Mind you, her fastidiousness did pay off. She always looked glamorous, or 'the cat's whiskers,' as they put it.

It was still raining when they left the shop, but the dark clouds were beginning to roll away, taking most of the thunder and streak lightening with them. They looked up as the Memorial clock struck the half hour, and decided they would have enough time to snatch a drink in Dimarco's Café before the next bus was due to leave. After making their way through the Arcade, they crossed the road and into the café, which was not quite as bustling as usual. They chose a window seat, from where they could monitor the comings and goings of the buses into Wellington Square, and as they were putting their bags down, Mr Dimarco came over to the table. After asking after mum as he always did, he took their order and in no time at all, they were sipping a hot sweet cup of tea.

They were ready and waiting when their bus lumbered into view, depositing a surprising number of passengers into the square. But then, not really surprising Sally thought to herself. It was unlikely that people would allow a mere storm to stop them performing their weekly ritual, when just a few short years ago they had faced up to a far, far greater and fiercer threat than this one. After all, what was a bit of rain, thunder and lightning in comparison to that bombardment from the old Luftwaffe.

They were tempted to linger a while, but they had a busy day ahead of them, with the peas to pick and shuck for dinner, and shopping to fetch from the village. Hopefully the rain would have stopped or just dwindled to a bit of a mizzle by then. Anyway, it was sausage and mash for dinner today, accompanied by thick gravy and lots of cabbage and peas, Sally reminded her sister as they boarded the bus. She always topped her mashed potato with a smidgen of the juice from the sausages and a sprinkle of Sifta salt, delicious. For pudding, it was baked semolina, another favourite dish, and they thanked their lucky stars that mum was such a good cook.

Sally turned her head towards the clock ticking away slowly on the schoolroom wall. There was still a good half hour to go before home time, she calculated and returned to her scribbling with a sigh of resignation. She was not bored far from it, but it was Wednesday, Hilary's half day, and she could not wait to vacate her desk and make her way to the front of the school where she knew her friend would be waiting. Since Hilary's dad had moved out of the family home, the two girls had made the journey into Hastings nearly every Wednesday afternoon, to meet him from work and have tea with him. The protracted and eventual disintegration of Mr and Mrs Elkins' marriage had caused a lot of distress within the family, with Hilary and Ronald being particularly affected by it. Yet they had coped somehow. As Hilary had remarked only a couple of days ago, 'life has to go on and so forth.'

Sure enough, Hilary was waiting at the railings and Pat who had beaten Sally to it, was beside her. They walked and ran down through the village, on along the main road, and were home in time for a quick turnaround before catching the number 12 into Hastings for their rendezvous with Mr Elkins.

Hilary and Sally hopped off the bus beside the White Rock Pavilion, and crossed over the road for a quick look out over the sea. They calculated they had twenty minutes or so before Mr Elkins finished work, enough time to peruse the beach and surrounding area before making their way along and into Robertson Street to meet up with him. They leaned over the railings along the promenade, screwing up their eyes against the glare of the sun as it glittered on the water, and contemplated the scene in silence for a few moments. Today the sea was calm, benevolent almost, the waves rippling across the sand and breaking onto the foreshore with barely a sound. It could be very different though as they well knew. It was a moody, unpredictable entity, and fisher folk with their long and intimate association with the sea, treated it with the greatest respect and rightly so. Their lives and livelihoods depended upon it.

After a while, they turned reluctantly away from contemplation of sea and sand and juxtaposition of movable objects, re-crossed the road, and dawdled towards Robertson Street. They paused a couple of times to look in shop windows, and just as they approached the corset shop, they spotted Mr Elkins walking towards them, a large carrier bag dangling from his left arm. They knew at once that packed away inside that bag would be a delicious selection of cakes, fresh from the bakery in which he worked, one or two for tea, the rest to take home with them. He was a Master Baker. Not only did he produce a delicious daily feast of bread and rolls and confectionary, but the celebratory cakes he created were legendary. After the usual greetings, they set off towards the White Rock gardens, their favourite route through to Bohemia Road where Mr Elkins now lived. Hilary and her dad were now talking nineteen to the dozen, or rather Hilary was talking and Mr Elkins was giving her his undivided attention. They were very close those two Sally thought as she listened, noting the ease with which they communicated. These meetings were so important to them.

There were only insects and the occasional butterfly hovering over the flowers and clumps of wild thyme in the well-tended though not overly fussy gardens, with no sign whatever of a wraithlike fairy. Ah well you couldn't have everything Sally thought as she sprinted a few paces to catch up with the other two. Really, life was not half bad one way or the other she reckoned, and had a feeling that the elusive little creature would not hide from her forever.

By the time they reached the house in Bohemia Road, they were ready for the cup of tea and refreshment they knew would be waiting for them. Sure enough, once they were through the door, Mrs Ingram, Mr Elkins' Landlady came forward to tell them that tea was ready. Her timing was faultless. She always greeted them formally with just a soft handshake, and though she waited on them hand and foot, she never joined them at the table.

Between mouthfuls, they chatted and giggled their way through ITMA, one of their favourite radio programs, with Mr Elkins, whose powers of mimicry were on a par with dad and his brothers, doing most of the talking. Mrs Mopp's, 'can I do you now sir?' slipped as easily and believably from his lips as Colonel Chinstrap's, 'I don't mind if I do.' And the mock formality of: 'After you Cecil. No after you Claude,' had the girls in stitches. Once the characters and catch phrases in ITMA had been done to death, they moved from the ridiculous not exactly to the sublime but onto something a bit more reflective. Mr Elkins was asking, and Hilary was updating him on what had occurred in and around Sedlescombe over the past week. He had always been active within the village, helping to arrange whist drives, jumble sales, dances and other fund raising events, and had taken a major part in the arrangement of the yearly school outing events. And although Mr Gregory had initiated the appearance of the Billy Cotton Band Show in the village, Mr Elkins had also been involved in this popular event. It was obvious he missed the camaraderie, the close relationship he had had with the locals hence his avid interest in what was now occurring within the village. Eventually and inevitably, the conversation moved onto a discussion on Old Thyme Dancing, with the girls vying with one another to hog the verbal high ground. 'The Lancers,' the reason for the purchase of those new knickers, was discussed in great detail, and Mr Elkins listened, a smile hovering around his mouth and emphasising the deep creases around his eyes. After a while, Sally just had to mention the long frock Betty was making for her to wear when she went to special dances. It was in a soft cream coloured material, gathered in at the waist, and with a frill around its boat shaped neckline. It would be hers this weekend her sister had told her so, and Betty always kept her promises. It might just need a slight adjustment here and there but that was all. Hilary's frock was next. She had already chosen a style similar to her own, and Betty had managed to find a length of pale blue satiny material with which to make it. They would also be getting one of Betty's special padded hangers, made up from left over scraps of material to go with them. She was a dab hand when it came to needlework was Betty.

They continued to chat, pausing briefly to gather together cups, saucers and plates for Mrs Ingram to take away to the kitchen, then relaxed back into their seats and carried on talking. The time passed by in a flash as it always did on these visits, and all too soon it was time to gather together their belongings ready for departure. Particular care and attention was paid to the bag of goodies, always carried to the bus stop by Mr Elkins and passed to Hilary as she stepped up onto the bus. There was never any chance that this particular package would get left behind. "Back shortly Kay," Mr Elkins called out as they left the house, and in no time at all they were standing at the bus stop awaiting the number 12.

"Look after yourself dad," said Hilary, holding her hand out for the precious package as the bus pulled up in front of them. "I will, it's being so cheerful as keeps me going," he replied, and "ta, ta," his parting comment as they stepped up to and onto the bus, and they grinned. There was in that ITMA programme, a character or saying appropriate to any eventuality it seemed.

Hilary was quiet for the first part of the homeward journey, then the natural order of things reasserted itself and they were soon chatting away as normal. Mum, they decided was getting a bit low on wood for the copper, so sometime this weekend, they must replenish her stocks. They would take Dora and Jacky to the big wood with them, they decided and perhaps they could persuade Betty to come along too. The old Rexine covered pram would go with them that was for definite, it was surprising how much wood could be packed into and across the old thing. It was worth its weight in gold they reckoned, and tried to calculate the number of miles it had done, often being pushed or dragged over challenging ground, with both Dorothy and Jacky on board. Hilary remembered the time she had walked a fretful Jacky to Wayside in that pram, and had arrived back home with a bag of duck eggs in the time it had taken Sally to hem up a couple of dresses. Mum could not believe it. It had done the trick though, and had settled Jacky down a treat.

Something that kept both Jacky and Doro entertained for hours on end Hilary was saying, was the ticklish art of daisy chain making. There were masses of these bright little flowers around, and once the two had chosen and eaten their cake, there should be just about enough time to make up a couple of bracelets before bed time, she reckoned. Finding ones with decent stems would be no problem. They all knew where they were. The usual garlanding from top to toe was out of the question of course, which was just as well Sally thought to herself. Fixing delicate chains, particularly around the ankles of a couple of wriggling dervishes was challenging to say the least. Another favourite past time, and a definite maybe for the weekend, was a cheesy bob hunt. There were masses around if you knew where to look. The youngsters would lay on the ground with their noses just inches above it, and with a delicate touch, turn the mini segmented bugs into a good impersonation of a small ball bearing. It kept them quiet for ages. Hunting for and finding a web of baby spiders however, was their all-time favourite. They would creep up and gently touch the web, and in a split second, the speckle of animated dots would turn into a tightly packed, inert ball. They would wait for the few minutes it took for the little creatures to re-emerge, then they would touch and watch all over again.

After ringing the bell as the bus passed Brown's old place, the girls left their seats and as they waited for the vehicle to come to a halt, spotted a movement along the lane. The little ones were up to their usual tricks. Best humour them they thought. With studied nonchalance they walked the short distance to the bottom of the field, and as Hilary put her hand on the gate to open it, they popped up from behind the hedge, emitting what they considered a blood-curdling shriek. A good impression of shock horror from the older girls had them in stitches and it was a while before order was restored.

Once indoors, some of the special cakes were handed around, the rest packed resolutely away in one of mum's large cake tins and they munched away contentedly. Soon residual crumbs were being licked from sticky fingers, and the rest washed away with the aid a bit of mum's Sunlight soap and a trickle of water from the scullery tap. Then the youngsters were off, out of the door and into the field like rockets. They were anxious to make the most of the short window of opportunity between now and bedtime, knowing that that dreaded hour was creeping up on them. The older girls followed rather more leisurely, with mums, "don't get them too excited now," ringing in their ears. By the time they caught up, avoiding the fresh pancakes over which a few ginger dung flies were still hovering, the little ones were already immersed in the serious business of daisy chain making. With a combination of supple fingers and a bit of expertise, the operation flowed, and by the time mum called them over the youngsters were decked out in an impressive array of flower jewellery. Dad's only comment as he opened the gate for them to pass through was, "better than all them diamonds," and the words of Mr Smith from the Manse suddenly popped up into Sally's mind. She had once heard him describe her dad as a gruff but honest man of integrity, and that just about summed him up she reckoned.

Later, as Sally walked down the field arm in arm with Hilary, she looked up into the Heavens and spotted the crescent of a new moon and breathed a sigh of relief. Her luck was in. If there had been glass between her eyes and that mysterious object, she would have been a bit anxious for the next few weeks, which was absurd really. She treated mum's habit of bowing and scraping to the thing as a bit of a joke, but still felt uneasy when certain rites and rituals were not carried out. It was a 'just in case' sort of thing she supposed. Hilary was on her way home and as it was still light, Sally was walking as far as the end of the lane with her. They paused for a while beside the cottages to make arrangements for the Old Thyme Dancing on Friday, and once these had been made to their satisfaction, went their separate ways. Sally ran back along the lane, up the field and on to the underground tank to wave to Hilary who was already standing beside Pay Gate corner waving to her. As she hopped back off the lump of concrete and up and into the scullery, she caught the aroma of hot cocoa. Hooray for Rosebud, she thought. There was always plenty of milk around these days.

In spite of that bedtime beverage, deep sleep evaded her. Each time she drifted away from conscious thought, she floated off and into the fantastical, Technicolor world of Oz and other strange, mythological spheres. She would wake in a daze, struggle to adjust from unreality to the real and believable, then when she'd relaxed and managed to doze off again, the pattern would repeat itself. What occurred in the land of Nod was weird and disjointed, unexplainable and unpredictable she thought as she rubbed the sleep from her eyes the next morning. It was puzzling, but was just a case of passing through one gateway in the mind to another, she told herself. She just wished she had some control over it.

Chapter 16

It was going to be a lovely day. Even before she'd opened her eyes early this morning, Sally had been aware of that strange, unearthly silvery light, associated with a spell of fine weather and had drawn her own optimistic conclusions. Chanting Gran Powell's magic words, 'black hares' at night and 'white rabbit' first thing in the mornings, seemed to be working - so far so good.

It was Saturday, Pat had finished the milking, and once she had finished her breakfast, she and Sally would be taking the two containers mum had already filled with the warm liquid along to Hazel and her Mother in law, Mrs Soan in the village. The list for the shopping mum needed was already in her dress pocket. Hazel was expecting a baby later in the year and Sally was thrilled to bits that her sister had already asked her to be a God Mother to the child. It was a daunting responsibility, she realised.

As the girls walked briskly up Crazy Lane, the milk in the containers sloshed rhythmically to and fro in time with their footsteps. When they reached the brow of the hill, they paused briefly beside Farrow's gate and looked out over the countryside. The sky was clear but for a few wispy clouds dotted here and there, prompting Pat's comment, 'rare as quick setting string, a Saturday like this,' and Sally nodded in agreement. After pointing out various landmarks in the far and middle distance, they moved away from the five bar gate and continued on their way. It was just a case of putting one foot in front of the other down Chapel Hill. Gravity did the rest.

As they walked across the bridge, Sally suddenly remembered the shopping list tucked away in her pocket, and hastily retrieved it. If they popped it into the shop now, the groceries mum needed would be ready for them by the time they returned from their milk deliveries. Freda would make sure of that. Reg Phillips delivered groceries to mum on a regular basis, but at this time of year in particular, when friends and family arrived at Sylvian non-stop, extras were needed. The Elvine family, Mrs Elvine, daughters Doreen and Joan, the latter with her husband and daughter, had departed yesterday having spent the past couple of weeks at Sylvian. Those two weeks had been so much fun. Pete, Joan's husband in particular, with his boundless energy and enthusiasm, had had them all running around playing tip it and run, rounders, and some other games they'd never even heard of, all played without visible rule or regulation. It was Pete who had pulled a dripping Peggy Doe from the stream that early morning after she'd slipped while they were fleeing from an irate farmer whose mushrooms they had been scrumping. They still laughed about it even now. Still Aunty Ethel, Uncle Cecil and Stephen were due to arrive here by late afternoon, and they were all looking forward to seeing them again; Stephen, Dorothy and Jacky got on particularly well together. In fact it was because Sally was chatting about them and relating one incident in particular that had occurred while they were visiting earlier in the year, that had put that note in her pocket right out of mind. Aunty after a deal of persuasion, and clearly against her better judgement, had agreed to accompany Hilary and Sally to a dance on the Saturday evening. Bad decision. After an hour or two of feeling completely out of place, she had decided to take herself off home, not realising how dark it had become. Down through the village, with a lighted window here and there, it was not too scary she said. However, once she reached the bridge and began to make her way along the main road in pitch darkness, she reckoned she'd never felt so scared in all her life. She was in a right old state, shaking like a leaf when she had burst through and into the kitchen, mum said. She looked for all the world like the old Googly Moosh himself was after her. Although Sally could empathise, knowing what a scary guts she was, she still found the whole thing amusing. Even Aunty had seen the funny side of it the following morning - in the bright light of day of course.

Once the shopping list was sorted, they made their way towards the cottage just above the village hall where Mrs Soan lived. They chatted to the old lady for the time it took her to empty the contents of the container into a couple of jugs, rinse the thing out and pass it back to them. Then they were off, covering the short distance to the little cottage where Hazel and Albert now lived in the blinking of an eye. Hazel as always, anticipated their arrival, and in no time at all they were sitting and chatting around the kitchen table with her, a mug of cocoa held comfortably between clasped hands. They loved it here.

After a while, they stood up and moved reluctantly away from the table, picked up the bags, and began to think about their next port of call, Phillips' shop, where the weight of the milk they had now delivered, would be more than compensated for by the shopping they'd be collecting. Also, as Pat reminded Sally, they had other jobs to do when they got home, the picking of the late ripening fruit from the bushes around by the greenhouse, ready for mum to turn into pies and crumbles, for instance. The bulk of the fruit had been picked and processed earlier on, while Aunty Nellie had been here. She often arrived when the soft fruit season was at it height and she and mum spent hour upon hour, making jam and bottling fruit; with the aid of the old Primus stove, of course. Another talent of theirs, a skill inherited from Granny Sansom no doubt, was their ability to turn a gross pigs head into the most succulent, delicious brawn. 'Just remember to wipe its nose and clean its ears, that's all. Leave its eyes in and they'll see you through the week,' Aunty had commented once, accompanied by that characteristic giggle of hers.

The girls were level with the Pump House when they spotted Old Fred and Bangy emerging slowly from the track leading to the allotments. The two men paused beside the green, lowered the Hessian bags they were carrying onto the grass, and stood looking down towards the river bridge. Old Fred was smoking one of his roll ups they noticed, and as he half turned his head towards his mate, they saw him pick a bit of tobacco idly off his tongue. As the girls moved closer, their footsteps muffled by the grass, they heard him voice an amusing bit of doggerel.

"Jest like assoles be lettuce. Everyone's got 'em," he said, then turned around his face a picture as he suddenly became aware of their presence. "Blindo flippin top me, frit the bloody life out er me yer did," he exclaimed, then paused for a few seconds, momentarily lost for words. Sally stifled her giggles as best she could, looking away from his startled face and onto the bags on the ground as she sought to compose her features. Noting her redirected gaze with relief, he began to regale them with the merits of the contents within.

"Jest look at me unyons. Me en Bangy jest got em from yon allotments, see? I were jest saying how's some of em be thet big, they be needin a jock strap fer support, specially thet en on top there," he said, pointing to a particularly large specimen that even dad would have been impressed by. "Good bit a soil over dare, see? A sprinkle o sultanas, en it could be yer actual Dundee cake," he added with a grin. "En o course we do ave a good awld army of deff adders over dare what clears up a lot o bliddy pests en all. Jest as well old Cokey Coleman from Cripp's ent ere to see em, me unyons. Make is bloody eyes pop out, en all. Allers goin on about growin unyons big as cocernuts, cept 'e's the only one what sees 'em. Bout as useful es a strainer without no oles in be owld Cokey, en I tells him so. Yer puts yer bliddy plants en seeds in arse uppards, thet be your trouble, I tells im, but e jest chuckles. E ain't a bad'n really, not when yer takes im all in all. Even though e do stretch truth till it be no more'n lies. Owes yer chickens then?" He asked after a short pause. "Gettin' plenty of eggs are e? Jest stick a feather in a tatty en it er lay you en egg at this time o the year, I allas says, cept awld Bangy ere told me thet un really." Bangy just chuckled, his eyes twinkling in that weather beaten old face of his.

The girls stayed listening to the chatter of the two old men for as long as they dared. The time was getting on now, and they had peas to pick and shuck as well as that fruit when they got home they remembered. They didn't mind shucking the peas and mostly sat on the underground tank to do so. They would chew on some of the sweet, empty husks as they worked, the rest would be taken around and deposited on dad's stinky old compost heap.

They collected the shopping and were just approaching cow shit corner, when they saw Basil Beeching freewheeling down Chapel Hill on his bicycle, and paused to pass the time of day with him. Uppermost in their minds and dominating their conversation of course, was the conversation they had just had with Old Fred and Bangy. At that precise moment, they were trying to memorise one of Fred's ditties, and Basil grinned as he listened to their feeble attempts to mimic that characteristic accent:

> *"Oi went round a straight crooked corner.*
> *And see'd a dead donkey die.*
> *Oi got out me pistol to stab it.*
> *En e it me one in the eye."*

After listening to them for a few moments, he offered up other snippets of wit and wisdom he had gleaned from them and other old villagers, most of whom he reckoned had experienced the loss of loved ones in wars or from disease. Also their living and working conditions had been pretty dire, yet they mostly glossed over these hardships, he said. The girls listened and nodded as he quoted a couple of these pearls of wisdom. 'Don't put your wishbone where your backbone aught to be,' and 'ah my child, if wishes were horses then beggars would ride.' And another, 'handsome is as handsome does.' All trotted out from time to time and when appropriate. These pearls of wisdom, when delivered by Bangy and his mates, were usually followed by tales of youthful experiences and exploits, that had the youngsters creased up with side-splitting laughter. And Battle Market it seemed had provided them with a fair few opportunities for mischief if not mayhem. The old organ grinder it seemed had come in for his fair share of teasing, his monkey distracted to say the very least, and they were not averse to creeping up on farmers with frisky animals, clapping loudly and then running away. One time, Old Fred told them, 'Little Shaky got so drunk e couldna see through a ladder, en we ad to carry the bugger ome. We warn't so appy thet day, cept Jessie Kenward were thar, en e were big en strong es a blidddy Oxe.' Luckily it seemed, Jessie had also been with them one particularly cold day, when several of them had been skating on the ice across the Brooks. Bunny had fallen through the ice and into the icy cold water, and it had been mostly down to Jessie that they'd got him home before he had frozen to death.

Before they went on their way, the girls persuaded Basil to recite their latest tongue twister, and giggled as the faster he went the more jumbled the words became. 'Red leather, yellow leather,' he chanted, stopping and starting as he tried to coordinate lips and tongue. Just to even the odds, they also had a go, with even more disastrous results. The girls were still practising the bit of nonsense when they got to Farrow's steps, without much success. Still as Sally remarked, what was that small thing when compared with the news that Bangy shared her aversion to Asparagus. 'Jest like eating a dead sock,' he said, echoing her own take on the stuff. Now that had really cheered her up.

As they walked up the field, the girls noticed the freshly washed bed linen, pegged out and flapping gently in the breeze, a testament to the fact that mum had not been idle while they'd been away. Pegged in somewhere alongside that lot she hoped were the skirt and bolero Betty had made for her, which was ideal for Square Dancing, amongst other things. She would be wearing this outfit until it dropped off her back she reckoned, just as she had with her favourite yellow sweater. She still missed that tatty old thing. Pat had a similar set, and said she always felt like the Cat's Whiskers when she wore hers. At least all the washing was drying nicely by the look of it and rightly so, she thought. Apart from those few mares tales up above, the sky was pretty well cloud free.

Hilary and Sally were standing at the bus stop at Black Brooks, all set for the Thursday evening Square Dance session on the Pier. Hilary was wearing a blouse and dirndl skirt, and Sally her beloved skirt and bolero. The first thing they did when the bus pulled up alongside them was to make sure Cecil Taylor was on board, and of course he was. They also knew that Ron Edwards would be waiting for the bus at Kent Street, possibly with his brother Ken and brother in law Alec Alexander alongside. Ken however, was courting and Alec who was married to Ron's sister Joyce, was now a proud father, so it was touch and go as to whether they would be there. A condition of the girls being allowed to stay to the end of the Square Dance session was that at least one of these young men would be there to see them home safely. If they were on their own, the girls would be obliged to leave the Pier early, in time to catch the last bus through to the village. When the men were there however, which was almost always, they would take a later bus as far as Westfield Lane and walk down Ebden's Hill, through Kent Street and on and into Black Brooks; and if push came to shove, would walk the whole way home.

Once the bus was over the hill, they saw Ron standing alone beside the bus stop, and were not surprised that the other two had not made it. He hopped up onto the bus, took the seat next to Cecil, and for a while the conversation was all about Square Dance routines with their precise and complicated foot work and ambiguous titles, which they all agreed was nearly but not quite as enjoyable as the Old Thyme variety. The two men, who had had a bit more practice than the girls, did most of the talking, and as Sally listened, tried to reassure herself that perhaps she had just about progressed beyond the two left feet stage. At least she was able to follow the dictates of the Caller, or the Task Master as she and Hilary called him, albeit with movements often just a split second behind those around her, she thought ruefully.

By the time the bus swung around the corner at the bottom of London Road, Cecil and Ron were on to comedy shows, Monsewer Eddie Gray and the Crazy Gang in particular. As Sally listened and chuckled alongside, she looked out over the sea and could not help but compare its calm aspect, its puny waves, with how it had been on the day of that frightful storm. She began to experience that same thrill of excitement and exhilaration as she had that day when she had watched those huge waves being whipped into a white foam by the off shore winds. She remembered how she and Pat had braved the elements, battling the length and breadth of Queen's Road as the storm had raged around them. Though soaked to the skin, they had revelled in the spectacle of Old Mother Nature flexing her muscles, she remembered and grinned to herself. Her sister was as crazy as she was she reckoned.

As soon as they set foot on the Pier, the low hum of preparation they could hear coming from the far end, meant that they had arrived before the start of proceedings. So far so good, Sally thought to herself. She always felt a bit awkward if they arrived when the dancing was in full flow; they always managed to get in some ones way. Also, as Hilary remarked, they needed a bit of time to compose themselves before the 'step to your partners' and so forth began.

Luckily, the dances so far this evening, were ones that Hilary and Sally recognised, and they had been able to follow the dictates of the Caller, even to anticipate his next directive. It was now coming up to the last dance before the interval, and as they heard the title, 'The Cumberland Square' announced, they grinned. Having participated in this particular routine in their Country Dance days, they left their seats with a measure of confidence and enthusiasm.

During the interval as they sat sipping cold drinks, there was the usual discussion on performance and progress, with Cecil as always the chief protagonist. He delighted in mulling over the nights occurrences, insisting on going through every dance routine and their performance within it with a fine tooth comb. However, he always parried his observations be they of a complimentary or critical nature, with a grin and a chuckle, and this was always, always followed by a few words of encouragement. Hilary and Sally, grateful for the welcome bit of breeze coming from open windows and doors, listened with half an ear to what he was saying. Luckily, the occasional nod or shake of the head was all that was really required of them, so they relaxed back into their seats to re-energise and prepare themselves for the second half.

After the break, the routines were less familiar to the girls and they were grateful for the ongoing guidance of Ron and Cecil, also they had to admit, for the ongoing precise instruction from the Caller. There seemed to be many more head spinning twists and twirls, and strange backward and forward movements in these dances, and by the end of the session they felt quite giddy, or swipey as Gilbert Carter would have called it. It did not occur to them to sit out a dance here and there, though the flash of a nervous grin did accompany the announcement of the more obscure routines.

By the time they left the Pier, the sun had dipped down beneath the horizon, with barely a glimmer of orange glow visible to pronounce its departure. On the way to the bus stop, the girls paused beside the railings, leaned over and listened to the waves lapping gently over the sand and pebbles. It was pleasantly cool now, and after the noise, toil and sweat of the past hour or two, they found the experience very therapeutic. Once they'd had their moment or two of silent contemplation, they linked arms and wandered over to Ron and Cecil, who were now on the subject of Friday evening's Old Thyme Dance session.

The faithful old bus drew up beside them, with an appreciable number of passengers already on board. Once they'd found seats and the Conductor had clipped their return tickets, they leant back in their seats to make the most of the breather before they undertook the last and longer part of the journey on Shanks Pony. Their rest and relaxation was short lived as they knew it would be. In no time at all Wayside had come and gone, the old bridge was looming, and it was nearly time for them and the old bus to part company.

They hopped off the bus at the top end of Westfield Lane and stepped lightly onto Ebden's Hill, grateful that from now on it was nearly all downhill. It was easy to see through the dark of a summer night, not like in winter when you'd be hard put to see a hand in front of your face, Sally thought as she looked around her. Even the knarled, gargoyle decorated trunks of the ancient Oaks in the woodland here were thrown into sharp relief by the curious play of light and shadow. She blinked, and an image of Herne The Hunter, that mysterious stag horned apparition, popped up behind her eye-lids. Suddenly the absolute certainty she'd had that he was just a creature of legend, thought up by some medieval dreamer, melted away. She was beset by a weird, oddly compelling impression of a benign, ever watchful presence that existed somewhere in that realm between myth and reality, an entity in harmony with the forests complex fauna and flora. Maybe this was just a flight of fancy, but for a fleeting moment she had felt a strange connection with some watchful Sentinel, whose singular quest for balance and harmony, give or take the odd aberration, extended beyond wild places and into the world of mankind. She did not envy him the task. However, she found this enigmatic encounter strangely comforting.

Her attention suddenly switched from the realms of fantasy and into the here and now when she heard the expression, 'bless 'is little toffee toloured titfer,' and grinned knowing full well to whom Cecil was referring. Bill Holmes had got a new hat. It was a cross between a trilby and a tammy in style, tawny in colour and with a definite vernacular look about it: and he wore it everywhere. Having sussed that out she was all ears as Cecil continued to talk about this eccentric fellow. When he began to tell the tale about the time Bill had been persuaded, against his better judgement, to accompany some of the local lads to the Battle bonfire celebrations, she grinned wryly, knowing exactly what was coming.

"The Jumping Jacks and rookies scared him half to death, then when the Battle rousers got going, they reckon he went rigid with fear. At one point there, they thought they'd lost him," said Cecil. He paused here to usher the girls out of harm's way as a car approached, before continuing. "Anyway, they carried him into the back room of the pub on the corner there, and sort of brought him round a bit, but he never what you might call recovered properly and in the end they had to carry him home. They were sorry you bet they were. He's not fat but he's pretty solid is our Bill."

Sally could empathise and how. She hated those 'bangers' with a vengeance. Yet she always attended these displays, immediately regretting it and spending the whole evening in a state of fear and with her fingers stuck firmly in her ears. She was a bloody fool she told herself.

At the bottom of the hill, the wooded area gave way to a more open aspect, where during the day, the fields and roadside verges would be alive with butterflies and bees, lightly supping nectar and pollen from the wide selection of wild flowers here. By now of course the night shift would have taken over, and she thought about and tried to picture the creatures within this shadowy world. Small rodents for instance, potential victims of prowling foxes and the silent barn owl. And secretive moths would be hovering silently, mysteriously over the dusky landscape, sharing this domain with those mice and voles and their nemeses. She could not see or hear these creatures, but she knew they were there.

She pricked up her ears, relinquishing thoughts of secret night and the odd fantasy, when she heard the name Tony mentioned. Cecil was talking about his brother, and in particular the change a spell of discipline in the Army had made to the little miscreant who prior to this sobering experience, had been full of fun and devilment, his youthful pranks legendary.

"He ran rings round mum and dad when he was a kid did our Tony," Cecil was saying. "I remember dad being particularly upset when the little devil ran off with his razor and ruined the thing, whittling wood and goodness knows what else with it. But that never stopped him. He just shrugged off the odd clout here and there and even seemed to take the few canings he got at school in his stride. Tough little bugger he was. Of course he had to grow up once he got into the Army. What really put him on the straight and narrow though as far as we're concerned was discovering he had a natural flair for playing musical instruments. Well he didn't discover it exactly. It was pointed out to him by one of the senior officers. He could play the Bugle like nobody's business, and he even became a Drummer Boy, and you've got to be good to be given that responsibility," he added, clearly fond and quite proud of that brother of his. He paused here for a quick mental check before adding for good measure. "And, he's still got that old Vesta case granddad gave him all those years ago."

The girls chuckled as they thought about other tales of mischievous deeds they'd listened to over the years, carried out by this and earlier generations of village youth and at times, the not so very young. Some of these tales were so old, they were probably more imagination than substance, purely anecdotal, but when chronicled by natural story tellers like Bangy and Fred and Mercy Dengate, they were pure magic. Sally remembered with amusement, old Fred's expression and exclamation when he had seen Philly Brooman walking down across the village green towards them that time. 'Blind o flippin top me. If er 'air done look loik a barse broom in a froit,' he'd said. And she'd known exactly what he meant. She allowed her imagination to linger for a few moments on Fred, then Bangy, with his bow legged stance and bright twinkling eyes, and then on Mercy Dengate, who's brogue and smile warmed the very cockles of your heart; mum's expression, not her own. She suddenly realised how lucky she was, and how important it was that another generation was ready and able to carry on the tradition of tale telling when these old villagers shuffled off the mortal coil. She felt reasonably optimistic that this would be so as she listened to the flow and content of the conversation taking place around her, and was more than satisfied that this would happen by the time Ron had finished telling the tale of Mr Freddie Stuart's winning of the Sedlescombe Marathon. He was up there with old Bangy and his mates when it came to telling a tale was Ron, combining the amusing detail and drama of an incident, and adding just that obligatory bit of poetic licence here and there for good measure. The annals of the village would be safe in the hands of these two young men she reckoned, alongside the likes of Albert Soan of course.

She was suddenly aware that they were coming up alongside the entrance to Gotways Farm, only moments away now from the farm track leading to Ron's house where he and they would be parting company. They moderated their pace as they approached the track, then paused briefly at its entrance to discuss the Speedway fixtures for the weekend. It was Saints versus Wolves on Sunday afternoon, and with the team they'd got, plus Diggie Fuller as their Mascot, it was odds on that Sedlescombe would beat Westfield this time. That having been said and decided, Ron bade them farewell. "Got to be up bright and early for work in the morning," he said as he began to make his solitary way down along the track.

From the top of Whydown Hill, Sally could hear the steady plop, plop of water as it dripped from the pipe at the side of the bank and into the mini reservoir below. This pipe had been positioned so, by some enterprising soul, possibly an occupant of one of the isolated cottages around here, to harness and control the flow of water from the natural springs in the fields above. There were many such springs in these parts, as she well knew. From as far back as she could remember, she and Pat had watched the water from the ones in the field at home, bubbling up out of the ground like mini cauldrons, and had been utterly fascinated by this puzzling phenomenon. According to Mr Collins, most of those seemingly bottomless wells around here that scared her half to death owed their very existence to these natural water sources. In the rainy season when the water here was in full spate, Ellen Brown would fill bucket after bucket of the soft spring water, and trot off home to use for her various household chores. She still visited the watering station periodically even when the flow was reduced to a mere trickle. She would pause for a brief inspection and either tut-tutt her way back down the hill empty bucket in hand, or place the receptacle carefully beneath the sluggish drip and return when the thing was full. Her timing was uncannily accurate they'd noticed.

They were soon up to and passing Lucks Ness cottage, with Blackbrooks cottages now just a few easy steps away. As they turned off the main road and into the lane, Sally's sensitive nose picked up a bit of a whiff from the stagnant water in the ditch alongside. She had no problem with this however, remembering only too well, how much worse that indescribable stench of raw sewage along here had been before the lavvies in the cottages nearby had been given a bit of major surgery. It had been a case of holding your breath as you ran towards the field, and hoping that by the time you took your next gulp the pong would have been diluted with a bit of fresh air.

They paused beside the bottom gate for the usual last minute briefing, before parting company. Then Sally made her way across the field while Hilary and Cecil stayed where they were, awaiting her usual salutation from the security of the top gate. She did not rush indoors immediately like a frightened rabbit as she usually did, but lingered beside the gate listening to the low hum of their voices, the click clack of their footsteps as they retreated back along the dusty, pot-holed track. Even when all human sound had ceased, she stayed where she was, reluctant to relinquish the mood of magical fancy that had been with her since that strange, compelling experience she'd had with Herne the Hunter. She closed her eyes momentarily, and the whimsicality of this curious night closed in around her. The rustle from the fruit trees in the orchard was some Will – o – the Wisp or Jack – o Lantern, while the light breeze across her face, was the touch of Queen Mab and her entourage passing by. Then she opened her eyes as the cat, having appeared out of nowhere, wound itself slowly around her ankles. Damn, she muttered. She had been in the magical world of Moonshine's watery beam, of wing of grasshopper and smallest spiders web. Still, an image of that 'small grey coated knat, not half so big as a round little worm, picked from the lazy finger of a maid,' remained along with those curious little atomies, and for that she was grateful. The spell had been interrupted but not severed, she thought as she bent down to stroke the furry assassin.

She stood up and looked out across the field and beyond, her eye resting for a moment on the solitary light over the pump in Blackbrooks Garage, then over towards the village where just a sporadic twinkle suggested that most of the villagers were in the land of nod. Perhaps at this very moment, Cecil was walking up to and into his little cottage beside the Green, she thought. Then she turned and made her way along the path and up and into the scullery.

Dad was sitting in his customary seat beside the kitchen table, and looked up as she entered. A large cushion was propped up beside him, a threaded circular needle to hand, which suggested he'd been doing a bit of a repair job on the thing. He and mum were never idle for long, their motto, 'use time in time while time lasts. For all times no time when times past,' very much adhered to. He had abandoned the task a while ago now though she reckoned as she observed his facial tiredness and the way his body had sunk down and into his comfortable old chair, and who could blame him. He had been up since the crack of dawn she realised, and suddenly felt a wee bit guilty.

"Don't get up dad. I can see myself round to the lavvy," she said as he roused himself, then grinned as she saw a look of surprise cross his face. "Well that's a first I must say," he replied as he absentmindedly moved the cushion away from his legs. "Off you go then and be quick about it. I'm ready for my bed even if you're not." And he began to stow away the other bits and pieces around him.

As she made her way to the lavvy, the cat at her ankles, she looked over towards mum's little bit of garden. Not that she could see much of its content in this light. She could see it in her mind's eye though, the predictable peonies, poppies and yellow loosestrife, surrounded by a colourful, haphazard selection of both cultivated and wild flowers, that appeared there year on year as if by magic. And of course, that homely selection of clay pots stacked higgledy-piggledy alongside. She moved forward, opening the door of lavvy and entering into its fuggy interior without the usual night time fear and trepidation. She knew without any shadow of doubt that she was protected in some way on this strange magical night. She was immune from danger, real or imagined.

She paused momentarily before stepping up into the scullery, reluctant to abandon this night of curious sensation. Then common sense prevailed. She knew that at this very moment, Dad would be standing beside the table, trusty torch alongside, ready and waiting to close down for the night, and he was. He was standing exactly where she knew he would be and turned as she walked inside. "Off to bed with you now then," he said quite predictably, and she dutifully began to make her way across the room. He waited till she had reached the bedroom door, before drawing the flickering lamp towards him, and she watched as he turned down the wick, cupped his hand around the tall glass cover, and then with a singular puff of well-practised expertise, he had extinguished the flame. A very satisfying ritual, she reckoned as she followed the beam of his torch through and into her bedroom before the residual whiff of paraffin vapour hit her nostrils.

Chapter 17

The girls sat around the kitchen table playing the 'funniest word game' as they munched away at their breakfast. Many of the words chosen by Dorothy and Jacky, though amusing and inventive in their own way, were obscure to say the least. Their effort to come up with the most curious and unlikely combination of syllables did cause a few chuckles here and there, but it was Pat's pronunciation of the word, 'visibility,' that caused the little ones to fall about laughing. It was during the furore that ensued, that mum walked in with a rather official looking envelope in her hand, which she passed over to Pat, and the general cackle ceased immediately. A missive like this, addressed to Patricia L Cotton could only be one thing they knew as they gathered around her. She examined the envelope, then moved slightly away to open and examine its contents, and they knew immediately by the wide grin that spread across her face that she had passed the entrance exam to the Bexhill Grammar School. Goody, goody, she'd now have a whole new set of books to borrow and read, was Sally's first thought and reaction in the split second it took her to absorb the news. Then she felt guilty as she joined with the others to congratulate her sister for having taken the first and very important step towards fulfilling her ambition, to become a

State Registered Nurse. The question of books and special uniform would have to be discussed and addressed at some time of course, but right now all Pat needed was a bit of time and space to allow the news to sink in. One of the first things she'd do though once she got her breath back she said, was to write to Betty and Ron who had been so supportive throughout. And she could not wait to tell Hilary.

It was going to be another fine day, Sally decided as she peered through the bedroom window early on Sunday morning. Though the trees edging the big wood were wearing a halo of pale pink, there was no ominous red sky, and that faint mist hanging over the village was just a heat haze of course, she told herself.

It was now early afternoon, the girls were on their way to Sunday School, and true to Sally's earlier prediction, it had become a fine and very warm day. As Mrs Smith was on Missionary work in Africa, it was Olive who would be looking after the little ones, with a bit of assistance from her brother Daniel and the older girls of course. This fine weather boded well for an open air session in Farrow's field, Sally reckoned. It was Olive who had taken the group to the primrose secret earlier in the year, and the little ones had been enchanted by the place. She like her parents and Miss Smith reckoned that youngsters learned more about God and his astonishing creations by exploring the world about them, than by sitting between four walls and just reciting prayers.

As they trooped up Crazy Lane, Dorothy, Jacky and Janet Powell who was with them, were in and out of the hedgerows searching for ladybirds, and chanting the ditty with which they'd serenade the little creatures when or if they found one: "Ladybird, ladybird fly away home. Your house is on fire and your children are gone. All except one, her name is Ann. She hid behind a frying pan." The older girls listened with half an ear as recital of this well-worn bit of nonsense continued with monotonous regularity, their attention mostly on the piano accordion Hilary was carrying, and which Olive Smith would be playing for them this afternoon. She had bought this strange musical instrument from Tony Powell recently, who preferred to use his old squeeze box these days. Not only was it very nearly as versatile he said, but was a lot lighter and a darned sight easier to carry around. It was certainly a weighty object this instrument, no doubt about that. Without the aid of the thick, decorative strap attached to its casing and which was now yoked securely across Hilary's shoulders to support the bulk of the thing, she would have struggled.

They were not the first to arrive at Chapel, and as they walked through the doorway, they heard Olive asking Alfie Goble where his brother was. "E be sick miss. E be bad in bed en worse up, en mum reckons it be the lurgies 'e got, like what I ad thet time," he replied all in one breath. Then he turned and looked around. "Swop me blimmin bob. What be thet bliddy thing? he asked, pointing towards the accordion Hilary was carrying, his eyes nearly popping out of his head.

The girls giggled, he looked so comical, and it was left to Olive, who had mastered the two handed technique of this complicated musical instrument, to explain its function. After giving Hilary a hand to extricate herself from the thing, she placed it around her own shoulders and gave a demonstration of its sound and harmony. Very satisfactory and daunting at the same time Sally thought as she listened, knowing full well that she would never, ever reach that standard of expertise. Once the brief demonstration was over, Olive passed the accordion back to Hilary, and after busying herself with the register, followed by a swift gathering up of the few but necessary bits and pieces she needed, she ushered the youngsters outside.

After accessing Farrow's field by the top gate, they made their way down towards the orchard, Hilary and her musical curiosity now surrounded by excited youngsters. "She looks for all the world like the Pied Piper of Hamlin," Olive remarked to Pat and Sally, who grinned in agreement. "It's just as well she really likes and gets on so well with the little ones," she added.

They milled around the chosen site for a few moments, ignoring and ignored by the chickens scratching around in the orchard. Then a measure of order was brought about by Olive's calm but firm direction, and all at once as if by magic, they were sitting around in a large and reasonably neat circle. After offering up a short prayer, Olive reached for the accordion, and a session of singing began. The first request was for 'Jesus wants me for a sunbeam,' and after that, several other well-worn and favourite songs and hymns were played and sung. It was in a brief moment of quiet, as the notes of a song faded away, that the characteristic piping song of a skylark could be heard. They all looked upwards and saw, and were silenced by the sound and sight of these magical songsters hovering high above their heads. The moment lasted mere seconds however, the spell broken by a loud sneeze followed by giggles as the culprit tried unsuccessfully to muffle a second one. Olive, noting a gathering mood of restlessness around her, decided that choral vocal chords had been exercised quite enough for one day, and lowered the accordion. The little ones, responding spontaneously to the signal, scrambled to their feet to seek out a more solid connection with God's work and creations. Wild flower gathering and bug hunts were soon under way. Sally noted with relief, the absence of fresh cow packs in the field. There were always a few moth eaten brained youngsters, who would be tempted to search for the flies and dung beetles that inhabited these smelly mounds, and she was not willing to share her hankie with dung smeared hands. No way. She did offer the use of it to Alfie though, who was trying to catch grasshoppers with his bare hands, but he was quite disparaging about it. "Bout es useful es a chocolate tea pot, thet thing, " he remarked, and just carried on with the cupped hand method. Ah well, you couldn't win 'em all she thought as she turned and followed Pat and Hilary over towards the orchard hedge, where Daniel, jam jar in hand, was bug gathering, a group of excited youngsters alongside.

"There's some decent hazel sticks over here, just about the right size for making arrows," said Sally running her hands along the straight, upright growth of fresh twigs. "We never did manage to get the tips sharp like your dad could, did we Hilary. I remember watching him blacken the ends in the fire and shave them off quick and sharp as you like. When we tried though, we just burned the darned things. We even caught them alight a few times, didn't we? Well I did anyway. I stopped trying in the end and just used me old pen knife to sharpen 'em off. We've not used bows and arrows for ages now, have we?"

"No, nor catapults neither, though the least said about those lethal blooming things the better I reckon. Duff shots the pair of us. Talk about cack handed," said Hilary, and Sally grinned and nodded in agreement, remembering only too well the close shaves they'd had with those slings. Apart from the Brookside and Windy Ridge windows they had broken with badly aimed missiles, one or two shed windows in the area had also come to grief courtesy of a miss placed shot. Time to get away from those embarrassing reminiscences they reckoned, and moved over to join the general search for creepy crawlies and wild flowers. Olive strolled over and joined them, and it did not take her long to spot and carefully extricate an interestingly marked spider from its web amongst the tall grasses, which she placed it in the palm of one hand, anticipating and controlling its movements from this to the other hand with split second timing. She soon had an admiring audience around her, some content to watch its antics from a distance, others vying excitedly for an opportunity to have the little creature within touching distance. Sally was somewhere in between. Worms were her pet hate. After a short while, noting the creatures increasing agitation, she replaced it carefully alongside its web, which it totally ignored, opting instead for the camouflage of undergrowth and tall grasses, though which it disappeared.

The foraging continued for a while, but eventually Olive was obliged to call time on the nature hunt. An inevitable show of opposition followed, but the youngsters were eventually persuaded to abandon the search. After taking a take a brief and last minute examination of the bugs before they were released, they gathered up their posies of grasses and wild flowers and joined together for the last hymn of the day, 'All things bright and beautiful.' If a little out of tune without the aid of the accordion, it was never the less offered up enthusiastically and pretty well word perfect.

After a perfunctory spit and wipe of grubby hands and a general tidying up of the area, they set off across the field. They had just reached the top gate, which Daniel was in the process of opening, when Olive felt a tap on her arm. She turned immediately and found Alfie on her heels, a rather anxious, troubled look on his face. "I need a thrutch Miss," he said, and as she looked incomprehensively at him, a voice from amongst the group behind piped up. "He means he needs the lavvy Miss, urgent like."

"Ah, of course," Olive replied, taking his hand and ushering him quickly through the gate and down towards the Manse. The others followed at a rather more leisurely pace, and waited beside the Chapel wall until the two re-emerged through the doorway, the crisis obviously dealt with. There was a general shuffling of feet until Olive took charge once again, then a sigh of relief when she announced that a brief outline of plans for next week's activities could be dealt with here and now; without rather than within the walls of the old Chapel. And then they were free to go.

Most of the youngsters headed off down towards the village, the sound of their noisy departure reduced to a dull echo by the time the others, moving off in the opposite direction, had reached the top of the hill. Brian Winchester was the first to reach the junction, with Dorothy, Jacky and Janet close on his heels. As they waited for the older ones to finish their protracted and boring conversations, they amused themselves with a recitation of one or two ditties, most accompanied by manic hand movements. Once the girls had temporarily abandoned their posies of course.

'Rub-a dub-dub, three men in a tub, and who do you think they were. The butcher, the baker the candlestick maker, they all jumped over a rotten potato.' Then, 'Little Tom tiddle mouse, lived in a little house. And he caught fishes in other men's ditches.' These were followed immediately by several garbled attempts at 'Red leather, yellow leather,' which they soon abandoned for the more rhythmical 'Sky blue pink with a finny anny border.' The latter bit of nonsense, which seemed to go on ad infinitum, eventually had the desired effect. Eileen Lawrence and Sylvia Gain had got the message. After bidding a brief farewell to the girls, they turned and set their sights on home, heading briskly into and along Cottage Lane. Once Hilary had hoisted the accordion more comfortably across her shoulder and the girls had retrieved their posies, they set off down Crazy Lane, the youngsters now well into a game of 'I spy.' "It's down the twitten," Hilary called out to them, as having moved ahead, they were now approaching the entrance to the short cut. "I want to pop me accordion back home and you've got to let your mum know you're staying with us for a bit longer Janet. We'll wait at Windy Ridge for you all," she added. With just a nod of acknowledgement, the youngsters moved towards and onto the track, and in no time at all, they were down and onto the main road at the bottom, where they turned and disappeared from sight. The older girls paused half way down, then they turned and made their way across the rough bit of pasture, and into Hilary's back garden. Once they were through the door and into the kitchen, Hilary lowered her giant sling bag carefully onto the floor with a sigh of relief. "That's better. Now we can sit down and relax for a bit before they get back," she said as she began pulling the chairs away from the table. "Vera or Gran Powell are bound to give them a drink and a biscuit and so forth while they're there, so they'll be a minute or two." Pat and Sally, who were more than willing to comply, sat down and relaxed back into the proffered seats. As they waited, chatting idly about this afternoon's activities, Sally had one of her grasshopper moments.

"Just think, in a few weeks I'll have left school for good and all, then by the time you go to Bexhill Grammar Pat, I'll be working for Claude Button," she suddenly declared. "That's the plan anyway though I do feel a bit strange about the whole thing. Well mum's always got her groceries from Mr Phillips, so we've hardly set foot in the top grocers, have we? But he's offered me a job, so I'll just have to get used to it I suppose." The other two, used to her sudden changes of mind and subject matter, fell in with her observations, and by the time the little ones returned, were well into a discussion on these and other life changing experiences that were taking place. However, the sudden entry of this proverbial whirlpool, put paid to further discussions of a serious and meaningful nature, and after a moment's hesitation, Hilary pushed herself up and out of her seat. "No peace for the wicked," she remarked, as she began to move away from the table. "Come on then, time and tide wait for no man, remember? Nor woman either if it comes to that," she added and grinned as she noted the pained expression on the faces of the other two as they rose from their seats.

Once outside, they paused briefly beside the back gate while Brian re tied his shoelaces. Then with Dorothy and Jacky clutching their lightly crushed posies, the girls stood and watched as he ran across the rough strip of grass towards home. "Be up later," he called back over his shoulder. And then he disappeared, taking his grass stained knees with him.

***

The Wood family, who had been staying at Sylvian for the past two weeks, were preparing to depart, their mood and that of the Cotton's, rather more sombre than when they had first arrived. From the moment she'd set eyes on them, Sally had known they were a wee bit special. She had watched their arrival from the top of the underground tank, with a mixture of curiosity and excitement, noting their exuberance and zest for life, which with the three boys in particular was obvious right from the start. The first clear sighting she'd had of the boys was when they had run through the bottom gateway and into the field, Gavin the youngest in the lead, followed closely by Hamish and Donald. They had been pursued with single minded determination by Meg their beloved Bull Terrier, albeit at the end of a straining leash held doggedly by Mrs Wood. Dad and Mr Wood, cases in hand, had followed at a rather more leisurely pace, closing the gate securely behind them. The focus of the boy's attention was Rosebud who'd been grazing close by. As they moved up alongside her, she had raised her head from her grassy feast, and rewarded them with a brief glance from her lash fringed eyes before lowering it again. From then on they admitted, they had been hooked, and throughout their stay, had taken a keen interest in her and all that went on around her.

The early morning cuppa mum provided as a matter of course was sheer indulgence according to Mr and Mrs Wood.

She thought back to that first morning, and how after opening the top gate for dad to pass through with the laden tray, she had watched him carry it across the grass and up to the large window at the side of the shed. After carefully balancing the tray on one arm, he tapped on the window, and by the time he had rebalanced the load, the large glass aperture had been pulled across, open arms had reached out and within moments the tray and its contents had disappeared inside. As he turned, she had run inside and up to the kitchen window, and was just in time to see the door of the shed open. Gavin was the first through the opening, followed closely by Meg the dog, then Hamish and Donald appeared. The arrival of the tray with their mum and dad's early morning tea and biscuits, was the trigger they'd been waiting for. They had spotted Pat immediately; in the process of enticing Rosebud into the milking shed with the usual rattling of cow cake in a galvanised bucket. Dorothy was with her, the large apron she was wearing over her blue dress and red cardigan swamping her slight frame. As the boys ran over to join them, Sally left her vantage point and followed, then stood behind the boys at the doorway of the shed. They had watched in silence as Pat tethered Rosebud, cleaned her udders with a smear of Udsal, and after positioning her stool and bucket, had rewarded them with a demonstration of her deceptively simple milking skill. She had been so nervous that first time they'd watched her Pat said, though luckily it got marginally better as time went on. Just as well Sally thought to herself. They had not missed a single morning session and very few evening ones all the time they had been here.

Sally had missed out on something that very first day though, that walk through to and exploration of Battle. And all because she'd been too embarrassed to say she needed a wee. All she would normally have done was to step behind a bush or tree, but with the boys there she had been reluctant to do so, and Hilary, who had turned back with her, had also missed out on that particular adventure. Still she had been back several times since then, not only to walk and explore the woods, but also to visit Deffy and Bill. From the first meeting, the boys had been totally captivated by the tales told, and the lifestyle of these two old men. It was late afternoon before the wanderers had returned, not on foot this time but by taxi. They had missed the path a couple of times on the way to Battle, and did not want to risk the same thing happening on the way back, especially as exploration of this ancient town had taken longer than anticipated. The boys had been full of it, the old Abbey in particular, which they planned to re visit at the earliest opportunity. As they talked, Sally got the impression that their interest in these ancient stones lay to a certain extent within the history lesson provided by the guide, whose unique brogue and articulation seemed to fascinate and amuse them in equal measure. 'Arrold looked up, n got a harrer in is eye and collopsed,' was a favourite and much loved quote. Pity their teachers did not have the knack of whittling down lessons to bare essentials like he did they said, and just leaving their imagination and the occasional reference to history books to fill in the detail.

Her watchful reminiscence continued as these last minute checks took place around her, and as her eye rested on Mrs Wood, she was reminded of the first time she had heard her sing. She'd been on her way across the field to persuade those last few recalcitrant chickens to call it a day, when from the direction of the old shed, came the strains of a song from a voice so hauntingly beautiful, that it had stopped her in her tracks. Although she had listened to that amazing voice several times since then, it still had the power to make her skin prickle.

The boys now captured her attention. They were fussing around Rosebud whose response was immediate and predictable. As they stroked her neck and bid her farewell, she lifted her head, rewarded them with a blank gaze, then munching throughout, lowered it again. That automatic chewing of the cud was it seemed, as automatic to this docile creature as breathing. As she stood there, memories of the past two eventful weeks continued to crowd in on her. She remembered in particular the expression of sheer pleasure and appreciation, on the faces of the boys as they looked upon the food mum prepared and dished up for them each day. 'Every meal a winner, and fresh cakes every day. You girls don't realise how lucky you are,' was a regular cry from one or other of them. They had certainly done justice to the meal mum dished up to them when they'd returned from one particular trip. After having undertaken the arduous up hill and down dale walk from Hastings to Rye, they had spent the day exploring countless places of interest, and had it seemed, investigated every nook and cranny in and around this historical town. 'On a par with Battle but more so,' was the rather ambiguous way they described the place. This statement however, followed by a more detailed account of the day's experiences, was delivered after they had fallen upon and devoured the feast of food mum had prepared for them. Not only were they willing and able to place their empty, scraped clean plates on their heads, thus passing dad's vigorous waste not want not test, but they had devoured the best part of a large coffee sponge mum had then placed before them as well.

Then she grinned as she remembered how easy it had been to coerce the boys into helping out with chores, the dreaded water pumping one in particular. For that chore, mum always insisted that they wind a piece of rag around their hands to protect them from the vicious brick housing at the back of the pump. Failing to do that would result in bloodied knuckles she warned them, and Sally had backed her up on that one. It had caught her out a few times in the past she remembered ruefully.

She was certainly going to miss those long conversations that had taken place around the kitchen table most evenings, she thought as she continued to watch the final preparations for departure taking place. They ranged from accounts of the days' activities to other wider issues and experiences. What she'd been particularly interested in were those tales about India, where dad had served during The First World War, and where the Wood family had lived for a few years prior to the second. The grownups had talked in depth about Mahatma Gandhi, about his astonishing life and the legacy he'd left behind, and about what the future held for this fascinating country. She'd never heard her dad speak quite so passionately about the place and its people before. As she stood there, visions of teeming, colourful Bazaars, where wealth and poverty went hand in hand, popped up into her mind and imagination, joining other images. She could almost smell the mixed aroma of those lively exotic places, so vividly described by Mrs Wood, who though clearly troubled by the stark inequalities that prevailed, as was her dad, still missed the fascinating Country she'd grown so fond of. She had she said, been particularly upset at having to leave their beloved Ayah behind, as had Donald and Hamish who like herself, had shed a few tears at the time.

Yes Sally would miss them all, especially Hamish for whom she had a special fondness. She would miss the walks, those long conversations in which they had discussed anything and everything. But he and his family would be back sometime in the not too distant future he had assured her.

Well, that was it, Sally thought as she walked up the field on her way home from her last day at School. Her life was changing and all of a sudden she was not quite so absolutely sure she was up for the challenge. Still, best not to dwell on something over which it seemed she had very little control. She would just have to try and grin and bear it like her older sisters and Hilary had done; and like everyone else of course really. One thing in her favour was that she was pretty good at mental arithmetic, and no wonder she thought when you considered how much emphasis had been put upon this particular subject at school. One of the reasons for this she supposed was that shop work, where quick calculation was particularly useful, was always available to school leavers, not just here in the village but also in Hastings and Battle and other nearby towns. Strangely, donning that white overall with its curious detachable buttons also helped, she reminded herself as she remembered how different, how much more confident she'd felt the first time she had shrugged it on over her summer frock. Anyway, however she felt about this whole new experience, uniform and all, she knew that on Monday, she would be walking to the village as usual, not to school this time, but up to and into Button's Grocery Store, just a short distance away.

She paused and turned when she reached the top gate, screwing up her eyes against the glare of the sun as she looked back over the field. She was thinking about Pat now, for whom life or the educational part of it anyway, was soon to change. There was a quiet determination about her sister though, which when she thought about it had always been there; and she was well organised. She would need both these attributes in the very near future when as well as homework she would still have Rosebud to milk mornings and evenings. Sally did not envy her that last chore. Still thankfully some things never changed she thought, as having moved from gate to doorstep, she began to sniff the delicious aroma of mum's cooking up and into her nostrils.

Later, having prepared herself and her handbag for the trip to the village for this evening's Old Thyme Dance session, her attention switched for moment, onto Dorothy and Jacky and the imaginative game they were playing. Their favourite characters, Mole, Ratty, Badger and Toad it seemed were once again locked in battle with their nemeses, the cunning Stoats and Foxes and Weasels. The former were enacting the most unlikely acts of bravery and comradeship, while the latter were using every dastardly trick in the book to try to outwit them. It took her right back to when Rupert had been the centre of her world, when she had anguished over the dangers he faced, especially when it had involved deep, dark dungeons. Then just as she was really getting into the sheer fantasy of it all, they stopped mid-sentence, and in moments were through the kitchen door, then the top gate, and were running down the field to meet Hilary.

Shortly afterwards, the two older girls were on their way to the village, in the company of Ron Edwards and his Aunt and Uncle, Mrs and Mr Taylor. As they passed by Luff's farm, they noted the usual activity in and around the old farmhouse. There was never a dull or idle moment for Mr and Mrs Farrow, who seemed to take, to the enth degree, the ethos in the old saying: 'Use time in time while time lasts. For all times no time when times past.'

There was the usual activity in and around the Village Hall when they arrived. Chairs were being pushed to the outer edge of the floor, the Gramophone was in place with a stack of records placed alongside, and from the kitchen area, the rattle of cups, plates and glasses, suggested that Mrs Bishop and Mrs Woollett had arrangements for the interval refreshments well in hand. And the windows had already been dealt with. Each one was open wide, firmly secured and held in place with that holey metal bar.

After one or two announcements, Dulcie and Bill Lavender moved on to the floor to lead the first dance, a Waltz, and after the usual salutation of a bow from the men to their prospective partners, others joined them. Sally was dancing with Cecil, who along with Ron, were her favourite partners. Not only were they excellent dancers, but were also very patient when dealing with the two left feet syndrome, a particular blessing for Sally when it came to the Polka. No matter how hard she tried, she just could not get the rhythm of that blooming dance from her head to her feet, no matter how hard she tried.

In spite of the warmth of the evening, it was quite an energetic programme. After participating in the County Cotillion and the Lancers, the two dances leading up to the interval, they were more than ready for a rest, a long cold drink and a slice of energising fruit cake. As they ate and drank, there were exclamations of gratitude and appreciation towards the ladies who had provided them with this homemade feast. The lemonade was particularly good this evening, and it was agreed unanimously, that Mrs Bishop was top of the class when it came to the creation of this refreshing drink.

The second half started off with the announcement of a new dance, and after a demonstration from Dulcie and Bill, most people took to the floor to try their luck; with mixed results. A brief interlude followed, just long enough for people to catch their breath, and then a spontaneous cheer went up as the Gay Gordon's was announced. Just about everyone took to the floor for this popular dance, which most folk were satisfyingly at ease with. When it finished with the usual twirls, a bow and a curtsey, there was a breathless sigh of contentment all round.

At home time, there was the usual chatter and clatter as a general tidying up process took place. Chairs were rearranged and records were moved from the table to Dulcie and Bills little car, parked right alongside the entrance to the hall. Lastly, after having gathered up bags, cardigans and jackets, the windows and doors were secured, and the mini mass exodus, centred for a moment around the doorway, soon melted away. A sizable proportion of folk made their way down through the village, reducing in number as individuals or small groups peeled off along the way. By the time they reached cow shit corner, only a few remained, three making their way up Chapel Hill, the others, Hilary and Sally amongst them, taking the main road through to Black Brooks. As they passed Farrows steps, Sally glanced up towards the hushed farmhouse, its occupants now it seemed enjoying a well-deserved rest. They'd be up again at first light no doubt and the daily grind would begin all over again.

After parting company with the others at the bottom of the field, she followed the well-trodden path up towards the top gate. The smell of fresh cow dung hung in the air, its smell, she'd noticed before, subtly different from that of sheep's treddles. Thankfully, no matter how dark it was, she and her sisters had always managed instinctively to avoid close contact with these smelly objects over the years; apart from when they'd collected the latter for dad's tomato feed of course. It wasn't that dark this evening, but better not tempt providence she thought as she quickly crossed her fingers behind her back.

As she walked into the kitchen, dad appeared through the front room doorway, followed by a whiff of fresh furniture polish. Pat had been giving the big old round table in the front room its regular spit and polish she thought as she sniffed the not altogether unpleasant aroma up into her nostrils. When accompanied by the residual heat from the Rayburn, lit and used summer and winter for cooking and hot water purposes, it smelled a bit like perfume really.

"Saw you coming up across the field," he said as he closed the door behind him. "Not been indoors that long myself if it comes to that. Had the devil's own job getting the chicken in tonight, the usual culprits. All I'm trying to do is protect them from that wily old fox who I tell them, likes nothing better for his supper than a tasty hen, but it made no odds. Did they take any notice? No. Bloody stubborn, ungrateful birds, I told them. Drive me mad they do. Anyway, best get your teeth cleaned then off to bed with you," he said as he removed his trusty clock from its day time position on the mantelpiece and placed it on the side of the table ready for its night-time role. "I'll just check around the place and then I'll be on me way. I'm ready for me bed."

She lingered beside the side window for a few moments once he'd disappeared through the scullery door, and watched his shadowy figure move towards the old sycamore trees. Old memories stirred within her mind and imagination. Amongst them, was his fearless search around the place when one or other of her sisters had awoken with the night time terrors, convinced a murderer was roaming around outside. She remembered her overwhelming sense of relief when, after what seemed an endless wait, he had walked back through the copper-house door accompanied by that characteristic sniff if his. Even now, the memory had the power to make her shiver. He was small and wiry her dad, and brave. He was gruff too no doubt about that, but he was kind when it mattered. She thought about his gentle nursing of frozen fingers back to life beneath his arm pits in that 'when icicles hang from the wall, and Dick the shepherd blows his nails,' sort of weather. And his gentle bathing of grazed knees. She grinned as for a few more moments she indulged in these long ago and far away memories, then she moved away from the window and scuttled off to the scullery to give her teeth a cursory brush.

She was in bed by the time he returned. She heard the slight click of the door as he made his way through to his bedroom that was all. Then she turned on to her side and even as she prepared her body for its journey into the land of nod, knew full well that her mind and imagination were not quite ready to follow. She dwelt for a few moments on

Monday, wondering how she would cope with the grown up world with which she was about to be confronted, but that was life, she supposed. And she was not the only one to be confronted by change, not by any means. Pat was also about to take a step out into the unknown and as far as Sally could tell, was taking the whole thing in her stride. Whether she was as truly unfazed by the whole thing as she seemed, was hard to tell. Her sister had always been less vocal, less moany than she was. She just had to thank her lucky stars for the blessing of continuity she told herself. For the consolation that jogging alongside and absorbing the impact of most sudden, dramatic changes in life, were all those other everyday occurrences. This did not apply when it came to wars and other such drastic, life threatening occurrences of course, she reminded herself hastily. That was of a different magnitude, in another category altogether. The here and now was not the place and time to allow those particular deep and consequential issues to dominate her thoughts though. She'd never get to sleep.

Songs and poems were a much better choice, she reckoned as she turned her mind towards this satisfactory, soothing medium.

'Three Gypsy's stood at the Castle gate. They sang so high they sang so low. A Lady sat in her chamber late. Her heart it melted away as snow,' she recited. And 'Brave Lochinvar,' The Lady of Shallot,' or as much as she could remember of them, and other favourites, moved like quicksilver through her mind.

Then after a while, she began to recite the words of a recently discovered poem, experiencing over again that strange connection she'd felt the first time she'd encountered the poem.

'I will arise and go now, to Innisfree. And a small cabin build there of clay and wattles made.
   Nine bean rows will I have there and a hive for the honey bee.
And live alone in the bee-loud glade.
   And I shall have some peace there, for peace comes dropping slow.
Dropping from the veils of mourning to where the cricket sings.
   There midnight's all a glimmer, and moon a purple glow.
And evening full of the linnet's wings.
   I will arise and go now, for always night and day.
I hear lake water lapping with low sounds by the shore.
   While I stand on the roadway or on the pavements grey.
I hear it in the deep heart's core.'

She sighed. She was relaxed and sleepy now, her mind and imagination ready to relinquish conscious thought. She felt herself begin to float away, into a strange and secret other worldliness, with Herne The Hunter at its heart. Her last conscious thought however, was of the veiled Lady of Pevensey, shrouded not in grief now but in an aura of peace and tranquillity.